Instructor's Edition

Ear Training
A Technique for Listening

Fifth Edition

Bruce Benward
University of Wisconsin

J. Timothy Kolosick
University of Arizona

Brown &Benchmark
PUBLISHERS

Madison Dubuque, IA Guilford, CT Chicago Toronto London
Caracas Mexico City Buenos Aires Madrid Bogota Sydney

Book Team

Publisher *Rosemary Bradley*
Acquisitions Editor *Christopher J. Freitag*
Production Editor *Jane C. Morgan*
Proofreading Coordinator *Carrie Barker*
Designer *Katherine Farmer*
Production Manager *Beth Kundert*
Production/Costing Manager *Sherry Padden*
Visuals/Design Freelance Specialist *Mary L. Christianson*
Marketing Manager *Kirk Moen*
Copywriter *Jennifer Smith*

Basal Text *10/12 Times Roman*
Display Type *Helvetica*
Typesetting System *Muse/Macintosh™ QuarkXPress™*
Paper Stock *50# Courtland*
Production Services *A-R Editions, Inc.*

Brown & Benchmark
PUBLISHERS

President and Chief Executive Officer *Thomas E. Doran*
Vice President of Production and Business Development *Vickie Putman*
Vice President of Sales and Marketing *Bob McLaughlin*
Director of Marketing *John Finn*

A Times Mirror Company

Copyedited by Mark Thomas Tobey; proofread by Rose R. Kramer

Library of Congress Catalog Card Number: 95–75719

ISBN 0–697–28785–8

Printed in the United States of America by Times Mirror Higher Education Group, Inc.,
2460 Kerper Boulevard, Dubuque, IA 52001

10 9 8 7 6 5 4 3 2 1

Contents _____

Unit 4

Unit 5

Unit 6

Unit 7

Unit 8

Unit 9

Unit 10

Unit 11

Unit 12

Unit 13

Unit 14

Unit 15

Unit 16

Preface

Scope

The text, *Ear Training: A Technique for Listening*, is designed to accompany most undergraduate music theory courses and may be used in two semesters, although some instructors may extend its use to three or even four semesters.

Extent of Melodic Study. From the identification of a single interval to the comprehension of melodic organization in two-part and three-part forms of moderate length.

Extent of Harmonic Study. From the identification of a simple triad to the recognition of nondominant 7th chords, modulations, secondary dominants, and augmented 6th chords.

Extent of Rhythmic Study. From simple rhythmic units containing whole-beat and half-beat values to the perception of complicated patterns with subtriplets, syncopations, and changing meters.

New in this Edition

Reordering of Sections. The sections have been reordered to facilitate locating particular drill types. A list of units that reflect this reorganization is given under Organization in this preface. A chart showing the derivation of each section is given in an appendix to facilitate changes in syllabi based on previous editions.

Rewritten Chord Function Identification Drills. The Harmony A units have been completely rewritten. The new examples are easier to play and allow the instructor to improvise textures based on those progressions. Across each line of examples, the progressions can be played continuously, allowing the instructor to play longer progressions of up to twenty chords for the class.

New Chords in Music Literature Section. In this new section, the instructor plays short segments from musical compositions by famous composers. The students recognize the chord progressions used within a multiple choice format. These materials can help establish a link in the student's mind to listening analytically in concerts and rehearsals.

Changes in Melody Sections. Error Detection sections now include printing error, performance error, and missing accidental drills. New melodies were written for certain Melodic Dictation units. Recorded Interval sections now include both ascending and descending intervals.

Organization

The text consists of two books, *Ear Training: A Technique for Listening* for the student, and the *Instructor's Edition for Ear Training: A Technique for Listening*. The latter book (this book) contains the music for dictation and lists suggestions and procedures for class presentation and discussion.

Each book contains sixteen units. The units are graded from basic and uncomplicated (Unit 1) to complex and sophisticated (Unit 16).

Each unit is divided into four skill areas: (1) Melodic Sections, (2) Harmonic Sections, (3) Rhythmic Sections, and (4) a Transcription Section. Each skill area represents a logical progression of skills and musical complexity throughout the sixteen units of each book. All ear training curricula can make use of these materials, but each instructor's approach may vary.

The instructor may choose to introduce melodic, harmonic, and rhythmic materials concurrently; that is, assignments in Melody Unit 1, Harmony Unit 1, and Rhythm Unit 1 during the first week of the semester or quarter, continuing in like fashion throughout the year. Alternatively, the instructor may wish to begin the study of certain materials later in the semester. For example, harmonic studies could commence when chords and harmonic function are discussed in written theory classes.

Each skill area is organized consistently by ear training drill types. This organization is shown below.

Melody Units

Section	Drill Type
A	Melodic Dictation
B	Mode Identification
	Melodic Error Detection
C	Scale Degree Identification
	Melodic Figure Identification
	Two-Voice Dictation
	Phrase Relationships
	Musical Form
D	Intervals
E	Models and Embellishments

Harmony Units

Section	Drill Type
A	Chord Function Identification
B	Chords in Music Literature

C	Harmonic Rhythm
	Nonharmonic Tones
	Cadence Types
	Aural Analysis
D	Triad Position Identification
	Harmonic Dictation
E	Chord Quality Identification
	Harmonic Error Detection
F	Support Drills for Harmonic
	Dictation
	Units 1, 2, and 15 only

Rhythm Units

Section	Drill Type
A	Rhythmic Dictation
B	Rhythm Error Detection

Transcription

Taped dictation examples for independent work

Goals and Objectives

Ear Training: A Technique for Listening is designed to provide students with a seeing ear—an ear that can perceive and identify patterns both large and small in music. Most students entering higher education will have performed much music and will have listened to an even larger quantity. Yet, in their previous experience the listening has probably been passive, directed more toward perfunctory indulgence than to the patterns, shapes, and structures inherent in the music. This is not to presume that beginning students have no capacity for understanding, but that the capacity has not as yet been developed.

Thus, in an ear-training class, it is the instructor's task to encourage students to focus attention on those configurations, groupings, and characteristics of music that generate organization and continuity. The emphasis on ear training should be at least equal to that on theory, sightsinging, and keyboard harmony, and must be of sufficient intensity to ensure lasting results. To summarize, the goal of an ear-training course is to produce a student who listens intelligently to music and who can provide an accurate analysis of a composition in at least modest detail through listening alone.

Approach

The book represents two different types of exercises: (1) fundamental drill (microlistening) emphasizing note-to-note and chord-by-chord relationships, and (2) larger and broader aspects of music (macrolistening) emphasizing melodic, harmonic, and rhythmic patterns. Fundamental drill is supplied by exercises requesting identification of intervals, scale and modal patterns, triad types, basic key relationships, and chord-by-chord harmonic analysis. From fundamental drill the book progresses through embellishments of intervallic and chordal models to larger patterns and relationships such as sequences, phrase relationships, harmonic rhythm, and small forms (two-part and three-part forms). Transcription drills, appearing at the end of each unit, can be used throughout the course to reinforce both microlistening and macrolistening skills through recognition and notation of examples from music literature.

The authors caution that thorough training in the fundamentals is a prerequisite for the study of larger relationships, the structural forces in music. Students who cannot identify a perfect 5th are incapable of perceiving a modulation to the dominant in a two-part or three-part composition.

Students should be encouraged to explore musical sound freely *outside* the aural skills classroom. Recognizing learned patterns and their embellishments in actual musical compositions can be a joyful learning experience and can establish a strong link between academic work and professional music making. Each student must find his or her own path to aural skill development and should realize that such learning never ceases.

The text includes a wide variety of exercise types, thus developing and maintaining student interest and eliminating the danger of stereotyped dictation as the only ear-training class activity.

Melody

1. Straight dictation of melodic lines
2. Identification of errors in a given melodic line
3. Multiple choice exercises—selecting correct notation for a melodic line
4. Identification of intervals
5. Identification of scale and mode types
6. Identification and notation of embellishments based on a given model
7. Identification of melodic groupings such as sequences, rhythmic repetition, and through composed excerpts from music literature
8. Identification of phrase relationships
9. Two-part dictations
10. Addition of correct accidentals to melodies from music literature
11. Identification of binary, rounded binary, and three-part forms

Harmony

12. Identification of triad types
13. Identification of triad factors in the soprano and bass voices
14. Harmonic analysis and/or four-part dictation based on chorale phrases

15. Common harmonic progressions for chord identification
16. Identification of nonharmonic tones
17. Identification of harmonic rhythm
18. Identification of errors in four-part writing
19. Identification of harmonic progressions in homophonic music
20. Identification of modulation to closely related and foreign keys
21. Identification of 7th chord types, added-tone chords, and 9th chords
22. Identification of nondominant 7th and secondary dominant chords
23. Identification of common progressions in popular song styles

Rhythm

24. Straight dictation of rhythm on a neutral pitch
25. Multiple choice exercises—selecting correct notation for a rhythmic line
26. Identification of errors in rhythm

Transcription

27. Notating single line examples
28. Notating multivoice examples with moderate rhythmic complexity
29. Notating multivoice contrapuntal examples
30. Notating examples with chromatic alterations and altered chords

Using Supporting Materials

Three types of supporting materials are available for *Ear Training: A Technique for Listening*. A **transcription tape,** packaged with each student manual, contains all of the transcription units and can be used for dictation drill outside class.

Additional cassettes, containing a large number of the printed examples, are available for purchase from the publisher. Examples included on the tapes are marked (*R*) in each section. These cassettes are available through Brown & Benchmark Educational Resources, 25 Kessel Ct., Madison, Wis. 53711. Institutions that purchase such tapes may allow students to copy these cassettes for their own private use. The **computer software** for this textbook contains most of the written exercises. Drills are interactive and friendly, allowing students to concentrate on developing their musical skills without frustration with the technology. These materials allow instructors to use this book in any of the following ways:

1. *Exclusively as a programmed text.* Since the *Instructor's Edition* contains all material presented as well as the correct answers to all exercises, copies may be placed near recorded materials in order that students can check answers as each exercise is completed. Computer software for the text gives this same type of feedback on the screen.

2. *Both as a text for use in the classroom and for supplementary study* with the tapes and software. The instructor can establish correct listening procedures in class. In the listening laboratory students may set their own pace, hear taped versions of exercises as many times as needed, and check their answers with the *Instructor's Edition.* Working with the computer software provides students with instant feedback for drills in most units of the book. Such independent student work allows the instructor to concentrate class time on special problems that result from work outside class. The authors prefer this approach.

3. *Exclusively as a classroom tool.* Sometimes, through lack of listening facilities or for pedagogical reasons, the book may be used in class only. Sometimes students prefer to get together in small groups and play material from the *Instructor's Edition* for one another.

Suggested Classroom Procedures

The directions for presenting each unit are given in this manual. Although they represent the methods used by the authors, other instructors may wish to augment them with their own procedures. The piano is perhaps the most convenient medium for ear training, and is generally available in the classroom; however, other instruments played by students offer a refreshing diversion and should be used as often as possible. Recent developments in portable electronic synthesizers make it easier than ever to add new timbres to ear-training examples.

Since listening for specific musical conventions requires considerable concentration and direction, the instructor should always ensure that students are thoroughly familiar with the concept under study before sending them to the listening laboratory for supplementary work in ear training. Tapes and computer software in a laboratory are very useful, but students cannot obtain maximum results from such facilities without prior guidance. Such technological tools provide unlimited drill and independent exploration of musical structures, but teaching comes best from a human musical role model.

If you have questions or comments about *Ear Training: A Technique for Listening,* contact the publisher or call Dr. Benward at (800) 564–9273.

Unit 1

Melody 1A

Melodic Dictation: Scalewise (Conjunct Diatonic) Melodies

Student text: Page 1.

Each exercise consists of a short melodic phrase. Listen to the phrase as it is played. Complete the phrase on the staff in notation.

1. As you listen to each melody the first time, immediately try to memorize its sound and melodic shape.
2. Do *not* try to write the melody until you have completely memorized it. You will learn almost nothing by trying to write the melody too early.
3. Before you hear the melody a second time, sing as much of it as you can.
4. A second or third hearing should provide the pitches you missed. Outside class, listen as many times as you need in order to memorize the entire melody.
5. Analyze the melody in your mind, identifying the scale degrees and rhythmic values of each note. Use solfeggio syllables or numbers as directed by your instructor.
6. Only after you have memorized the sound of the melody and have analyzed the structure of the melody, should you attempt to write anything on paper!
7. Observe that when the melody is memorized, you can slow it down in your mind sufficiently to write the notes on the staff as you sing (or preferably *think*).
8. Write the melody on the staff in music notation.

To the Instructor:

Progress in identifying scale degrees is vital to melodic dictation skills. See Section C of Melody Units 1 through 4 for scale degree recognition exercises.

This section provides a large number of simple melodic dictation examples. Many of these can be skipped if the students are doing well. Students in need of extra work will have ample opportunity to practice. These examples help develop major scale fluency in a variety of keys. Ask the students to identify the portion of the major scale that is used in each of the melodies. Request that students identify and sing all the scale degrees used in a melody. Then, have them sing the melody itself.

16.–30. (R)

* Note or rest in workbook.

Melody 1B

Mode Identification: Major and Harmonic Minor Scales

Student text: Page 3.

1. Your instructor will play melodies based on major and harmonic minor scales. Before listening to the melodies, play **major** and **harmonic minor scales** on your instrument or piano until you know their sound well.
2. Sing the same scales until you can sing both major and harmonic minor from any given **pitch.**
3. Now, listen to the melody once and capture the last pitch in your mind by matching its pitch immediately after it is played. Most of the melodies in this section end on the **tonic** (first) pitch of the scale.
4. Try to reconstruct the scale by remembering the notes of the melody and forming the scale from your recollections. You may need a couple of hearings before you have all the pitches in your mind.
5. Circle the correct answer (major or minor).

To the Instructor:

Before assigning this section, illustrate the procedure described above and make sure class members understand it well. More talented students may be able to skip some of the steps. Encourage them by all means, but at first play each melody as many times as needed by the poorest student in the class. Whenever possible, all students should achieve correct answers! All students should eventually outgrow the need for such structured procedures.

Melody 1C

Scale Degree Identification: Single Notes

Student text: Page 3.

First you will hear a C-major scale, followed by one of the pitches of that scale. Write the number (1 to 7) or syllable (do to ti) of the one pitch played.

1. Sing the scale (using numbers or syllables) until it is familiar to you.
2. If you have difficulty remembering the pitch of *all* scale degrees, be sure to remember at least 1 and 5 (do and sol). These two can be used as reference tones—landmarks that will help to locate other scale degrees.
3. When you hear the single pitch (after the scale is played), sing (or *think*) it immediately.
4. Then, relate it to one of the reference tones, tonic (first scale step) or dominant (fifth scale step)—whichever is closest, and sing stepwise to that reference tone.
5. You will know the identity of the pitch played by the number of scale steps you sang to get to the reference tone.
6. When you are sure of your answer, write it in the appropriate blank.

To the Instructor:

When this assignment is presented in class for the first time, permit students to sing out loud a short time because it is so helpful in scale degree orientation. Nevertheless, encouragement to switch to silent singing (thinking) should be persistent.

The first ten tones are within the scale played:

1.	2.	3.	4.	5.	6.	7.	8.	9.	10.
5	6	2	7	1	4	3	5	1	6
sol	la	re	ti	do	fa	mi	sol	do	la

These tones exceed the scale played:

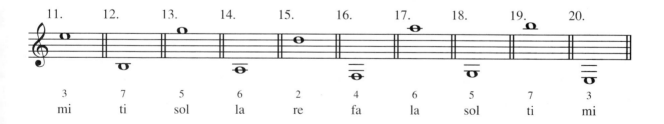

11.	12.	13.	14.	15.	16.	17.	18.	19.	20.
3	7	5	6	2	4	6	5	7	3
mi	ti	sol	la	re	fa	la	sol	ti	mi

Melody 1D

Intervals: m2, M2, m3, M3

Student text: Page 4.

Each exercise consists of a single interval.

1. You can use your knowledge of the major and harmonic minor scale in recognizing intervals. Think of the intervals in this section as pitches of a major or harmonic minor scale:

   minor 2nd (m2) = sounds like the **leading tone** to tonic (scale degrees 7 to 8 or ti to do) of a major scale

   Major 2nd (M2) = sounds like the tonic to **supertonic** (scale degrees 1 to 2 or do to re) in the major scale

   minor 3rd (m3) = sounds like the tonic to **mediant** (scale degrees 1 to 3 or la to do) in the minor scale

   Major 3rd (M3) = sounds like the tonic to mediant (scale degrees 1 to 3 or do to mi) in the major scale

2. When you have related the sound of an **interval** to pitches found in the major or harmonic minor scale, then you are ready to write the answer.
3. Write the missing note of the interval on the staff.
4. Write the name of the interval in the space provided.

To the Instructor:

Before beginning this section, carefully lead students through the steps listed above. If you have a system for identifying intervals that you find superior to the one printed here, by all means use it.

The lower note of the interval is given.

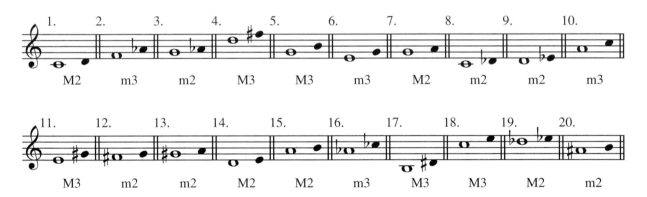

The upper note of the interval is given:

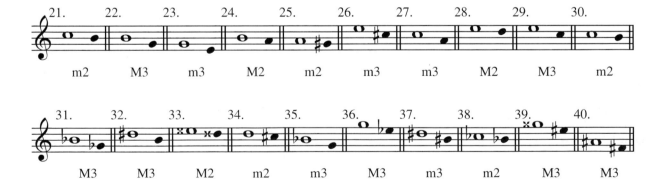

Melody 1E

Models and Embellishments: Short Melodic Structures

Student text: Page 5.

1. Before coming to class, play and sing the melodic structures in the models. Your instructor will review those structures at the beginning of this lesson.
2. Your instructor will play the given musical structure followed by embellishments of that structure. Notice how notes and rhythms are added to the melodic structure.
3. Memorize the sound of each melody and repeat its sound in your mind. Write the notes of the melody on the numbered staves provided below each model.
4. As you proceed through the lesson, the embellishments will be more elaborate. Keep the structure in mind as you listen to each embellished melody. Try to hear that structure "through" the embellishments.

To the Instructor:

1. Have the students sing one of the melodic structures in the first line of this section.
2. Proceeding down the page, have the students sing the model and an embellishment to discover the relationships between them before, after, and during their notation of the melody.
3. For these melodic embellishments, it may be useful to play the harmonies given with the left hand in order to provide a strong harmonic context for the melodies.
4. It may be helpful to discuss simple themes with variations in class to introduce the type of elaboration represented in "Models and Embellishments" exercises throughout this book.
5. The last melody is from the Messiah and may be familiar to the students. You may be able to find other melodies in music literature that are based on these models.

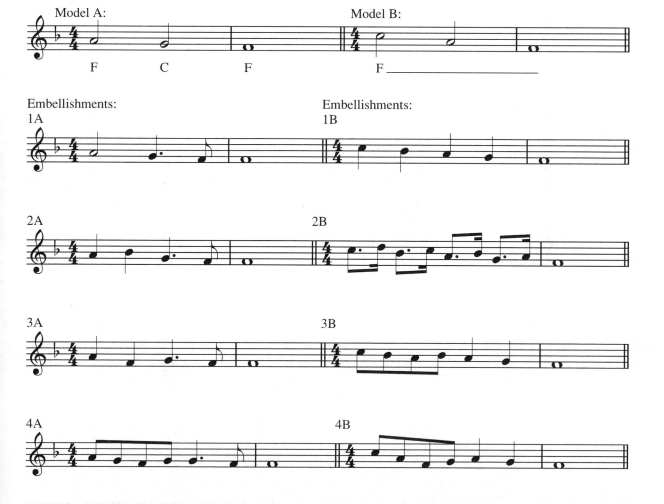

One additional example based on these models. See G.F. Handel: The Messiah, "And he shall purify."

Harmony 1A

Chord Function Identification: I and V Triads

Student text: Page 7.

1. Make sure you can hear the bass note of four-voice triads in root position. Outside of class, play the following triads and match the pitches of the bass notes by singing them in your own voice range.

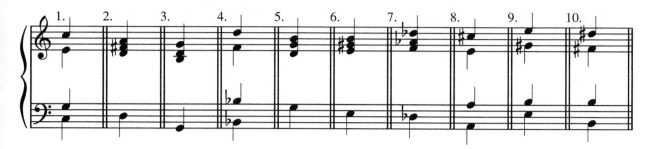

Practice singing the root of chords that you hear in your daily listening.

2. In this section, listen to the four triads in each of these exercises. In class, your instructor may wish to combine certain exercises to challenge you with longer chord progressions. All examples are in the key of C major. Be sure to keep the tonic pitch (C) well in mind.

3. In examples 1 through 15, all chords are in root position. It will help you to isolate and identify the scale degree (by number of syllables) of each bass note by singing it. These examples use the following chords:

4. Write the roman numeral analysis in the blanks for the chords played. In examples 1 through 15, the number or syllable used to identify the bass can be translated to a roman numeral as shown below:

Scale Number		Syllable		Roman Numeral
1	or	do	=	I
5	or	sol	=	V

To the Instructor:

1. Make sure the instructions are understood before students start this section.
2. Have the class sing a C-major scale.
3. Have the class sing along with the bassline for a few exercises.
4. Each line of exercises is written as a continuous chord progression. You are therefore not limited to exercises with only four chords. For example, you could tell the students, "I'll play from the first chord in example 7 through the third chord of example 8." Challenge your students to recognize longer progressions.
5. If difficulty is encountered, adjust the tempo or play the bass somewhat louder.

6. Students may find these exercises more interesting if you play the examples using a keyboard texture rather than only block chords. Here are some simple textures based on the first example.

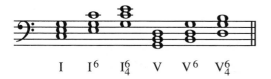

C: I V V I   V I V I   V I V V   I V I I   V I V I

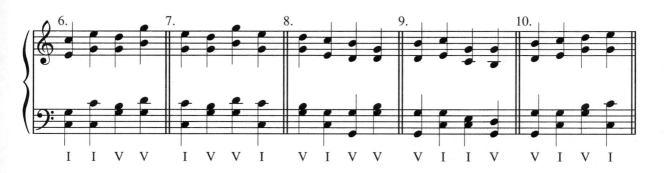

I I V V   I V V I   V I V V   V I I V   V I V I

11–20 (R)

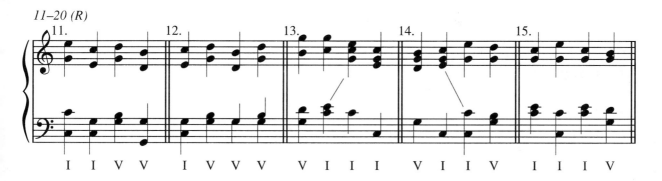

I I V V   I V V V   V I I I   V I I V   I I I V

Examples 16 through 25 contain chords in inversion. In inverted chords, the root of the chord is not the lowest note. The exercises in Harmony 1D will help you to identify inversions. Practice them with tapes or play chords in inversions on a keyboard instrument. The chords in these examples are chosen from the following harmonies:

$$I \quad I^6 \quad I^6_4 \quad V \quad V^6 \quad V^6_4$$

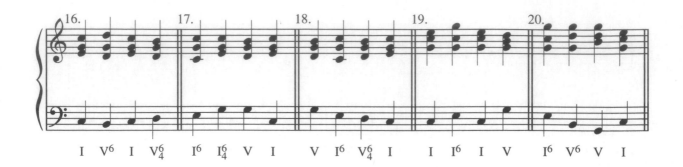

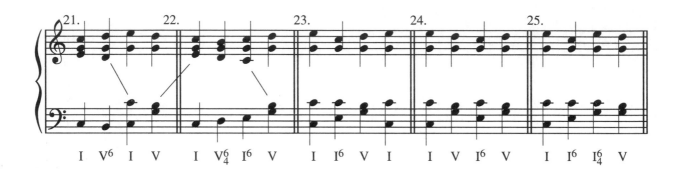

Harmony 1B

Chords in Music Literature: I and V Triads

Student text: Page8.

1. Each exercise consists of four examples from music literature which include a variety of harmonic rhythms and nonharmonic tones.
2. Below you see four models (A through D). Your instructor will play each of these four models. Listen carefully and try to distinguish each—one from another.

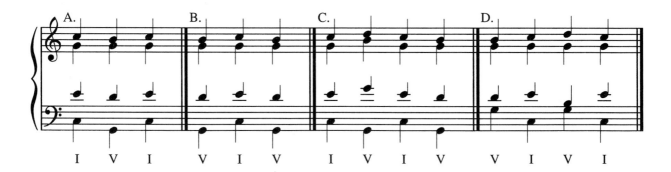

3. When the procedure described in No. 2 above, is completed, your instructor will play an example (1 through 4—be sure to announce the number) from music literature. The music literature example contains the same chords and the same inversions as one of the four models above.

---

1. Reichardt: Jägers Nachtlied

V   I   V

2. Schubert: Waltz No. 6, D. 145

I   V   I   V

3. Kuhnau: Biblical Sonata No. 1: Victory Dance and Festival

V   I   V   I

4. Mozart: Piano Sonata, K. 332, I

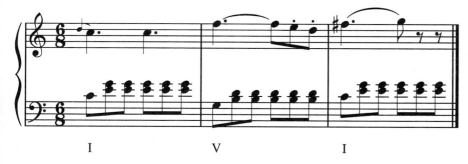

I   V   I

4. Your instructor will tell you how many times he or she will play the music literature example. When you have matched the literature example with one of the four sets of chords (A through D), place the letter in the appropriate blank below, and prepare for the next example from music literature.

5. There are four examples from music literature. Enter the correct letter (**A through D**) as the instructor plays each:

1. _____   2. _____   3. _____   4. _____

6. When the first four examples are completed, use the same procedure for models 5 through 8.
These (E, F, G, H) are the remaining four models. Pair them up with the examples from literature (5, 6, 7, 8).

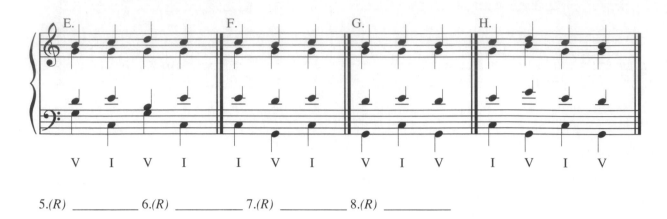

5.(R) _____ 6.(R) _____ 7.(R) _____ 8.(R) _____

5. Haydn: Piano Sonata, Hob. XVI/7, II

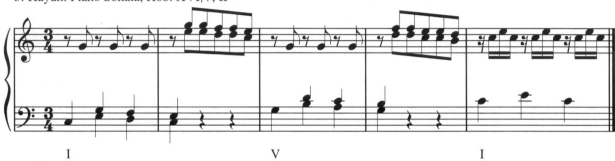

6. Haydn: Piano Sonata, Hob. XVI/9, III

7. Haydn: Sonata, Hob. XVI/9, II

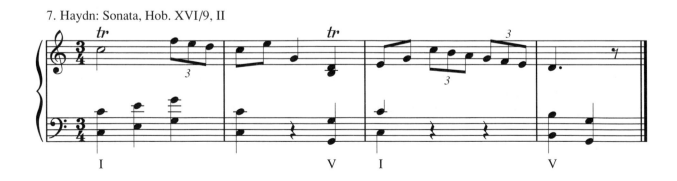

8. Haydn: Piano Sonata, Hob. XVI/G1, I

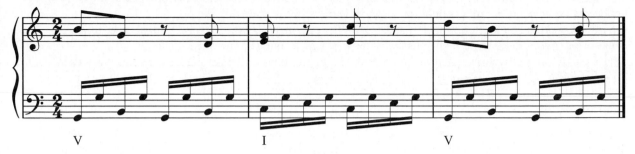

V   I   V

To the Instructor:

Adjust the number of playings for each example to suit the ability of your class. Students with years of experience may be able to match examples after two or three playings, while a less experienced class may require many repetitions. Remember that students learn absolutely nothing until they can identify correct answers.

At the beginning of this drill, point out the similarities in the models (four-voice chords). How many of A through D end with the tonic chord? Or, how many begin with the tonic? Let students themselves discover the resemblances and correlations, and do not move on to the playing of the music literature examples until the study of the examples is complete.

In the classroom, announce answers and spend whatever time is needed to determine why each error occurred—why did student no. 7 choose **C** when the correct answer is **B?**

As a preview to these ear-training exercises, you may wish to analyze one or more of these examples with the students in a music theory lecture. This can help establish a strong relationship between music analysis and ear training.

The difficulty level of this unit may be altered by the instructor (to suit local situations). To make this unit easier in classroom situations, you might continue playing the models (at the request of students) after you have begun to play excerpts from literature.

To make this unit more difficult, do not play the models (four-voice chord examples) at all, but ask students to write down the analysis of each example from literature as soon as you have played it.

Incidentally, for those who wish to acquaint their students with harmonic rhythm, these excerpts from literature provide an excellent source of examples. Diagram the rhythm of the example on the blackboard, and ask students to determine where the harmony changes.

Harmony 1C

Harmonic Rhythm

Student text: Page 9.

Each exercise consists of a short excerpt of music.

1. In this section you will apply your listening experiences to a composition from the literature of music. The strategy is simple to explain but often difficult to put into practice—place an "X" at each point in the music when you hear most (or any) chord factors change enough to form a different harmony.
2. In the first five examples you can follow the melody and note possible changes simply by assessing the melodic pitches.

3. The remaining five excerpts require concentration on the quality and make-up of each harmony.
4. This is your first opportunity to listen especially for harmonic rhythm, do not be discouraged if you make a few mistakes. Review each error carefully, and try to determine what confused you.
5. If you are working outside of class, and make a number of errors, play the exercise several times *after* answering. Assessing the cause of a mistake is the best way to avoid similar errors later on.
6. Place an "X" at each point in the melody where the harmony changes. The examples indicates the correct procedure.

To the Instructor:

This is intended as an exploratory section to encourage students to become more aware of harmonic schemes and relationships in music literature. The application of ear-training skills to practical problems helps to assess the present level of improvement and lets students try out their new-found competence. Instructors may wish to present this section simply as a learning experience for class members—a shared time for discussing common errors and techniques for improvement. Numbers 1 and 4 contain root-position triads only and may be desirable as an introduction to the remainder of the section.

Example:

Beethoven: *Ecossaise* in E Flat

1. Chopin: Mazurka, op. 33, no. 2

2. Schumann: Album for the Young, op. 68

Schalkhaft ♩ = 96

p   *giocoso*

cresc.   *f*

3. Mozart: Piano Sonata, K. 284

Tema

p

p

4. Chopin: Mazurka, op. 17, no. 1

Vivo risoluto ♩ = 160

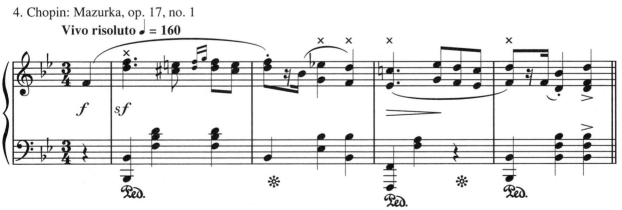

f   *sf*

Ped.   ✱   Ped.   ✱   Ped.

5. Mozart: Piano Sonata, K. 284

7. In the following exercises, the melody is replaced by melodic rhythm only. Circle the numbers that represent chord changes. If a chord change occurs at another point, place the circle between the numbers.

6. Beethoven: Violin Sonata, op. 12, no. 3

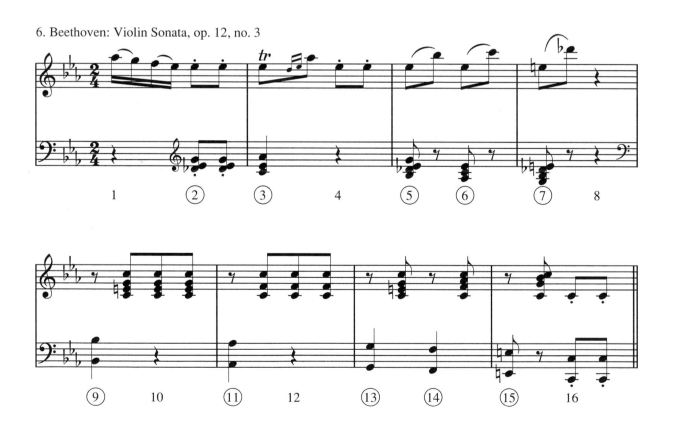

7. Schumann: Album for the Young, op. 68

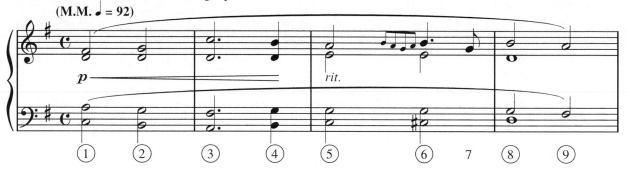

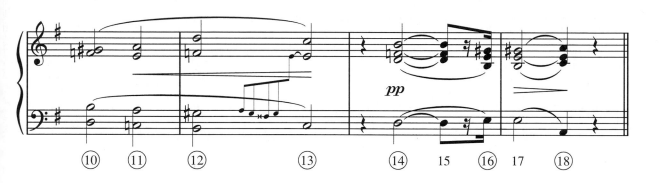

8. Schumann: Album for the Young, op. 68

9. Mozart: Piano Sonata, K. 309

Allegretto grazioso

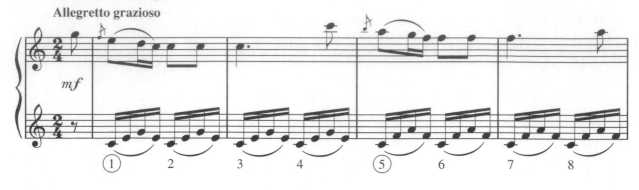

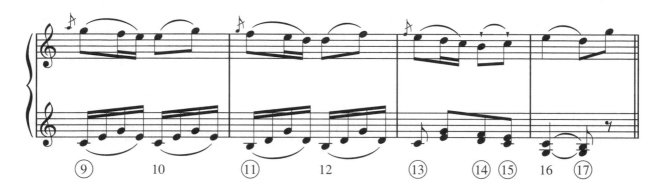

10. Chopin: Mazurka (posthumous)

Harmony 1D

Triad Position Identification: Major and Minor Triads

Student text: Page 11.

Each exercise consists of the three positions of the same triad in any order. Before you begin your instructor will acquaint you with the 1–3–5–3–1 pattern, which is an essential aid in identifying the triad in root position.

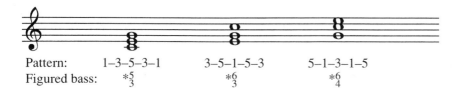

| Pattern: | 1–3–5–3–1 | 3–5–1–5–3 | 5–1–3–1–5 |
| Figured bass: | *$^5_3$ | *$^6_3$ | *$^6_4$ |

* Indicates intervals above the lowest sounding tone.

1. Listen until all three positions have been played. Locate the one in root position by relating it to the 1–3–5–3–1 pattern. Remember that 1–3–5–3–1 means that the 3rd and 5th are above the **root**—thus, **root position.**
2. When you have located the root position version write $\frac{5}{3}$ in the appropriate blank (1, 2, or 3).
3. Now that you have identified the root, 3rd, and 5th, listen a second time and sing (better yet, *think*) the 3rd of the triad. When the 3rd you are singing coincides with the lowest-sounding tone of an example, that example is in *first* inversion. Write $\frac{6}{3}$ below it.
4. Repeat the process as described in number 3, above, but this time sing the 5th of the triad. When the 5th you are singing coincides with the lowest-sounding tone of an example, that example is in *second* inversion. Write $\frac{6}{4}$ below it.
5. As you become more experienced you will discover that you can determine each position simply by listening to it as a unit—your elaborate mental calculations become automatic!

To the Instructor:

This is the first assignment introducing the triad positions. If you prefer a method other than the one presented above to students, by all means apply it. In the initial presentation, play the examples slowly, giving class members plenty of time to make mental calculations. If students have difficulty, direct them through the entire process several times—until the procedure is quite clear. You may wish to introduce this section before encountering numbers 16–25 of Harmony 1A.

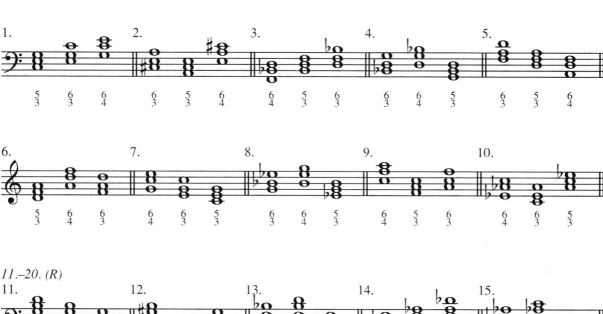

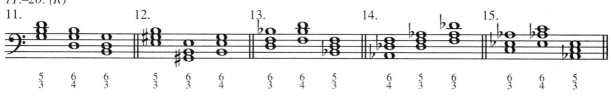

11.–20. (R)

Harmony 1E

Chord Quality Identification: Major and Minor Triads

Student text: Page 12.

Each exercise consists of a single triad. Recognize the quality of these major and minor triads.

1. For numbers 1–20 (triads in a simple position):
   1. Write large M for major or small m for minor in the blanks provided.
   2. If your instructor requests it, also write the triad on the staff. The roots of the triads are given.
2. For numbers 21–40 (triads in four voices—a few inversions)
   1. Circle either large M or small m indicating the sound of the triad played.
   2. Your instructor may ask you to spell the triad orally in class.

To the Instructor:

Play each triad two or three times and arpeggiate them only if students have considerable difficulty. As an added drill for spelling, a staff with the triad roots is provided for numbers 1–20. This is optional and will consume more class time, but will afford valuable practice in placing the triads on the staff.

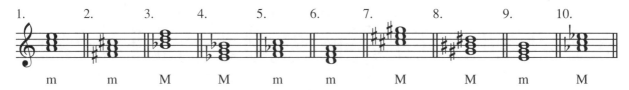

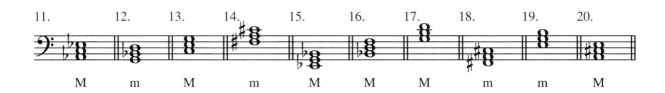

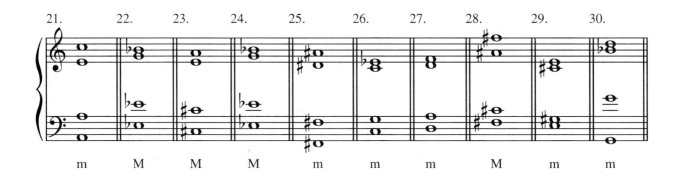

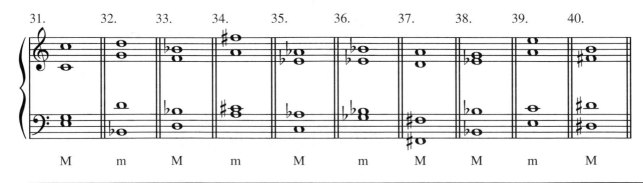

Harmony 1F

Triad Factors in the Soprano

Student text: Page 13.

Each exercise consists of a single chord. Write the number of the chord factor (1, 3, or 5) in the soprano voice.

1. First, you will hear a triad in simple (closest possible) position. Sing it—1–3–5–3–1.
2. Then, the same triad will be played in four-part harmony. Remember that the root will be the bass note, but aside from that the chord tones in the tenor, alto, or soprano voices may be in any order.
3. After the four-voice triad is played, the soprano note will be repeated alone. Sing or *think* it immediately! Keep its pitch in your mind.
4. Recollect the sound of the simple triad first heard (number 1, above) and determine whether the soprano pitch is the root, 3rd, or 5th.
5. When you are convinced, write 1, 3, or 5 in the blank provided.

To the Instructor:

Help class members get accustomed to the various suggested steps above before the section is assigned. If needed, demonstrate with a few triads.

1. Play the triad in simple position. Ask class members to sing the triad.
2. Then, play the chord in four-part harmony.
3. Finally, play the soprano tone separately and ask class members to sing it.
4. If students still have difficulty identifying the soprano factor, ask them to sing the factor and then on down to the root (in simple position)—5–3–1 if the soprano factor is 5, and 3–1 if the soprano factor is 3, and 1–1 if the soprano is the root of the triad.

Rhythm 1A

Rhythmic Dictation: Rhythm Including Half-Beat Values

Student text: Page 13.

Each exercise consists of a two-measure melody. Complete the **rhythm** (only) of each exercise on the lines provided below.

1. As you hear the preparatory measure(s), count the meter. If the meter is 4/4, count 1–2–3–4.
2. After the first hearing: Say or clap the rhythm immediately.
3. After the second hearing: Say meter beats and clap rhythm immediately. If you are sure of the rhythm by now, write it on the appropriate line.
4. If a third hearing is needed, use it to verify rhythms you have written down or to clear up any misconceptions.

Listen to the rhythm as many times as needed to get the right answer! Do it in three hearings if you can, though accuracy is the most important item for the moment.

To the Instructor:

Help students with the above steps at the time this section is assigned. In extreme cases, playing the melodies slower, tapping the meter during dictation, or drastically emphasizing the accented meter beats often helps. When class members feel more secure, these temporary concessions may gradually be removed.

Transcription 1

Single Melodic Lines and Melodies in Octaves

Much can be learned by transcribing recorded performances into musical notation. Because transcription requires the listener to specify entire compositions on paper, he or she develops a strong bond between written notation and the sounds it represents. During this process, you can develop your own strategies for listening, recognizing, and notating these recorded performances. To get you started, here are some general techniques:

1. Listen to each musical example several times before you start writing its notation.
2. Conduct along with each selection, establishing the meter and rhythmic relationships in your mind.
3. Sing or play along with the musical compositions. Internalize the sound of each composition.
4. If helpful, use a keyboard or other instrument as you listen to the tape.
5. If necessary, write each selection by dividing it into small sections, double checking your work on each section as you proceed. Try to work with increasingly longer sections and learn how the form of the composition (e.g., the return of principal themes) can help you transcribe it.
6. Certain musical events in each composition are provided for you in the worksheets. Use these musical "guideposts" to aid you in the transcription process.

To the Instructor:

Each musician takes a slightly different approach to listening and musical skills development. Students tend to learn about music in three principal ways. Their approach to transcription (and ear training in general) will be based on their orientation to music making and listening.

1. Some musicians possess a strong relationship between musical sound and specific motions used to play their instrument. In such cases it can be helpful for them to play along with the tape on their instrument or on a small keyboard to give themselves the "feel" of the music. Musical notation can be derived from that kinesthetic "analysis" of the music.
2. Other musicians have a strong aural and intuitive sense about music, recognizing general relationships between parts of a composition as *sonic* events. Such students may wish to write down the contour of melodic lines, indicating the rhythmic position of striking musical events. They can make up their own preliminary notation for these sonic events, notating the piece in a general way before trying to write down each detail.
3. "Visual" learners tend to approach music by studying the notation first and then translating it to sound. Without a strong relationship between sound and notation these students may be hesitant to transcribe an unfamiliar set of sounds. Along with the exercises on the tape, these students should study other musical scores while listening to a recording of the work. This will help reinforce the sound of the graphic image of the score.

Note: * = given material

Recorded Example 1

Recorded Example 2
Traditional Austrian: Posthorn–Signal

Recorded Example 3

W.A. Mozart: *Eine kleine Nachtmusik*

Unit 2

Melody 2A

Melodic Dictation: Melodies Using m2, M2, m3, M3

Student text: Page 17.

Each exercise consists of a short melody.

1. **Create an aural image of the melody.**
   After hearing each melody, immediately try to sing it in its entirety in your mind.
2. **Establish an understanding of the melody's structure.**
   After you can hear the melody in your mind, analyze the melody with solfeggio syllables or numbers.
3. Do not notate the melody until you have completed these two steps.
4. **Notate each melody on the appropriate staff below.**
   The first notes are given for the melodies in this section.

To the Instructor:

In addition to taking the students through each step (above), try the following exercise:

1. Before you play each melody, ask the students to sing the scale on which that melody is based.
2. Write the pitches of the scale on the board. Point to pitches in that scale at random and have class members sing them. Also point to groups of notes that are found in each exercise so that students learn to recognize common melodic conventions.

Melody 2B

Mode Identification: Major and Three Forms of the Minor Scale

Student text: Page 18.

For each exercise write the type of scale you hear.

Exercises 1–10   consist of a major, natural minor, harmonic minor, or melodic minor scale

Exercises 11–20   consist of short melodic excerpts from music literature based on one of these scales.

Natural minor   follows the key signature.

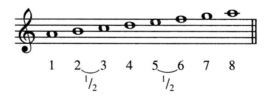

Harmonic minor   key signature plus raised 7th scale degree.

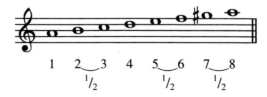

Ascending melodic minor   key signature plus raised 6th and 7th scale degrees.

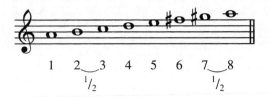

1   2   3   4   5   6   7   8
     ¹/₂   ¹/₂

Major   follows the key signature.

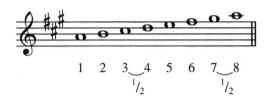

1   2   3   4   5   6   7   8
         ¹/₂   ¹/₂

To the Instructor:

Play each scale two or three times at a moderate tempo: $\circ$ = 72.

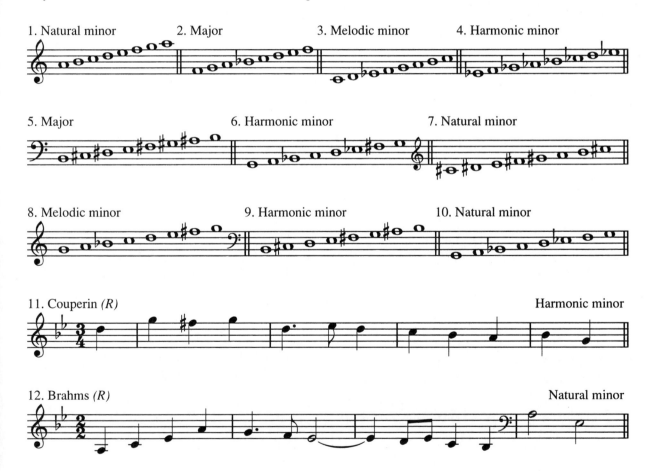

1. Natural minor   2. Major   3. Melodic minor   4. Harmonic minor

5. Major   6. Harmonic minor   7. Natural minor

8. Melodic minor   9. Harmonic minor   10. Natural minor

11. Couperin (R)   Harmonic minor

12. Brahms (R)   Natural minor

Play each melody two or three times at a moderate tempo.

Melody 2C

Scale Degree Identification: Two Notes

Student text: Page 19.

1. The instructor first plays a scale, then two tones of that scale.
2. Identify the two scale degrees played. The instructor will tell you whether to use scale numbers or syllables.
3. For additional help, review Melody 1C.

To the Instructor:

See the information provided in Melody 1C.

The instructor plays this scale.

These tones are in ascending order:

These tones are in descending order:

Melody 2D

New Intervals: P5 and P4

Student text: Page 20.

Intervals studied to date: m2, M2, m3, M3

Each exercise consists of a single interval. The first note is given.

1. Write the second note of the interval on the staff.
2. Place the name of the interval (P4, m2, M3, and so on) in the blank provided.
3. To help you recognize intervals, think of them as parts of a scale:

    P5 =   tonic to 5th scale degree of a major or minor scale
    P4 =   tonic to 4th scale degree of a major or minor scale
    M3 =   tonic to 3rd scale degree of a major scale
    m3 =   tonic to 3rd scale degree of a minor scale
    M2 =   tonic to 2nd scale degree of a major or minor scale
    m2 =   leading tone to tonic of a major or harmonic minor scale

Ask class members to sing the interval immediately after it is played. One particularly effective way to present intervals is to ask students to sing the scale degrees encompassed by an interval. Begin with the tonic note of a scale and sing each scale step up to the second tone of the interval. In the case of the minor 2nd, students will immediately note that beginning on the tonic will not prove successful. Students should listen for these leading tone relationships and sing "7–8" or "ti–do." If the interval happens to be a minor 3rd (not the 3rd scale degree of a major scale), students will usually discover that fact and quickly change to a minor scale.

Melody 2E

Models and Embellishments: Descending Thirds in Two Voices

Student text: Page 20.

1. Notice that the model in this section is a group of descending thirds. This model and its embellishments occur very often in Baroque period music. Listen for these in recordings and concerts. Before coming to class play and sing both parts of the model. Your instructor may choose to review this structure in class.
2. Your instructor will play the structure followed by embellishments of that structure. Notice how the thirds are embellished with additional notes and rhythms in each voice.
3. Memorize the sound of each embellishment and repeat its sound in your mind. Write the model's embellishments on the numbered staves provided.
4. As you proceed through this section, the embellishments will be more elaborate. Keep the structure in mind as you listen to each example. Try to hear that structure "through" the embellishments.

To the Instructor:

1. Have the students sing each voice of the model before the early examples.

2. Play the structure and embellishments in the order printed, or repeat the structure from time to time to remind students of the basis for each embellishment.
3. You may be able to find other embellishments of this two-voice model in music literature. Encourage students to listen for such embellishment while listening and performing music by discussing such examples in class.

Model:

Embellishments:
1.

2.

3.

4.

5.

6.

7.

Harmony 2A

Student text: Page 22.

Chord Function Identification: I, IV, and V Triads

1. Make sure you can hear the bass note of four-voice triads in root position. Outside of class, play the following triads and match the pitches of the bass notes by singing them in your own voice range.

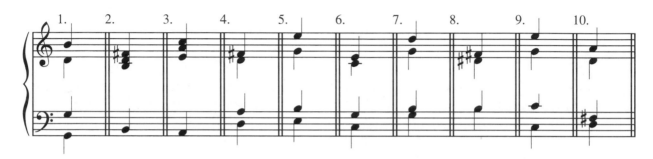

Practice singing the root of chords that you hear in your daily listening.

2. In this section, listen to the four triads in each of these exercises. In class, your instructor may wish to combine certain exercises to challenge you with longer chord progressions. All examples are in the key of A major. Be sure to keep the tonic pitch (A) well in mind.

3. In examples 1 through 15, all chords are in root position. It will help you to isolate and identify the scale degree (by number or syllables) of each bass note by singing it. These examples use the following chords:

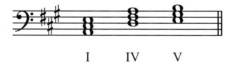

4. Write the roman numeral analysis in the blanks for the chords played. In examples 1 through 15 the number or syllable used to identify the bass can be translated to a roman numeral as shown below:

Scales Number		Syllable		Roman Numeral
1	or	do	=	I
4	or	fa	=	IV
5	or	sol	=	V

To the Instructor:

1. Make sure the instructions are understood before students start this section.
2. Have the class sing an A-major scale.
3. Have the class sing along with the bass for a few exercises.

---

4. Each line of exercises is written as a continuous chord progression. You are, therefore, not limited to exercises with only four chords. For example, you could tell the students, "I'll play from the first chord in Example 7 through the third chord of Example 8." Challenge your students to recognize longer progressions.
5. If difficulty is encountered, adjust the tempo or play the bass somewhat louder.
6. Students may find these exercises more interesting if you play the examples using a keyboard texture rather than only block chords. See Harmony Unit 1A for examples.

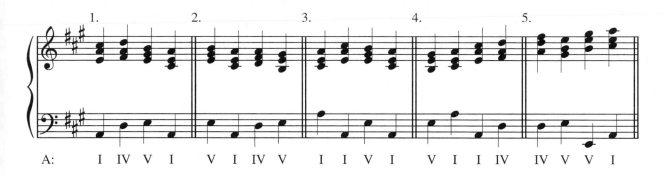

A: I IV V I   V I IV V   I I V I   V I I IV   IV V V I

I V I I   IV I I V   I I IV V   I IV V I   IV I V I

11. – 20. (R)

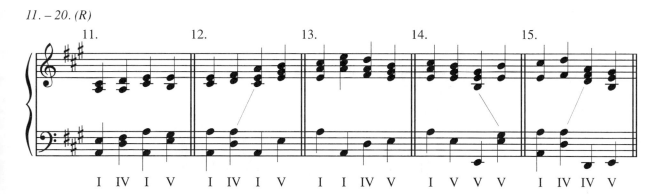

I IV I V   I IV I V   I I IV V   I V V V   I IV IV V

Examples 16 through 25 contain chords in inversion. In inverted chords, the root of the chord is not the lowest note. The exercises in Harmony 1D will help you to identify inversions. Practice them with tapes or play chords in inversions on a keyboard instrument. The chords in these examples are chosen from the following harmonies:

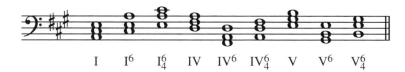

I I^6 I^6_4 IV IV^6 IV^6_4 V V^6 V^6_4

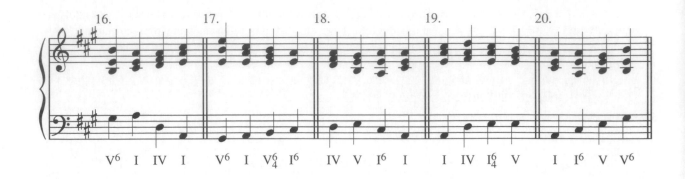

V⁶ I IV I V⁶ I V⁶₄ I⁶ IV V I⁶ I I IV I⁶₄ V I I⁶ V V⁶

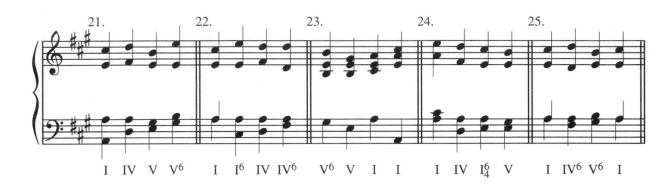

I IV V V⁶ I I⁶ IV IV⁶ V⁶ V I I I IV I⁶₄ V I IV⁶ V⁶ I

Harmony 2B

Chords in Music Literature: I, IV, and V Triads

Student text: Page 23.

1. Each exercise consists of four examples from music literature which includes a variety of harmonic rhythms and nonharmonic tones.
2. Below you see four models (A through D). Your instructor will play each of these four models. Listen carefully and try to distinguish each—one from another.

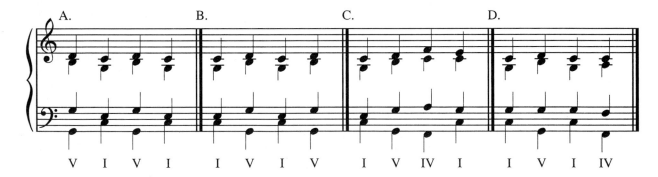

V I V I I V I V I V IV I I V I IV

3. Your instructor will play an example (1 through 4—be sure to announce the number) from music literature. The music literature example contains the same chords and same inversion as one of the four models.

1. Irish Jubilee

2. The Dark British Foes

3. Kitty Wells

4. Jordan's River I'm Bound to Cross

4. When you have matched the literature example with one of the four sets of chords (A through D), place the letter in the appropriate blank below.

   1. _____ 2. _____ 3. _____ 4. _____

5. When the first four examples are completed, use the same procedure for models 5 through 8.

These (**E, F, G, H**) are the four models. Pair them up with the examples from literature (**5, 6, 7, 8**).

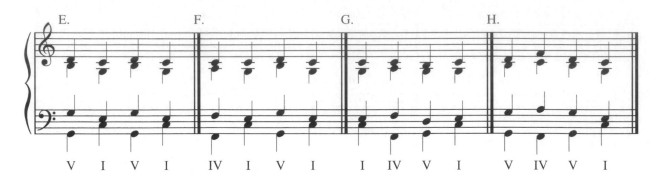

E.   F.   G.   H.

V   I   V   I   IV   I   V   I   I   IV   V   I   V   IV   V   I

5. (R) _____ 6. (R) _____ 7. (R) _____ 8. (R) _____

5. Jim Blake

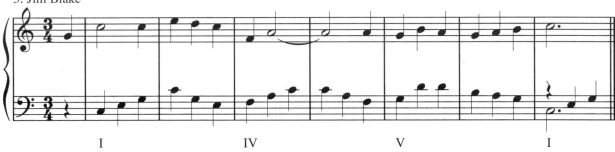

I   IV   V   I

6. Young Charlotte

IV   I   V   I

7. I Never Will Marry

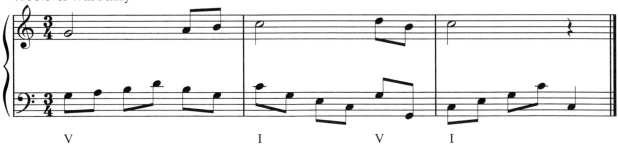

V   I   V   I

8. Oh Yah, Ain't Dat Been Fine

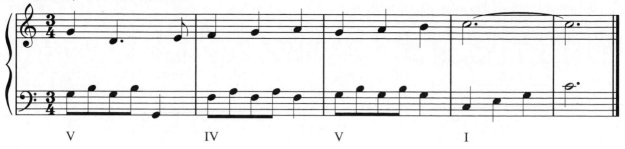

V   IV   V   I

To the Instructor:

A complete discussion of this type of exercise and suggestions for classroom use are provided in the "To the Instructor" section of Harmony 1B.

Harmony 2C

Nonharmonic Tones: Introduction

Student text: Page 24.

Each exercise consists of a nonharmonic tone in a two-voice setting. Write the name of the nonharmonic tone in the appropriate blank.

1. Nonharmonic tones played in this section are:

   Unaccented passing tone   **Accented passing tone**
   Unaccented neighboring tone   **Accented neighboring tone**
   Escape tone   **Suspension** (9–8, 7–6, 4–3, 2–3)
   Anticipation

2. Definitions of the nonharmonic tones played in this section are available in the Glossary (or consult your theory text).
3. A sound pattern is a three-note series of pitches, with the nonharmonic tone in the middle. The *sound pattern* of each nonharmonic tone is especially helpful in ear training.
4. Some items that are common to all of the above listed nonharmonic tones:
   a. The nonharmonic tone is always *dissonant* (9th, 7th, 4th, 2nd).
   b. The nonharmonic tone is always the *middle* note of the pattern.
   c. The two notes on either side are always *consonant*.
5. One nonharmonic tone can be distinguished from another by the pattern of movement—by (S)tep, by (L)eap, or by (R)epeated pitch. The pattern of movement helps to distinguish among all of the above listed nonharmonic tones except the passing tone and the neighboring tone.
6. Passing tones and neighboring tones can be distinguished only by the direction of the movement

   passing tone   =   down-down or up-up
   neighboring tone   =   up-down or down-up

7. The following example illustrates nonharmonic tones in a one-voice setting. Note that in all instances (1) the nonharmonic tone is dissonant, (2) the nonharmonic tone is the middle note, and (3) the first and third notes are consonant.

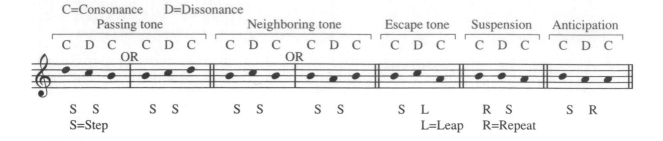

8. Practice playing these patterns until you know them thoroughly.
9. Before playing the two-voice illustrations, your instructor will play randomly some of the one-voice examples to help acquaint you with the distinguishing characteristics of each nonharmonic tone type.

Examples of the nonharmonic tones:

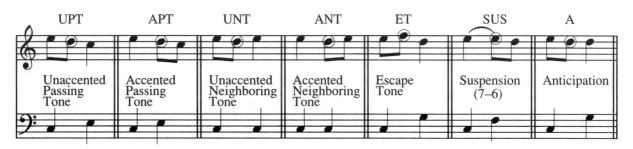

Circle the correct nonharmonic tone abbreviation:

To the Instructor:

When this section is assigned, go over the above steps one by one, and play (randomly) some of the one-voice nonharmonic patterns to illustrate the sound pattern of the three notes. When that is thoroughly digested, play some of the two-voice examples to show the added dimension of dissonance.

Nonharmonic tones are in the upper voice in numbers 1–10.

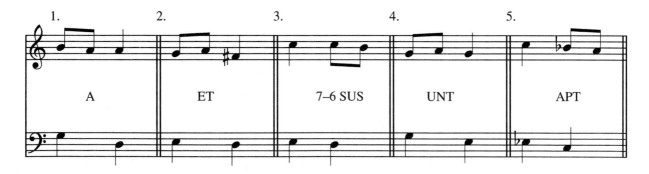

Nonharmonic tones are in the lower voice in numbers 11–20.

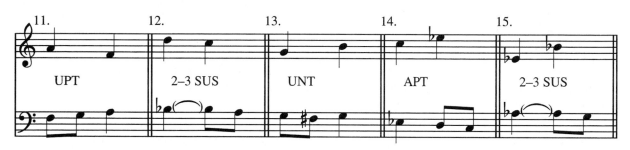

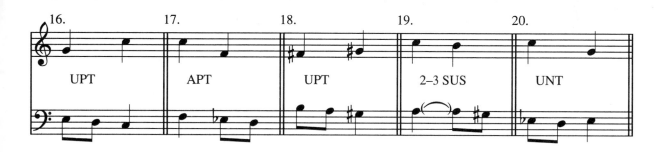

Nonharmonic tones may be in either the upper or lower voice in numbers 21–30.

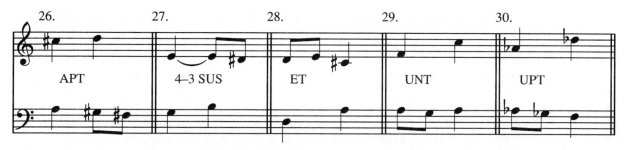

Harmony 2D

Triad Position Identification: Major and Minor Triads

Student text: Page 26.

Each exercise is a single triad in four-part harmony. Indicate the triad position. Your answers should be:

root position = $\frac{5}{3}$

first inversion = $\frac{6}{3}$

second inversion = $\frac{6}{4}$

The techniques in Harmony 1D will help you.

To the Instructor:

The step-by-step strategy in Harmony 1D is quite helpful here and should be rehearsed a few times before students are assigned this section. The goal is to abandon all listening "crutches" and recognize each triad position as a unified whole, a gestalt, a single sound functioning as an entity in itself.

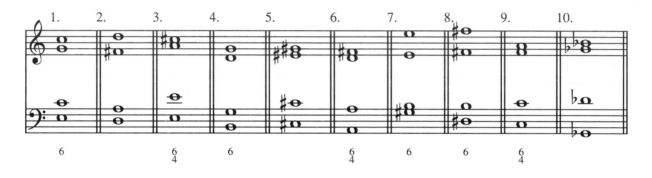

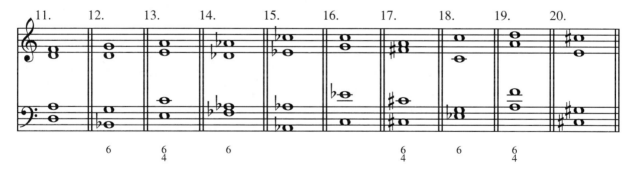

Harmony 2E

Chord Quality Identification: Major, Minor, and Diminished Triads

Student text: Page 26.

Each exercise consists of a single triad. Recognize the quality of each major, minor, or diminished triad.

1. For numbers 1–10 (triads in simple position):
    a. Write large M for major, small m for minor, and small d for diminished triads in the blanks provided.
    b. If your instructor requests it, also write the triad on the staff. The *roots* of the triads are given.

---

2. For numbers 11–30 (triads in four voices—a few inversions):
    a. Write large M, small m, or small d in the blanks provided.
    b. Your instructor may ask you to spell the triad orally in class.

To the Instructor:

Play each triad two or three times and arpeggiate them only if students have considerable difficulty. Shortcuts are often counterproductive. Students need to accept the fact that these triads must be identified by the interacting sound of the tones as a group. For added drill in spelling, a staff with the triad roots is provided for numbers 1–10. This is optional and will consume more class time, but will afford valuable practice in placing the triads on the staff.

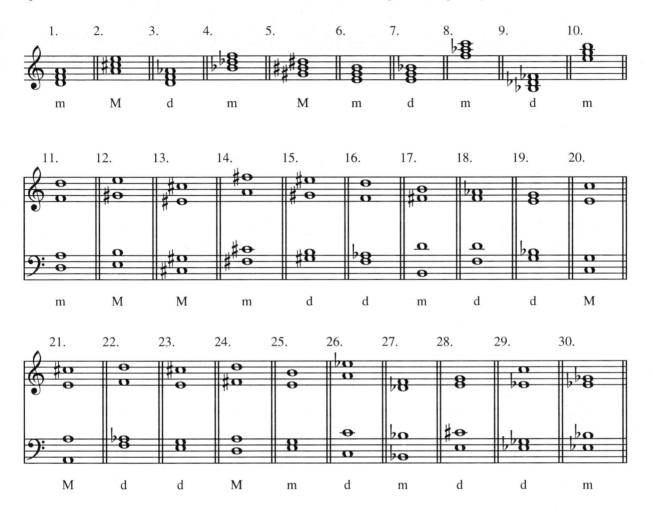

Harmony 2F

Triad Factors in the Soprano and Bass

Student text: Page 27.

Each exercise consists of a single triad played in four-part harmony.

1. Indicate the chord factor (1–3–5) in the soprano voice.
2. Indicate the chord factor (1–3–5) in the bass voice.

For the first few exercises, ask class members to sing each triad in root position, then the soprano tone, and finally the bass tone. Play each chord two or three times emphasizing first the soprano and then the bass tone.

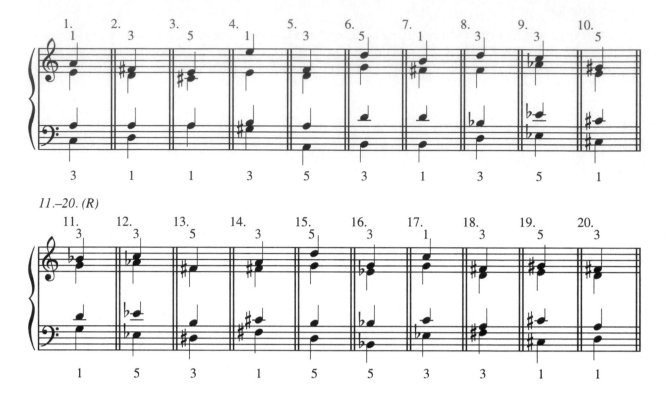

Rhythm 2A

Rhythmic Dictation: Duple and Triple Subdivisions of the Beat

Student text: Page 27.

Each exercise consists of a three-measure melody. Complete the rhythm (only) of each exercise on the lines provided.

1. As you hear the preparatory measure(s), count the meter. If the meter is 3/4, count 1–2–3.
2. After the first hearing: Say or clap the rhythm immediately.
3. After the second hearing: Count the meter beats and clap rhythm immediately. When you are sure of the rhythm, write it on the appropriate line.
4. If a third hearing is needed: Use it to verify rhythms you have written down or to clear up any misconceptions.

Listen to the rhythm as many times as you require to get the right answer. Accuracy is the most important item for the moment.

The following example indicates the correct procedure.

To the Instructor:

Help students with the above steps at the time this section is assigned. If necessary, play the melodies more slowly, tap the meter during dictation, or overemphasize the accented meter beats. Once class members feel more secure, these temporary concessions may gradually be removed.

Transcription 2

Two-Voice Examples

Refer to instructions found in Transcription 1 (page 25).

Note: * = given material

4. W. Byrd: "The Carman's Whistle"

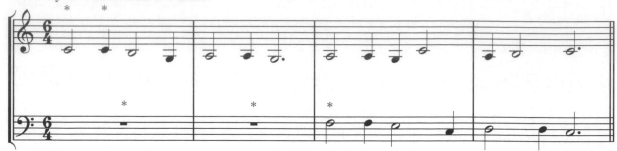

Recorded Example 5

5. Traditional Austrian: "Fanfare"

Unit 3

Melody 3A

Melodic Dictation: Melodies Using m2, M2, m3, M3, P4, P5

Student text: Page 31.

Each exercise consists of a short melody that begins on the tonic pitch.

1. **Create an aural image of the melody.**
   After hearing each melody, immediately try to sing it in its entirety in your mind.
2. **Establish an understanding of the melody's structure.**
   After you can hear the melody in your mind, analyze the melody with solfeggio syllables or numbers.
3. Do not notate the melody until you have completed these two steps.
4. **Notate each melody on the appropriate staff below.**
   The first notes are given for the melodies in this section.

To the Instructor:

It is critical that students memorize and sing, or better yet *think,* each melody with the correct solfeggio syllables or numbers. Hurdling the leap from singing to thinking (aural imagery) is often difficult and may require considerable amounts of class time. Nevertheless, singing the melodies out loud is indeed the first step toward aural imagery, and until that step is achieved, no further progress can be expected.

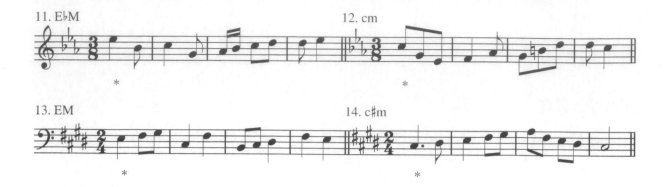

11. E♭M   12. cm

13. EM   14. c♯m

* Note or rest in workbook

(R) means recorded

Melody 3B

Error Detection: Scalewise Melodies with Errors

Student text: Page 32.

Each exercise consists of a short **melody** that your instructor will play. Each melody as played contains two pitch errors—pitches with letter names different from those printed in your workbook.

1.   Before listening to each melody, sing the printed melody over in your mind—or out loud if you are working outside of class.
2.   Each melody as played contains two pitch errors—pitches that have letter names different from those printed.
3.   The first pitch of each melody is correct, so you will always have a point of reference.
4.   As you listen to the melody played, concentrate on your original version as you sang it.
5.   When you hear a melody pitch that surprises you, circle the number above it.
6.   Check you answers while you hear the melody again.

To the Instructor:

Play each melody at a moderate tempo. As this section is assigned, make sure class members understand the procedures listed above. If students have unusual difficulty, play the melodies more slowly. In extreme cases play the versions in both the student's and this instructor's manual to permit easier comparison.

Errors are circled for your convenience:

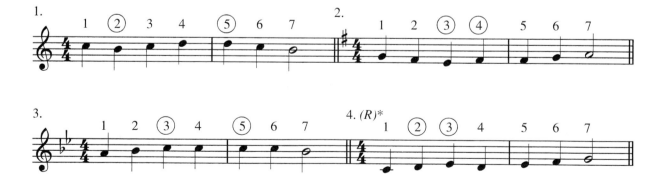

(R) means recorded.

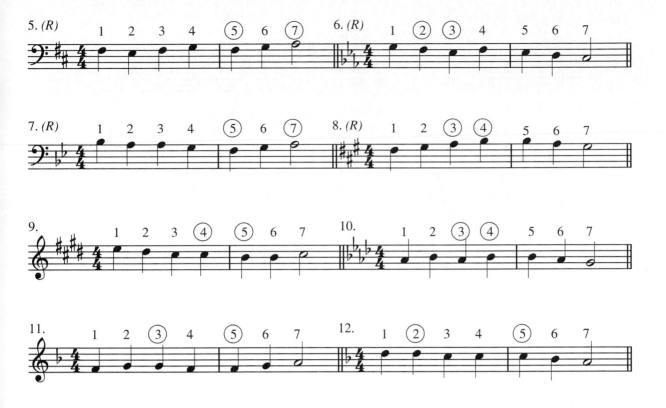

Melody 3C

Scale Degree Identification: Three Notes

Student text: Page 33.

1. The instructor first plays a scale, then three tones of that scale.
2. Identify the three scale degrees played. The instructor will tell you whether to use scale numbers or syllables.
3. The instructor plays this scale:

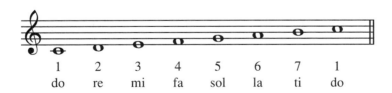

1	2	3	4	5	6	7	1
do	re	mi	fa	sol	la	ti	do

To the instructor:

See the information provided in Melody 1C.

These tones are in ascending order:

1.	2.	3.	4.	5.	6.	7.	8.
3 4 6	2 4 5	4 6 1	1 5 6	5 6 1	2 5 7	4 5 7	3 5 1
mi fa la	re fa sol	fa la do	do sol la	sol la do	re sol ti	fa sol ti	mi sol do

9.	10.	11.	12.	13.	14.	15.	16.
1 4 6	6 7 1	2 3 7	3 5 6	1 6 7	4 5 7	3 6 7	2 6 1
do fa la	la ti do	re mi ti	mi sol la	do la ti	fa sol ti	mi la ti	re la do

These tones are in mixed ascending and descending order:

17.	18.	19.	20.	21.	22.	23.	24.
6 5 3	4 2 5	3 7 2	6 5 1	5 7 1	7 6 2	1 6 5	5 2 6
la sol mi	fa re sol	mi ti re	la sol do	sol ti do	ti la re	do la sol	sol re la

25.	26.	27.	28.	29.	30.	31.	32.
2 7 3	6 4 7	1 6 4	5 1 4	2 1 7	3 2 6	4 1 7	2 7 3
re ti mi	la fa ti	do la fa	sol do fa	re do ti	mi re la	fa do ti	re ti mi

Melody 3D

Interval Review: m2, M2, m3, M3, P4, P5

Student text: Page 34.

Each exercise consists of a single interval. The first note is given.

1. Write the second note of the interval on the staff.
2. Place the name of the interval (P4, m2, M3, etc.) in the blank provided.
3. To help you recognize intervals, think of them as parts of a scale or triad:

    P5 = tonic to 5th scale degree of a major or minor scale
    P4 = tonic to 4th scale degree of a major of minor scale
    M3 = tonic to 3rd scale degree of a major scale
    m3 = tonic to 3rd scale degree of a minor triad
    M2 = tonic to 2nd scale degree of a major or minor scale
    m2 = leading tone to tonic of a major or harmonic minor scale

To the Instructor:

Continue asking class members to sing through each interval. Students often think that the system breaks down when the second pitch is below the first. But, thinking down can become as easy as thinking up if the procedure is practiced often enough. So, as soon as ascending intervals are mastered, considerable intensity should be directed toward descending intervals.

The given note is the lower note of the interval.

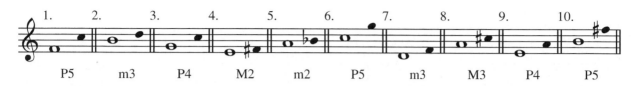

P5   m3   P4   M2   m2   P5   m3   M3   P4   P5

11.–30. (R)

M2   P4   m3   P5   M3   m2   P4   M3   m3   m2

The given note is the upper note of the interval.

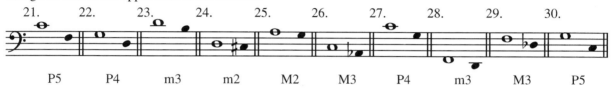

P5   P4   m3   m2   M2   M3   P4   m3   M3   P5

m3   M2   P4   P4   P5   M3   m2   P5   m3   P4

Melody 3E

Models and Embellishments: Simple Melodic Structures

Student text: Page 34.

1. Play and sing the melodic structure in the model before coming to class. Your instructor will review this structure at the beginning of this lesson.
2. Your instructor will play the given musical structure followed by embellishments of that structure.
3. Write the model's embellishments on the numbered staves provided.

To the Instructor:

1. Have the students sing the model and each embellishment and encourage them to discover structural relationships as they notate each melody.

2. Encourage students to listen for such structures in the other melodies in this book. Draw these structures to their attention at every opportunity.

Model:

Embellishments:

Harmony 3A

Chord Function Identification: I, ii, and V Triads

Student text: Page 35.

Each exercise consists of four triads in four-voice harmony.

1. Listen to the four triads in each of these exercises. All are in the key of G major. Make sure you have the tonic pitch (G) well in mind.
2. All triads in numbers 1–15 are in root position. Isolate and identify the scale degree (number or syllable) of each bass note by singing it.

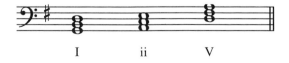

I   ii   V

3. Write the analysis of the four triads in the blanks by changing the numbers or syllables to roman numerals.

Scale Number		Syllable		Roman Numeral
1	or	do	=	I
2	or	re	=	ii
5	or	sol	=	V

Numbers 16–25 contain triad inversions.

$$\text{I} \quad \text{I}^6 \quad \text{I}^6_4 \quad \text{ii} \quad \text{ii}^6 \quad \text{ii}^6_4 \quad \text{V} \quad \text{V}^6 \quad \text{V}^6_4$$

To the Instructor:

Removing crutches, such as slower tempo or louder bass pitches, is often difficult to manage. A gradual withdrawal sometimes helps.

1. 2. 3. 4. 5.

G: I ii V I   ii V I I   V I V I   ii V ii V   I ii V I

6. 7. 8. 9. 10.

I V I ii   V I V I   ii V ii V   V I ii V   I V I I

Harmony 3B

Chords in Music Literature: I, ii, and V Triads

Student text: Page 37.

1. Each exercise consists of four examples from music literature which include a variety of harmonic rhythms and nonharmonic tones.

2. Below you see four models (A through D). Your instructor will play each of these four models. Listen carefully and try to distinguish each—one from another.

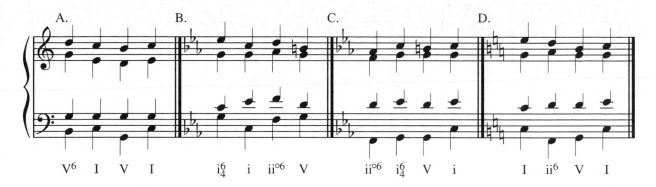

<pre>
A.   B.   C.   D.

V⁶   I   V   I   i⁶₄ i   ii°⁶ V   ii°⁶ i⁶₄   V   i   I   ii⁶   V   I
</pre>

3. Your instructor will play an example (1 through 4) from music literature. The music literature example contains the same chords and same inversions as one of the four models above.

1. Chopin: Valse Brillante, Op. 34, No. 1

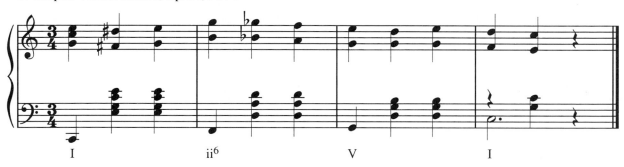

<pre>
I   ii⁶   V   I
</pre>

2. Chopin: Valse, Op. 69, No. 2

Play chords in rectangle only.

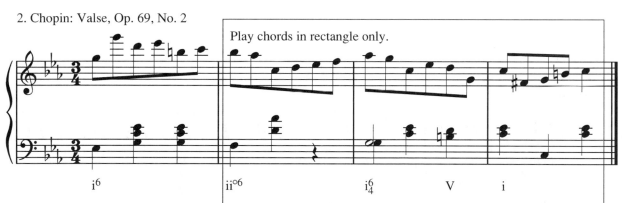

<pre>
i⁶   ii°⁶   i⁶₄   V   i
</pre>

3. Chopin: Valse, Posthumous

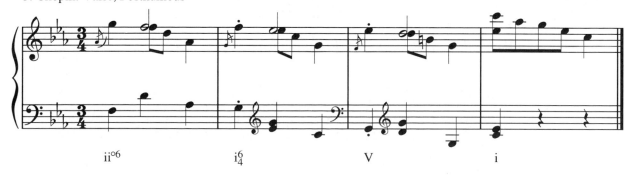

<pre>
ii°⁶   i⁶₄   V   i
</pre>

4. Chopin: Valse, Op. 69, No. 2

V⁶   I   V   I

4. When you have matched the literature example with one of the four sets of chords (A through D), place the letter in the appropriate blank below, and prepare for the next example from music literature.

1. _____ 2. _____ 3. _____ 4. _____

5. When the first four examples are completed, use the same procedure for models 5 through 8.

These (**E, F, G, H**) are the remaining four models. Pair them up with the examples from literature (**5, 6, 7, 8**).

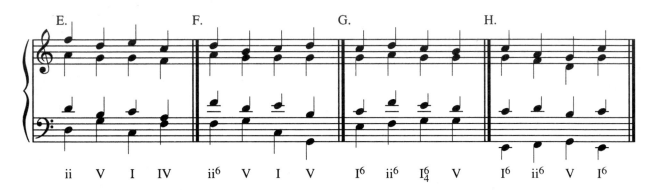

E.   ii   V   I   IV   F.   ii⁶   V   I   V   G.   I⁶   ii⁶   I⁶₄   V   H.   I⁶   ii⁶   V   I⁶

5. *(R)* _____ 6. *(R)* _____ 7. *(R)* _____ 8. *(R)* _____

5. Handel: Gigue, Suite in G Major

ii⁶   V   I   V

6. Handel: Gigue, Suite in G Major

ii   V   I   IV

7. Handel: Chaconne, Var. 22 (G228)

I^6 ii^6 V I^6

8. Handel: Chaconne in G Major, Var. 48 (G228)

Play chords in rectangle only

I^6 ii^6 I^6_4 V   I

To the Instructor:

A complete discussion of this type of exercise and suggestions for classroom use are provided in the "To the Instructor" section of Harmony 1B.

Harmony 3C

Cadence Identification: Cadence Types

Student text: page 38.

Each exercise consists of four chords in four-part harmony. The final two chords represent one of the traditional cadence types.

Cadence types:

PERFECT AUTHENTIC	V to I with both chords in root position. The tonic is the soprano note in the I chord.
IMPERFECT AUTHENTIC	V to I or vii°⁶ to I with at least one of the following circumstances present: (a) the V may be in inversion (b) the final soprano note is *not* the tonic
HALF	I, ii, or IV proceeding to V. The first chord of the two may be in inversion.
PLAGAL	IV to I
DECEPTIVE	In these exercises: V to vi (or VI)

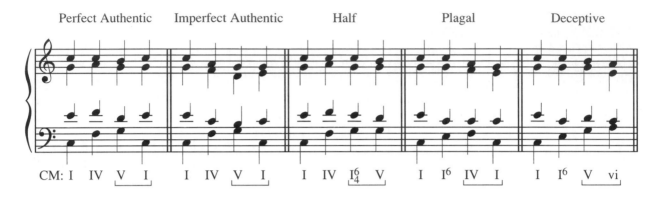

To the Instructor:

If you think your students will have difficulty with all five options in this section, try isolating only the perfect and imperfect authentic and half cadences. This will reduce the options to three, and accelerate understanding of the more common types. To assist in the culling process, note the numbers in parentheses (1–8). After spending class time with these cadences, add the plagal and deceptive.

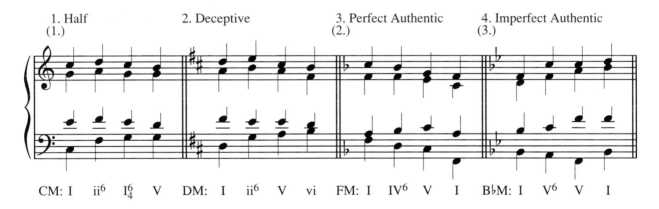

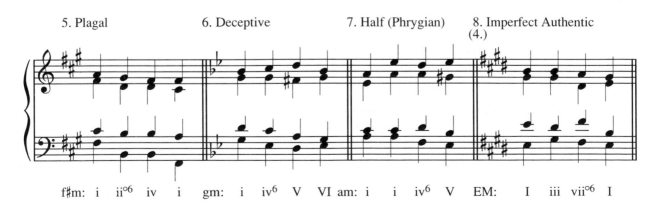

9. Plagal   10. Half   11. Plagal   12. Perfect Authentic
              (5.)   (6.)

dm: i VI iv i   em: i V⁶ i V   A♭M: I vi IV I   AM: I IV⁶ V I

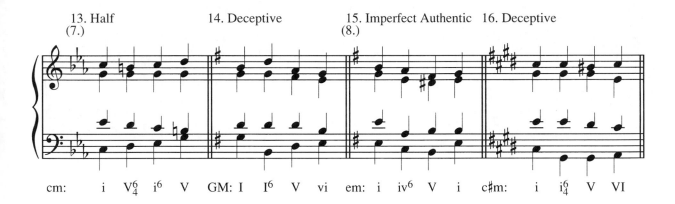

13. Half   14. Deceptive   15. Imperfect Authentic 16. Deceptive
    (7.)   (8.)

cm: i V⁴₃ i⁶ V   GM: I I⁶ V vi   em: i iv⁶ V i   c♯m: i i⁶₄ V VI

Harmony 3D

Harmonic Dictation: I(i), IV(iv), and V Triads in Four-Part Phrases

Student text: Page 38.

Each exercise consists of a phrase containing seven chords in root position.

Suggestions for practice:

1. Listen to the phrase. In this assignment the first triad is always the tonic and all triads are in root position.
2. Sing as you listen, matching pitches with the bass notes.
3. With as few listenings as possible, memorize the succession of bass notes. To test yourself, sing them without listening to the phrase.
4. Begin associating solfeggio syllables or scale numbers with the pitches. Remember, in this assignment the first bass note is always the tonic. Gradually you will develop skill in relating each pitch to a specific syllable or number.
5. Convert the syllables or numbers to actual pitches—do fa sol (or 1 4 5) in the key of C, means the notes C F G.
6. When the conversion process is complete, write the pitches on the **bass clef** staff in notation (remember, stems *down*).
7. Since all of the triads in this assignment are in root position, you can also write the roman numeral analysis in the blanks below the staves.
8. If your instructor requests, repeat the process with the three remaining voices (soprano, alto, and tenor).
9. If your instructor asks you to write out all four voices, you can check your choices by comparing them with the roman numeral analysis. Do the notes in all four voices match the triad analysis you selected earlier?

To the Instructor:

This type of assignment, occurring in almost all of the sixteen units of the text, may be used in any of the following ways:

1. Ask students only for roman numeral analysis—treating this assignment simply as an extension of Harmony 2A. This has the advantage of consuming less class time, but does not permit the correlation of harmonic and melodic elements of music.
2. Require soprano and bass melodies as well as the roman numeral analysis—correlating both harmonic and melodic dictation. A happy medium for many instructors.
3. Require students to write all four voices as well as the roman numeral analysis. This has many advantages for students, but can take inordinate amounts of class time. If a piano is the source of dictation, following inner voices is occasionally difficult, especially at this early stage of student development.

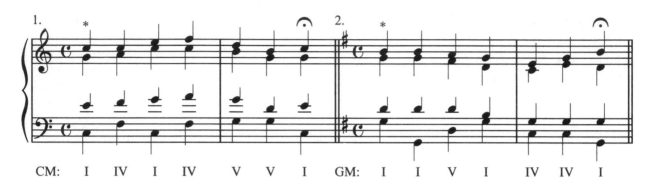

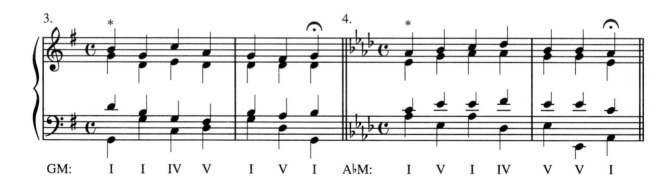

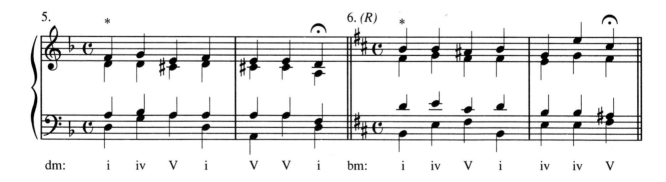

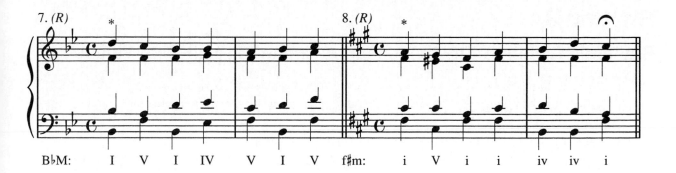

Harmony 3E

Chord Quality Identification: Writing Major, Minor, Diminished, and Augmented Triads

Student text: Page 40.

Each exercise consists of a single triad in four-part harmony. Each triad shown is correct except for the accidentals.

1. Write the type of triad (major, minor, diminished, augmented) in the blank below the staves.
2. Write the accidentals necessary to correct each triad.

The bass note is *always* correct.

To the Instructor:

Play each triad three or four times, but avoid arpeggiating.

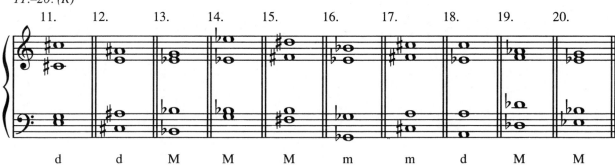

Rhythm 3A

Rhythmic Dictation: Rhythmic Figures Including Half-Beat Values

Student text: Page 41.

Most exercises consist of two measures in 2/4, 3/4, or 4/4 meter.

1. For numbers 1–10, the meter signature and first-note value(s) are given.
2. For numbers 11–16, nothing is given, but the instructor will provide the basic beat before beginning these exercises.
3. For helpful suggestions, see Rhythm 1A.
4. Complete the rhythm using a neutral pitch.
5. Write the meter signature and the rhythm using a neutral pitch. The instructor will provide the meter beat before beginning each exercise.

To the Instructor:

Play the exercises at different tempi—some fast, some slow. Three playings should suffice for most students. Beat or say one measure before beginning each exercise.

For exercises 11–16, the students have no meter signature or beginning note value. Be sure to provide the basic beat before beginning these exercises.

Rhythm 3B

Error Detection: Dotted Rhythm Values

Student text: Page 42.

1. Each exercise consists of six or eight measures of music, and contains errors in two measures (the notation does not correspond with what is played).
2. Before listening to each excerpt, clap, say, or *think* it through from beginning to end. Make sure that you know what the exercise sounds like as written.
3. Circle the measure number where the notation is different from that played by the instructor.

To the Instructor:

Play each exercise at about 100–150 per beat. Increase the tempo further if the class members have no difficulty. You may wish to ask class members to name the *exact* points of error within the offending measures.

Transcription 3

Two-Voice Folk Music Examples

Refer to instructions found in Transcription 1 (page 25).

Note: * = given material

Recorded Example 6

Traditional Lower Austrian: March

Recorded Example 7

Traditional Upper Austrian: Taps

Unit 4

Melody 4A

Melodic Dictation: Scalewise Melodies and Arpeggiations of I and V

Student text: Page 45.

Each exercise consists of a short melodic phrase. Complete the phrase on the staff in notation.

1. **Create an aural image of the melody.**
    After hearing each melody, immediately try to sing it in its entirety in your mind.
2. **Establish an understanding of the melody's structure.**
    After you can hear the melody in your mind, analyze the melody with solfeggio syllables or numbers.
3   Do not notate the melody until you have completed these two steps.
4. **Notate each melody on the appropriate staff below.**
    The first notes are given for the melodies in this section.

To the Instructor:

Singing back each melody and analyzing it with solfeggio syllables or numbers should become a part of the students' classroom routine. Encourage them to sing and analyze melodies they hear outside the classroom as well. Sometimes an assignment to transcribe a well known tune on the radio or a campus song, can be helpful in this area.

*Note or rest in workbook.

Melody 4B

Error Detection: Errors in Melodies Outlining the I, IV, and V Triads

Student text: Page 46.

Each exercise consists of a melody containing an error or errors in pitch.

1. Melodies 1–20 contain one printing error in pitch.
2. Melodies 21–25 contain three printing errors in pitch.
3. Circle each number representing the tone that is different from the tone played.

To the Instructor:

Give the students time to study the written melodies and imagine their sound before playing the instructor versions. Play each melody at a fairly fast tempo. Melodies 21 through 25 are taken from music literature. The instructor's manual has the melodies as they appear in their original score. The students are asked to recognize printing errors in their textbooks.

1.

2.

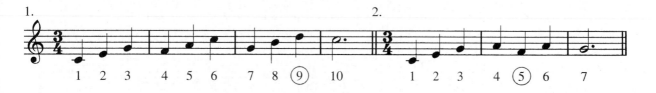

3.

4.

5.

6.

7.

8.

9.

10.

11.

12.

13.

14.

15.

16.

17.

18.

19.

20.

Each melody contains THREE errors.

21. Schubert: Allegretto in C Minor for Piano

22. Schubert: Military March

23. D. Scarlatti: Sonata in D Major

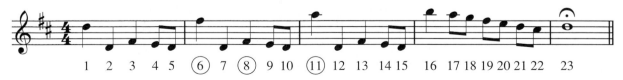

24. Haydn: Symphony in G Major

1 2 3 ④ 5 ⑥ 7 ⑧ 9   10   11   12 13 14   15

25. Haydn: Symphony in D Major

1   2   3   4   5   ⑥   ⑦   8   9   10 11 12 13 14   15   ⑯

Melody 4C

Scale Degree Identification: Three Notes

Student text: Page 48.

1. The instructor first plays a scale, then three tones of that scale.
2. Identify the three scale degrees played.
3. The instructor will tell you whether to use scale numbers or syllables.

To the Instructor:

See the information in Melody 1C.

The instructor plays this scale:

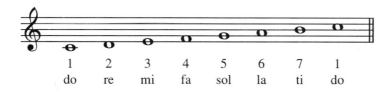

| 1 | 2 | 3 | 4 | 5 | 6 | 7 | 1 |
| do | re | mi | fa | sol | la | ti | do |

The tones of the first sixteen examples are within the range of the scale played.

1.	2.	3.	4.	5.	6.	7.	8.
5 6 1	6 4 3	2 4 1	3 2 6	1 5 4	7 2 6	4 7 3	2 7 6
sol la do	la fa mi	re fa do	mi re la	do sol fa	ti re la	fa ti mi	re ti la

9.	10.	11.	12.	13.	14.	15.	16.
1 4 2	6 4 3	7 3 4	2 1 6	4 1 5	3 1 2	6 7 4	7 1 3
do fa re	la fa mi	ti mi fa	re do la	fa do sol	mi do re	la ti fa	ti do mi

Some tones of these examples exceed the range of the scale played. Suggestion: Use these exercises to reinforce the study of compound intervals.

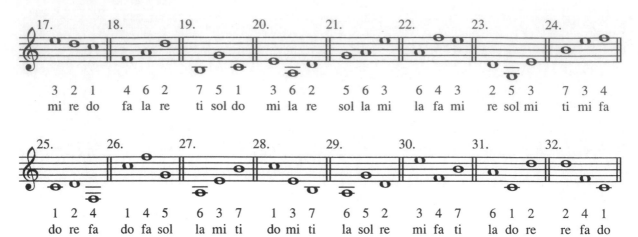

| 3 2 1 | 4 6 2 | 7 5 1 | 3 6 2 | 5 6 3 | 6 4 3 | 2 5 3 | 7 3 4 |
| mi re do | fa la re | ti sol do | mi la re | sol la mi | la fa mi | re sol mi | ti mi fa |

| 1 2 4 | 1 4 5 | 6 3 7 | 1 3 7 | 6 5 2 | 3 4 7 | 6 1 2 | 2 4 1 |
| do re fa | do fa sol | la mi ti | do mi ti | la sol re | mi fa ti | la do re | re fa do |

Melody 4D

New Intervals: m6, M6

Student text: Page 49.

Intervals studied to date: m2, M2, m3, M3, P4, P5

Each exercise consists of a single interval. The first note is given.

1.   Write the second note of the interval on the staff.
2.   Place the name of the interval (P4, m6, M6, etc.) in the blank provided.
3.   To help you recognize the new intervals, think of them as parts of a scale:

Second note ABOVE the first: M6   =   tonic to 6th of a major scale

Second note BELOW the first: M6   =   when you hear the second pitch, think of its as the tonic of a major scale

Second note ABOVE the first: m6   =   tonic to 6th of a minor scale

Second note BELOW the first: m6   =   when you hear the second pitch, think of it as the tonic of a minor scale

To the Instructor:

Identifying the intervals of a 6th (M and m) is more difficult than any studied to date because the 6th is a larger interval, and students tend to get lost filling it in (singing through). Some find it easier to use a common interval such as the perfect 5th as a measuring stick. Whenever they hear an interval larger than the P5th, they calculate the half or whole steps beyond the P5th and arrive at the intervals of a major or minor 6th—and later the major and minor 7th. Whatever temporary crutch is used, students should be encouraged to think of the 6th (as well as all other intervals) as a particular and discreet sound to be memorized per se. Until this is achieved, recognizing 6ths (and 7ths) will be slow and not always entirely accurate.

The given note is the lower of the two.

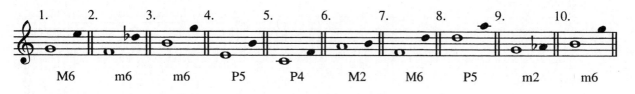

1.	2.	3.	4.	5.	6.	7.	8.	9.	10.
M6	m6	m6	P5	P4	M2	M6	P5	m2	m6

*11.–30. (R)**

11.	12.	13.	14.	15.	16.	17.	18.	19.	20.
m6	m2	m6	M6	P4	P5	M6	m6	P5	m6

The given note is the upper of the two.

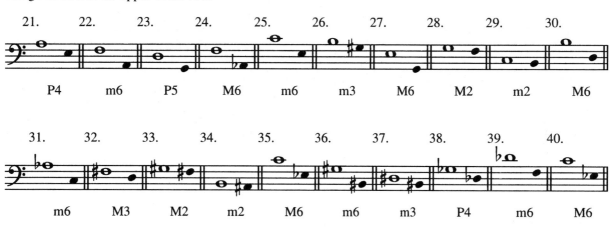

21.	22.	23.	24.	25.	26.	27.	28.	29.	30.
P4	m6	P5	M6	m6	m3	M6	M2	m2	M6

31.	32.	33.	34.	35.	36.	37.	38.	39.	40.
m6	M3	M2	m2	M6	m6	m3	P4	m6	M6

*(R) means recorded.

Melody 4E

Models and Embellishments: 5–6 Patterns in Two Voices

Student text: Page 50.

1. Notice that the model in this section is made up of two voices that ascend in oblique motion. Sing both parts of this structure before class.
2. Your instructor will play the structure, followed by embellishments of that structure.
3. Write the model's embellishments on the numbered staves provided.

To the Instructor:

1. Have the students sing each voice of the model before the early examples.
2. Play the structure and embellishments in the order printed, or repeat the structure from time to time to remind students of the basis for each embellishment.

Model:

Embellishments:

1.

2.

3.

4.

5. A five-measure example based on the same model.

Harmony 4A

Chord Function Identification: I, ii, IV, and V Triads

Student text: Page 52.

Each exercise consists of a harmonic progression of four chords in four-part harmony. The harmonies are limited to the I, ii, IV, and V triads.

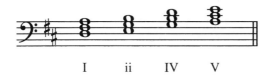

Write the roman numeral analysis of the triads in the blanks provided.

Numbers 1–15 contain root-position triads only.

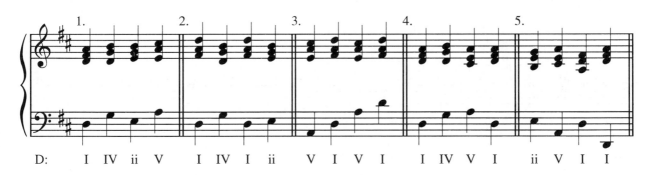

D: I IV ii V   I IV I ii   V I V I   I IV V I   ii V I I

   I IV I V   I IV ii V   I IV IV V   V I V I   IV ii V I

11.–20. (R)

| | | | | | | | | | | | | | | | | | | | |
|IV|I|ii|V|V|ii|V|I|IV|I|V|I|IV|ii|V|I|IV|ii|V|I|

Numbers 16—25 contain inversions.

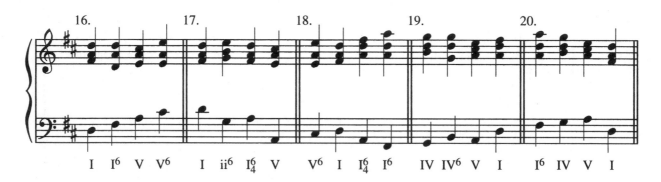

$I \quad I^6 \quad V \quad V^6 \qquad I \quad ii^6 \quad I^6_4 \quad V \qquad V^6 \quad I \quad I^6_4 \quad I^6 \qquad IV \quad IV^6 \quad V \quad I \qquad I^6 \quad IV \quad V \quad I$

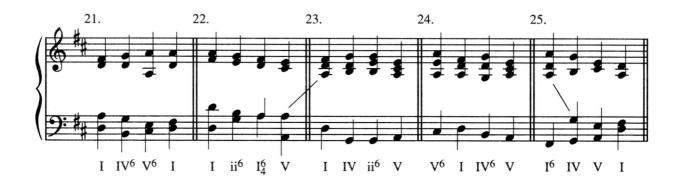

$I \quad IV^6 \quad V^6 \quad I \qquad I \quad ii^6 \quad I^6_4 \quad V \qquad I \quad IV \quad ii^6 \quad V \qquad V^6 \quad I \quad IV^6 \quad V \qquad I^6 \quad IV \quad V \quad I$

Harmony 4B

Chords in Music Literature: I, ii, IV, and V Triads

Student text: Page 52.

1. Each exercise consists of four examples from music literature which includes a variety of harmonic rhythms and nonharmonic tones.
2. Below you see four models (A through D). Your instructor will play each of these four models. Listen carefully and try to distinguish each—one from another.

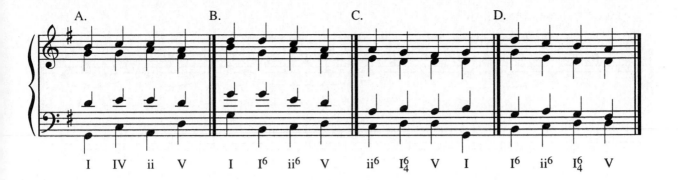

A.   B.   C.   D.

I   IV   ii   V   I I^6 ii^6 V ii^6 I^6_4 V   I I^6 ii^6 I^6_4 V

3. Your instructor will play an example (1 through 4) from music literature. The music literature example contains the same chords and same inversion as one of the four models above.

1. Schubert: Waltz

I   IV   ii   V

2. Beethoven: Six Variations on Nel cor non mi sento

I I^6 ii^6 V

3. Beethoven: Six Variations on Nel piu non mi sento

ii^6 I^6_4 V   I

4. Mozart: Die Zauberflöte, K620

I⁶   ii⁶   I$_4^6$ V

4. When you have matched the literature example with one of the four sets of chords (A through D), place the letter in the appropriate blank below.

1. _____ 2. _____ 3. _____ 4. _____

5. When the first four examples are completed, use the same procedure for models 5 through 8.

These (**E, F, G, H**) are the four models. Pair them up with the examples from literature (**5, 6, 7, 8**).

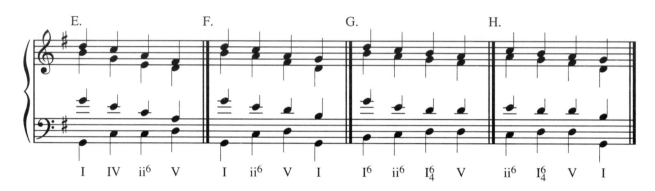

I IV ii⁶ V   I ii⁶ V I   I⁶ ii⁶ I$_4^6$ V   ii⁶ I$_4^6$ V I

5. *(R)* _____ 6. *(R)* _____ 7. *(R)* _____ 8. *(R)* _____

5. Beethoven: Trio, op. 121A

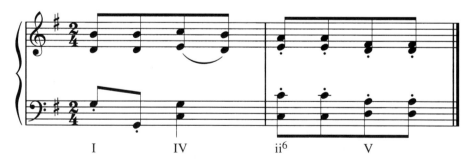

I   IV   ii⁶   V

6. Chopin: Mazurka, op. 33, No. 2

I   ii⁶   V   I

7. Beethoven: Piano Concerto IV, Op. 58

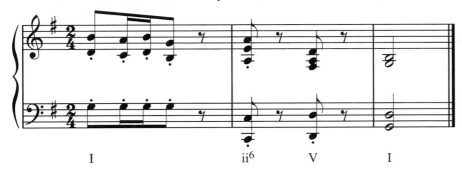

I   ii⁶   V   I

8. Haydn: Capriccio

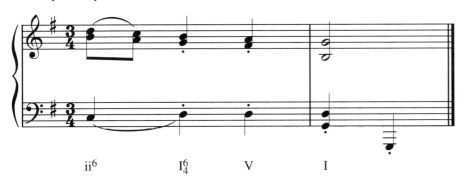

ii⁶   I$_4^6$ V   I

To the Instructor:

A complete discussion of this type of exercise and suggestions for classroom use are provided in the "To the Instructor" section of Harmony 1B.

Harmony 4C

Nonharmonic Tones: Two-Voice Examples

Student text: Page 53.

Each exercise (1–20) consists of a nonharmonic tone in a two-voice setting. Write the name of the nonharmonic tone in the appropriate blank.

1. Nonharmonic tones played in numbers 1–10:

Unaccented passing tone	**Accented passing tone**
Unaccented neighboring tone	**Accented neighboring tone**
Escape tone	**Suspension** (9–8, 7–6, 4–3, 2–3)
Anticipation	

2. Review Harmony 2C.
3. Write the name of the nonharmonic tones in the appropriate blanks:

To the Instructor:

A thorough review of the strategy presented in Harmony 2C is highly recommended at this point. The nonharmonic tones presented here for the first time (Appoggiatura, Retardation, Pedal Point, and Changing Tones) should be treated thoroughly, and the sound patterns (one-voice examples) played several times to insure comprehension.

In numbers 1–10 write the name of the nonharmonic tones in the appropriate blanks:

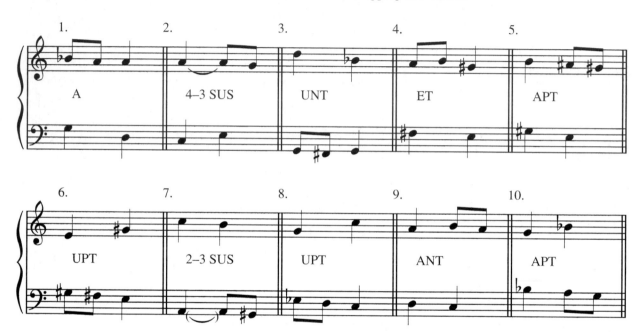

4. Additional nonharmonic tones presented in numbers 11–20:

Appoggiatura	**Retardation**
Pedal point	**Changing tone**

5. Observe the additional sound patterns provided by the **appoggiatura, retardation, pedal point,** and **changing tones:**

C = Consonance   D = Dissonance

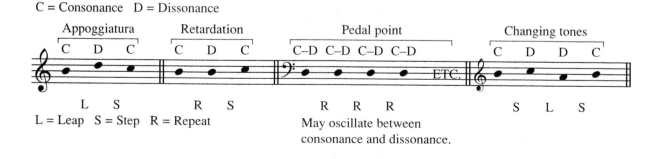

6. Only the appoggiatura and retardation are three-note patterns. Changing tones usually consist of a four-note pattern distinguished by two dissonances, and the pedal point may be of any length. For a more detailed description of the four nonharmonic tones listed, see the Glossary, your theory text, or the *Harvard Dictionary of Music*.

7. The following are nonharmonic tone examples in a two-voice setting:

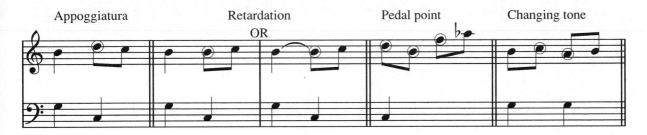

8. Numbers 11—20 include any of the eleven nonharmonic tone types studied. Write the name of the nonharmonic tone in the appropriate blank:

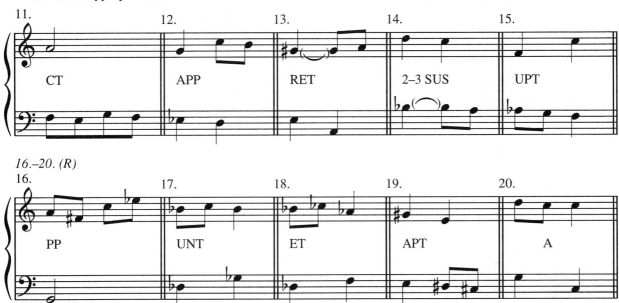

9. Numbers 21—30 are examples of nonharmonic tones in a four-voice setting. Write the names of the nonharmonic tones in the appropriate blanks:

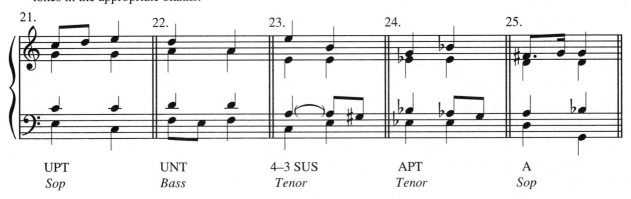

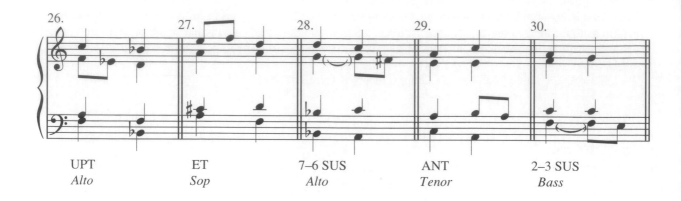

26.	27.	28.	29.	30.
UPT	ET	7–6 SUS	ANT	2–3 SUS
Alto	*Sop*	*Alto*	*Tenor*	*Bass*

Harmony 4D

Harmonic Dictation: I(i), ii, IV(iv), and V Triads in Chorale Phrases

Student text: Page 55.

Each exercise consists of a phrase from a chorale. Numbers 7–14 were harmonized by Bach.

1.

Numbers	Harmonic Vocabulary	Triad Positions	Nonharmonic Tones
1–6	I (i), ii, V	All root position	UPT and 4–3 SUS only
7–9	I (i) and V only	Root position and 1st inversion	UPT, APT, and 2–3 SUS
10–14	I (i), IV (iv), and V only	Root position, 1st inversion, 2nd inversion	UPT, LNT, and 4–3 SUS
15–16	I, ii, IV, and V	Root position and 1st inversion	UPT only

2. Indicate the roman numeral analysis of each triad in the blanks provided.
3. List nonharmonic tones beneath the harmonic analysis.
4. If the instructor requests it, give the melodic line of both the soprano and bass voices.
5. If the instructor requests it, give the melodic line of both the alto and tenor voices.

To the Instructor:

This set of chorale phrases may be used for any or all of the following purposes:

1. For class members to indicate the harmonic analysis only.
2. To indicate nonharmonic tones in addition to the harmonic analysis.
3. For numbers 1 and 2 above in addition to writing the soprano and bass voices on the staves.
4. For four-part dictation, including all above steps along with dictation of the inner voices as well.

The procedure for this type of dictation varies widely from instructor to instructor. Some prefer:

1. One playing for the soprano voice
2. One playing for the bass voice
3. One or two playings for the analytical symbols
4. An additional playing for each of the two (alto and tenor) remaining voices

Depending on the general level of the class, individual voices may be played slightly louder to assist students embarking on this type of dictation for the first time. Taking all four voices from dictation is perhaps the single most difficult task students will have. If at all possible, dictation, with a group of four class members playing instruments, will help to make this assignment more pleasant and considerably easier.

In numbers 1–6, all triads are in root position.

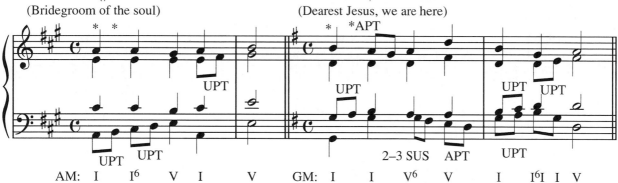

7. *Seelen-Bräutigam*
   (Bridegroom of the soul)

8. *Liebster Jesu, wir sind hier*
   (Dearest Jesus, we are here)

9. *Christe, du Beistand deiner Kreuzgemeine*
(Christ, Thou support of Thy followers)

10. *Wo soll ich fliehen hin*
(Whither am I to flee?)

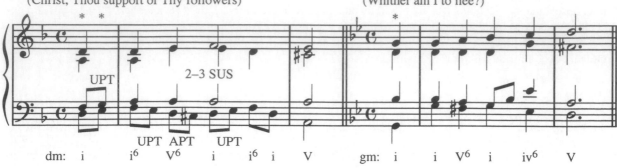

dm: i   i⁶ V⁶ i i⁶ i V   gm: i   i V⁶ i iv⁶ V

11. *Lobt Gott, ihr Christen, allzugleich*
(Praise God, ye Christians, all together)

12. *Nun danket alle Gott*
(Now let us all thank God)

AM: I V⁶ V I I⁶ I IV V I   AM: I   I I⁶ I IV IV⁶ IV I

13. *Ermuntre dich, mein schwacher Geist*
(Rouse thyself, my weak spirit)

14. *Christus, der ist mein Leben*
(Christ is my life)

GM: I⁶ IV V IV⁶ I V   I   GM: I I V I IV⁶ I⁶ I⁶₄ V V I

15. *Mach's mit mir, Gott, nach deiner Güt*
(Do with me as Thy goodness prompts Thee)

16. *Allein Gott in der Höh' sei Ehr'*
(Only to God on high be glory!)

DM: I I IV⁶ V⁶ I ii I⁶ V   AM: I I IV⁶ V ii I⁶ V I

Harmony 4E

Chord Quality Identification: Major, Minor, Diminished, and Augmented Triads

Student text: Page 57.

Each exercise consists of a single triad in four-part harmony.

1. The notes written are on the correct line or space, but may require accidentals to make them conform to what is played.
2. If the triad as written is not the same as the one you hear, add the necessary accidentals to make it conform.
3. The bass note is *always* correct.

The following examples illustrate the correct procedure:

EXAMPLES:

To the Instructor:

Play each triad three or four times, but avoid arpeggiating.

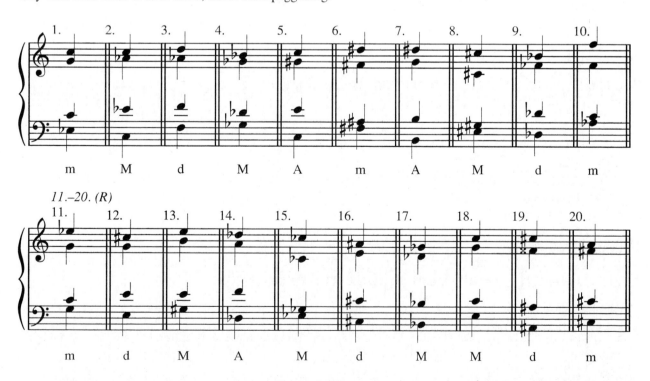

Rhythm 4A

Rhythmic Dictation: Half-Beat Values in Syncopation

Student text: Page 58.

Each exercise consists of a phrase of music.

Complete the rhythm (neutral pitch) on the staff in notation.

To the Instructor:

Play each melody three or four times at a comfortable tempo.

Rhythm 4B

Error Detection: Half-Beat Values in Syncopation

Student text: Page 59.

Each exercise consists of a phrase of music. On one beat, the written rhythm will be different from that played by the instructor.

Circle the number representing the beat that is changed.

To the Instructor:

Play these melodies at a moderate, continuous tempo. For diversion, try a modest rubato in a few places. These exercises contain half-beat values (duple division of the beat), except for the three in compound meter, which can be heard as having triple divisions of the beat, if the tempo is brisk enough.

Transcription 4

Two Austrian Dances (Two Voices)

Refer to instructions found in Transcription 1 (page 25).

Note: * = given material

Recorded Example 8

Traditional Burgenland: "Wedding Dance"

Recorded Example 9

Menuett (Styrian Folk Song)

Unit 5

Melody 5A

Melodic Dictation: Melodies Outlining the I, IV, V (and vii°⁶) Triads

Student text: Page 61.

Each exercise consists of a short melody.

1. **Create an aural image of the melody.**
   After hearing each melody, immediately try to sing it in its entirety in your mind.
2. **Establish an understanding of the melody's structure.**
   After you can hear the melody in your mind, analyze the melody with solfeggio syllables or numbers.
3. Do not notate the melody until you have completed these two steps.
4. **Notate each melody on the appropriate staff below.**
   The first notes are given for the melodies in this section.

To the Instructor:

Ask class members to sing and analyze each melody after it is played.

1.

2.

3.

4.

5.

6.

7. Mozart: Minuet in F Major, K. 2 *(R)*

8. Mozart: Concerto in C for Flute, Harp & Orchestra *(R)*

9. J. S. Bach: Fugue 21 *(R)*

10. Beethoven: Sonata *(R)*

11. J. S. Bach: Little Prelude *(R)*

12. Haydn: String Quartet, op. 76, no. 5 *(R)*

13. Beethoven: Sonata, op. 57 *(R)*

* Note or rest in workbook.

(R) means recorded.

Melody 5B

Error Detection: Excerpts from Music Literature

Student text: Page 62.

Each exercise consists of a short melody with *three* printing errors in pitch.

1. Review Melody 4B.
2. Circle the numbers representing the tones that are different from those played by the instructor.

To the Instructor:

Give the students time to study the written melodies and imagine their sound before playing the instructor versions. Play each melody from music literature at a moderate tempo. The instructor's manual has the melodies as they appear in their original score. The students are asked to recognize printing errors in their textbooks.

1. Bizet: *Carmen* (opera)

2. *Carmen*

1 2 3 4 5 6 7 8 ⑨ 10 11 12⑬ 14 15 16 ⑰   1 2 3 ④ ⑤ 6 7 8 ⑨ 10 11

3. Boccherini: Sonata no. 6 for Cello and Piano   4. Sonata no. 6

1 2 ③ ④ 5 6 ⑦ 8 9 10 11 12   1 2 3 4 5 6 ⑦ ⑧ ⑨ 10 11 12 13 14

5. Boccherini: Quintet in D, op. 37

1 2 3 4 5 6 ⑦ 8 9 10 11 12 ⑬ 14 15 16 17 18 ⑲ 20 21 22 23

6. Dvořák: Symphony no. 5 (from *The New World*) *(R)*

1 2 3 ④ 5 6 7 8 ⑨ 10 11 12 13 14 15 16 17 18 19 20 21 ㉒ 23

7. Dvořák: Symphony no. 5 (from *The New World*) *(R)*

1 2 ③ ④ 5 6 7 8 9 10 11 12 13 14 ⑮ 16 17 18 19 20 21 22

8. Dvořák: Symphony no. 5 (from *The New Word*) *(R)*

1 2 ③ 4 5 6 7 ⑧ 9 10 11 12 13 14 15 16 17 18 ⑲

9. Dvořák: Symphony no. 5 (from *The New World*) *(R)*

1 2 3 4 5 6 7 8 ⑨ 10 11 12 13 14 ⑮ ⑯ 17 18 19 20 21 22

10. Tchaikovsky: Symphony no. 6 op. 74 *(R)*

1 2 3 4 5 6 7 8 ⑨ ⑩ 11 12 13 14 15 16 17 18 ⑲ 20

Melody 5C
Melodic Figure Identification: Sequence and Rhythmic Repetition

Student text: Page 64.

Each exercise consists of a melodic excerpt from music literature that contains a sequence or a rhythmic repetition.

SEQUENCE

The immediate restating of a melodic figure at a higher or lower pitch so that the structure of the figure is maintained. Each unit is called a segment.

Tchaikovsky: Symphony no. 6

└──── Sequence Seg. 1 ────┘   └──── Sequence Seg. 2 ────┘

RHYTHMIC REPETITION   The rhythm of a significant portion of the excerpt is repeated. The pitches (at least a majority) are not repeated.

Weber: *Jubel Ouvertüre*

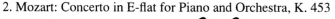

Listen carefully to each melody as played and circle:

SEQUENCE   when you hear a sequence
RHYTHMIC REPETITION   when you hear a rhythm repeated but no melodic sequence
NEITHER   when you hear neither a sequence nor a repeated rhythm

To the Instructor:

1. Ask class members to sing each of the examples at the beginning of this section.
2. Discuss the definitions and illustrations of sequence and rhythmic repetition.
3. Suggestion: Place the following excerpt on the board and ask individuals to improvise (by singing) examples of sequences and rhythmic (but no pitch) repetition.

4. Play the melodies at a moderate-to-fast tempo.
5. Some instructors may wish to provide the source of the melodies after each is played.

1. Mendelssohn: Symphony no. 4 op. 90 (Italian)   Rhythmic repetition

2. Mozart: Concerto in E-flat for Piano and Orchestra, K. 453   Sequence

3. Mendelssohn: Symphony no. 4 op. 90 (Italian) *(R)*   Neither

No melodic or rhythmic figures repeated or sequenced

4. Beethoven: Sonata for Piano (Waldstein), op. 53 *(R)*   Rhythmic repetition

5. Mendelssohn: Consoloation, op. 30, no. 3 *(R)*

Neither

No melodic or rhythmic figure repeated or sequenced

6. Mendelssohn: A Midsummer Night's Dream *(R)*

Sequence

⌐ Sequence Seg. 1 ⌐ ⌐ Sequence Seg. 2 ⌐⌐ Sequence Seg. 3 ⌐

7. Handel: *Alcina* (opera)

Rhythmic repetition

⌐————— Rhythm —————⌐ ⌐————— Same rhythm repeated —————⌐

8. Mendelssohn: "Wedding March" (from *A Midsummer Night's Dream*)

Neither

No melodic or rhythmic figure repeated or sequenced

9. Mozart: Minuet, K. 1, for piano

Sequence

10. Mozart: Overture to the *Marriage of Figaro*, K. 492

Sequence

11. Mozart: *Eine Kleine Nachtmusik*, K. 525

Rhythmic repetition

12. Mozart: Symphony no 39, K. 543

Rhythmic repetition

13. Mozart: Symphony no. 40, K. 550

Neither

14. Mussorgsky: Prelude to the opera *Boris Godunov*

Neither

Melody 5D

New Interval: The Tritone

Student text: Page 65.

Intervals studied to date: m2, M2, m3, M3, P4, P5, m6, M6

Each exercise consists of a single interval. The first note is given.

1. Write the second note of the interval on the staff.
2. Place the name of the interval in the blank provided.
3. The **tritone** (augmented 4th and diminished 5th) occurs in both major and harmonic minor from 4th to 7th scale degrees. Most musicians find it difficult to associate the sound with scales because melodic skips of a tritone are not very numerous.
4. The tritone occurs in the diminished triad as well, but it too is not as common as either the major or minor triad.
5. Imagine the sound of the P5th and diminish that interval by a half-step.
6. Memorize the unique sound of the tritone. Listen to it many times until it is firmly entrenched in your mind. This way you will have instant access to it and will not have to think of it in relation to other intervals. It's not easy to do, but the time spent will be well worth it.

To the Instructor:

Whatever temporary crutch is used, students should be encouraged to think of the tritone (as well as all other intervals) as a particular and discrete sound to be memorized per se. Until this is achieved, recognizing tritones will be slow and risky.

The given note is the lower note of the interval.

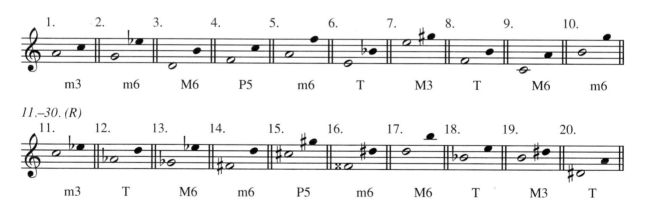

The given note is the upper note of the interval.

Melody 5E

Models and Embellishments: Descending 6ths in Two Voices

Student text: Page 65.

1. Notice that the model in this section is made up to two voices that descend in parallel 6ths. Sing both parts of this structure before class.
2. Your instructor will play the structure followed by embellishments of that structure.
3. Write the model's embellishments on the numbered staves provided.

To the Instructor:

1. Have the students sing each voice of the model before the early examples.
2. Play the structure and embellishments in the order printed, or repeat the structure periodically to remind students of the basis for each embellishment.

7.

8.

Harmony 5A

Chord Function Identification: I(i), ii(ii°), IV(iv), and V Triads and Inversions

Student text: Page 67.

Each exercise consists of a series of four chords in block harmony.

In the blanks provided, write the analysis of each of the four chords.

To the Instructor:

To prepare for this set of exercises:

1. For numbers 1–15, place the following chords on the chalkboard, or make an overhead acetate copy of this page:

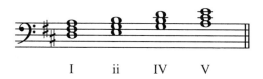

I   ii   IV   V

2. For numbers 16–25, place these chords on the chalkboard, or make an overhead acetate of this page:

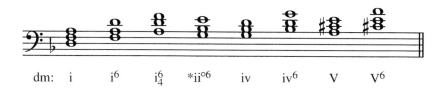

dm: i   i⁶   i⁶₄   *ii°⁶   iv   iv⁶   V   V⁶

*The diminished supertonic triad is seldom found in root-position.

3. As you point to each symbol or chord, ask class members to sing the triad in simple position, from lowest to highest tone. Improvise common progressions (such as I IV ii V) for class members to sing. When the chords are familiar and automatic, progress on to the exercises.

4. For the first three or four exercises, have class members sing the *root* of each chord as it is played. From then on, students should *think* the same procedure silently. For exercises 15–25, ask class members to sing first the root then the bass note of each chord. After the first three or four exercises, the chords should be identified silently.

5. At first, play each set of chords three or four times and very slowly. Then, increase the tempo slightly and decrease the number of playings.

Numbers 1–15 contain root-position triads only:

11.–20. (R)

Numbers 16–25 contain inversions.

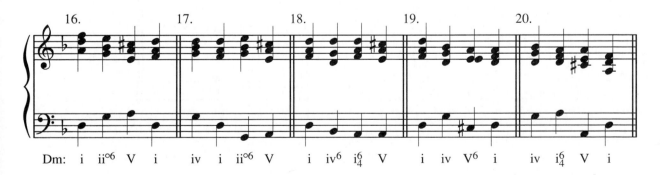

i ii°⁶ V i⁶   i iv ii°⁶ V   i i⁶ iv i   V⁶ i iv iv⁶   V i⁶₄ V i

Harmony 5B

Chords in Music Literature: I(i), ii(ii°), IV(iv), and V Triads

Student text: Page 68.

1. Each exercise consists of four examples from music literature containing a variety of harmonic rhythms and nonharmonic tones.
2. Below you see four models (A through D). Your instructor will play each of these four models. Listen carefully and try to distinguish each—one from another.

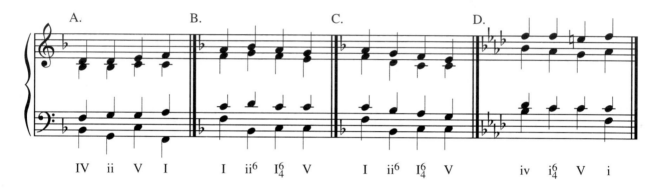

A.   IV ii V I   B.   I ii⁶ I⁶₄ V   C.   I ii⁶ I⁶₄ V   D.   iv i⁶₄ V i

3. Your instructor will play an example (1 through 4) from music literature. The music literature example contains the same chords and same inversions as one of the four models above.

1. Mozart: The Magic Flute, Act 1, No. 8

I   ii⁶   I⁶₄   V

2. Haydn: Piano Sonata, Hob. XVI/14

f minor

iv   i$^6_4$ V   i

3. Beethoven: Piano Concerto IV, Op. 58

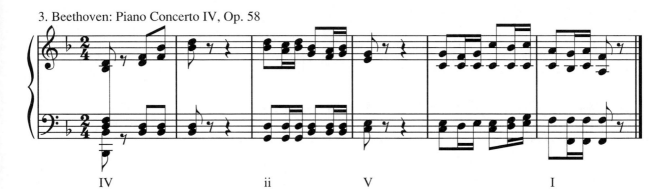

IV   ii   V   I

4. Haydn: Capriccio

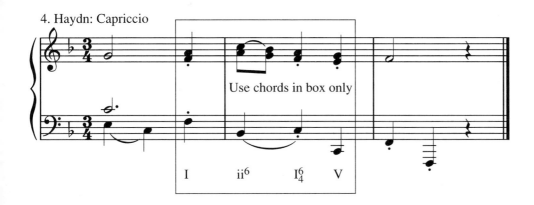

Use chords in box only

I   ii^6 I$^6_4$ V

4. When you have matched the literature example with one of the four sets of chords (A through D), place the letter in the appropriate blank below, and prepare for the next example from music literature.

1. _____   2. _____   3. _____   4. _____

5. When the first four examples are completed, use the same procedure for models 5 through 8.

These (**E, F, G, H**) are the remaining four models. Pair them up with the examples from literature (**5, 6, 7, 8**).

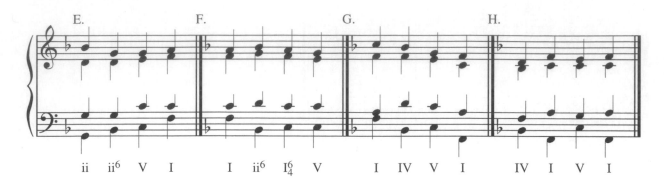

5. (R) _____ 6. (R) _____ 7. (R) _____ 8. (R) _____

5. Beethoven: Piano Concerto IV, Op. 58c

6. Chopin: Nocturne, Op. 37, No. 1

7. Boccherini: Cello Concerto in B flat Major

8. Beethoven: Romance, Op. 50

I   ii⁶   I$^6_4$ V

To the Instructor:

A complete discussion of this type of exercise and suggestions for classroom use, are provided in the "To the Instructor" section of Harmony 1B.

Harmony 5C

Harmonic Rhythm and Nonharmonic Tones

Student text: Page 68.

Each exercise consists of a phrase of **homophonic** music.

1. In each of the following five exercises you have been given the rhythm of the melody, numbers indicating the melody tones, and circles around each number indicating a nonharmonic tone.
2. Place an "X" above each melody note where the harmony changes.
3. Above the circled numbers, indicate the *type* of each nonharmonic tone.

To the Instructor:

Play each exercise two or three times at performance tempo.

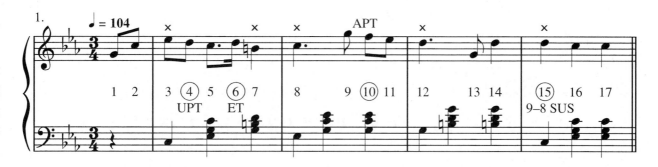

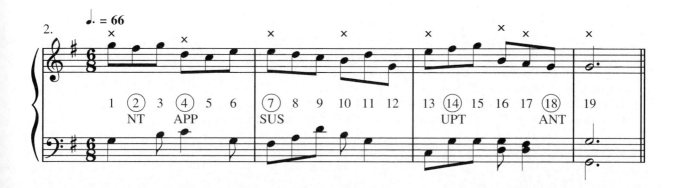

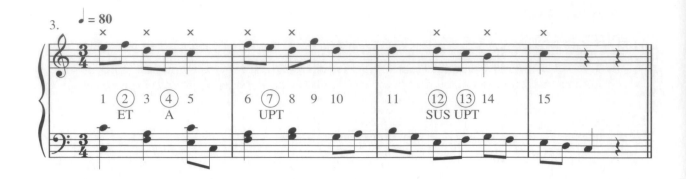

3.

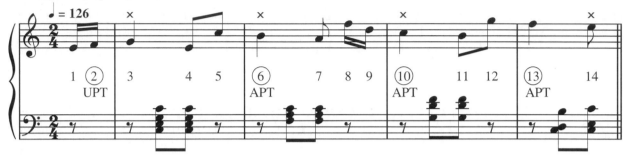

4. Haydn: Symphony no. 97

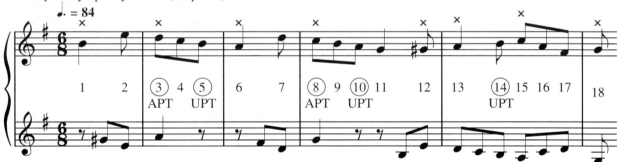

5. Haydn: Symphony no. 94 (Surprise!)

Harmony 5D

Harmonic Dictation: I(i), ii, IV(iv), and V Triads in Chorale Phrases

Student text: Page 69.

Each exercise consists of a phrase from a chorale.

    Numbers 1–6:   All triads are in root position.
    Numbers 7–10:   Triads may be in inversions as well as root position.

1. Indicate the roman numeral analysis of each triad in the blanks provided.
2. List any nonharmonic tones beneath the harmonic analysis.
3. If the instructor requests it, give the melodic line of both the soprano and bass voices.
4. If the instructor requests it, give the melodic line of both the alto and tenor voices.

To the Instructor:

For a complete discussion of this type of assignment, see Harmony 3D.

If numbers 7—10 seem too difficult for your class at this time, numbers 1—6 are intended as an introduction. All triads are in root position, and nonharmonic tones are confined to unaccented passing tones and an occasional suspension.

Harmony 5E

Error Detection: Single Triads in Four Parts

Student text: Page 70.

Each exercise consists of a single triad. The first five examples are triads in root position, and the remaining five are first inversions (the bass note is the third of the triad).

As played by the instructor, one of the four voices contains an error in pitch.

Indicate the voice containing the error:

S = soprano   A = alto   T = tenor (no errors in the bass)

1. Play each exercise on a piano with the damper pedal depressed. Try to match (by singing) the pitch of each voice (soprano, alto, tenor, and bass). Use an octave substitution for those voices out of your range.
2. When you can do this with accuracy, you are ready to try the exercises below.
3. In class, match the pitches of the voices by *imagining* rather than actually singing the pitches.
4. Reconstructing sounds in your mind is called *tonal imagery,* and mastering this trick is one of the most important skills you will acquire in an ear-training course!

To the Instructor:

Before presenting this section in class, play the triads as shown in the student text, making sure all voices are of equal intensity. Ask class members to pick out and sing any of the four voices. When students have achieved accuracy with this drill, they are ready for the exercises in this section. This section is particularly good for improving tonal imagery.

Play each four-voice triad as written—the circled note is the pitch found in the student text.

1. A   2. T   3. S   4. T   5. A   6. A   7. T   8. T   9. S   10. T

Rhythm 5A

Rhythmic Dictation: Introduction to Quarter-Beat Values

Student text: Page 71.

Each exercise is a short melodic phrase. Numbers 1—6 consist of two measures each and are intended to introduce quarter-beat values. Numbers 7—14 are taken from music literature.

1. Complete each rhythm on the single line provided.
2. The value of the first note is given in all exercises.

To the Instructor:

The two-measure examples at the beginning of the assignment should suffice as an introduction to quarter-beat values. Play each melody at performance tempo. If, however, that appears too difficult for class members, divide the melody into two sections and dictate each separately. Some of the melodies taken from music literature do not contain quarter-beat values. Counting through (an adaptation of singing through) each exercise may help some slower students at the outset. Instead of counting only the major beats (as in 3/4 meter counting 1–2–3), ask class members to divide each beat into four units (1–a–an–du–2–a–an–du, etc.) This usually requires a slower tempo but may speed initial progress.

7. Wagner: *Tannhäuser*

8. Rimski-Korsakov: *Capriccio Espagnol*

9. Rimski-Korsakov: *Scheherezade*

10. Wagner: *Die Walküre (R)*

11. Wagner: *Die Meistersinger von Nürnberg (R)*

12. Schumann: Concerto in A Minor for Piano and Orchestra *(R)*

13. Schumann: Symphony no. 3 in E-flat (Rhenish) *(R)*

14. Schumann: Symphony no. 1 in B-flat (Spring) *(R)*

Rhythm 5B

Error Detection: Quarter-Beat Values

Student text: Page 72.

Each exercise contains a melodic phrase with one rhythmic error.

Circle the number representing the section of the phrase containing the rhythmic error.

To the Instructor:

Play each exercise at performance tempo.

1.

2.

3.

4. Mozart: Concerto for Violin and Orchestra, K. 216

5. *(R)*

6. J. S. Bach: English Suite no. 3 *(R)*

7. Brahms: Symphony no. 1 in C Minor *(R)*

8. D. Scarlatti: Sonata for Harpsichord, Longo 108 *(R)*

Transcription 5

Piano Music with Pedal Point

Refer to instructions found in Transcription 1 (page 25).

Note: * = given material

Recorded Example 10

Robert Schumann: "Melody"

Recorded Example 11

Alexander Goedicke: *Hopak*

Unit 6

Melody 6A

Melodic Dictation: Intervals of a 7th

Student text: Page 75.

Each exercise consists of a short melody. Numbers 1—10 introduce the intervals of a 7th, while numbers 11—18 are excerpted from the works of J. S. Bach.

1. **Create an aural image of the melody.**
    After hearing each melody, immediately try to sing it in its entirety in your mind.
2. **Establish an understanding of the melody's structure.**
    After you can hear the melody in your mind, analyze the melody with solfeggio syllables or numbers.
3. Do not notate the melody until you have completed these two steps.
4. **Notate each melody on the appropriate staff below.**
    The first notes are given for the melodies in this section. Incomplete final measures are marked "inc."

To the Instructor:

The first ten melodies are constructed especially to contain one or two intervals studied recently. The remainder, numbers 11—18, place melodic dictation in the setting of music literature. Occasionally, some students will recognize melodies excerpted from literature, and may, thus, have a slight advantage. Insist that all class members sing the entire melody back to you and gradually add solfeggio syllables or numbers. Writing the melodies is a simple task if students have been prepared in this manner. Since this section contains intervals of a 7th, you may wish to present section D before starting this section.

9. English Suite no. 3 *(Musette)*

10. French Suite no. 6 *(Bourrée) (R)*

11. French Suite no. 5 *(Gavotte) (R)*

12. Suite no. 3 for Cello alone *(Bourrée) (R)*

13. Suite no. 3 for Orchestra *(Gigue) (R)*

* Note or rest in workbook

(R) means recorded.

Melody 6B

Error Detection: Schubert Melodies

Student text: Page 76.

Each exercise consists of a phrase of music by Schubert.

Circle the numbers representing the three pitches that are different from those played.

To the Instructor:

Give the students time to study the written melodies and imagine their sound before playing the instructor versions. Play each melody from music literature at a moderate tempo. The instructor's manual has the melodies as they appear in their original score. The students are asked to recognize printing errors in their textbooks.

1. Schubert: Sonata in A Minor for Piano and Cello

Melody 6C

Melodic Figure Identification: Sequence, False Sequence, and Rhythmic Repetition

Student text: Page 77.

Each exercise consists of a short melodic excerpt containing a sequence, a false sequence, or a rhythmic repetition.

Indicate which of the following devices is contained in each excerpt.

SEQUENCE   The immediate restating of a melodic figure at a higher or lower pitch so that the structure of the figure is maintained.

FALSE SEQUENCE   One or more notes of the figure is repeated and the remaining notes are sequenced.

RHYTHMIC REPETITION   The rhythm is repeated, but the pitches are not sequenced or repeated.

Listen carefully to each melody as played; circle the device contained in the excerpt.

1. SEQUENCE   when you hear a sequence
2. FALSE SEQUENCE   when you hear a false sequence
3. RHYTHMIC REPETITION   when you hear a rhythm repeated but no melodic sequence
4. NONE   when you hear none of the three devices listed above

To the Instructor:

To prepare for this section:

1. Ask class members to sing each of the examples at the beginning of this section.
2. Discuss the definitions and illustrations of sequence, rhythmic repetition, and false sequence.
3. Suggestion: Go back to Melody 5C and ask class members to improvise sequences, rhythmic repetitions, and false sequences. When students are thoroughly familiar with the terms and their applications, this assignment will be considerably easier.

4. Play the melodies at a moderate-to-fast tempo.
5. Some instructors may wish to play a recording of each melody in its original context after it is discussed.

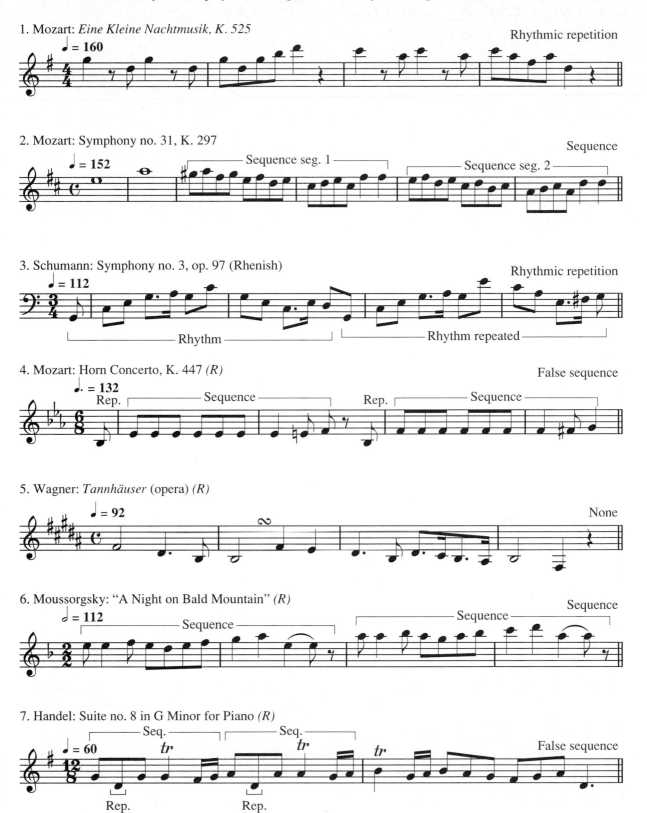

1. Mozart: *Eine Kleine Nachtmusik, K. 525*

Rhythmic repetition

2. Mozart: Symphony no. 31, K. 297

Sequence

3. Schumann: Symphony no. 3, op. 97 (Rhenish)

Rhythmic repetition

4. Mozart: Horn Concerto, K. 447 *(R)*

False sequence

5. Wagner: *Tannhäuser* (opera) *(R)*

None

6. Moussorgsky: "A Night on Bald Mountain" *(R)*

Sequence

7. Handel: Suite no. 8 in G Minor for Piano *(R)*

False sequence

8. Mahler: *Des Knaben Wonderhorn* — None

9. Beethoven: Sonata for Piano, op. 26 — Sequence

10. Beethoven: Sonata for Piano, op. 2, no. 3 — False sequence

11. Handel: Sonata in G, op. 1, no. 5 — Rhythmic repetition

12. Mozart: Serenade in E-flat, K. 375 — False sequence

Melody 6D

New Intervals: m7 and M7

Student text: Page 79.

Intervals studied to date: m2, M2, m3, M3, P4, P5, m6, M6, A4, D5

Each exercise consists of a single interval of a m6, M6, m7, or M7. The first note is given.

1. Write the second note of the interval on the staff.
2. Place the name of the interval in the blank provided.
3. The best way to identify both the major and minor 7th is to practice singing them above and below a variety of given pitches. Soon you will have them well in mind and can recognize their peculiar qualities without having to rely on a special system.
4. Another method, of short-term benefit, is to think of major and minor 7ths as inversions of minor or major 2nds—easier to identify. Sing an octave above or below (depending on the situation) to get into proper range. Then, sing up or down a half or whole step to complete the original major or minor 7th.

To the Instructor:

Whatever temporary crutch is used, students should be encouraged to think of the 7th (as well as all other intervals) as a particular and discrete sound to be memorized per se.

The given note is the lower note of the interval.

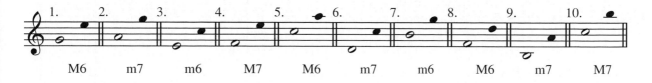

M6   m7   m6   M7   M6   m7   m6   M6   m7   M7

11.–30. (R)

m6   M7   M6   m6   M7   M6   m7   m6   M6   M7

The given note is the upper note of the interval.

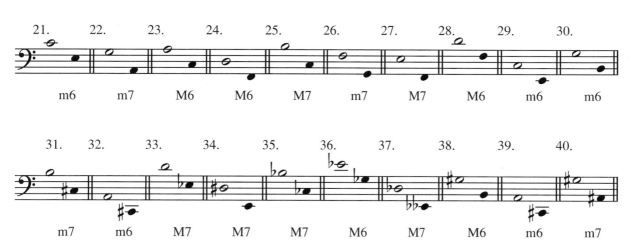

m6   m7   M6   M6   M7   m7   M7   M6   m6   m6

m7   m6   M7   M7   M7   M6   M7   M6   m6   m7

Melody 6E

Models and Embellishments: 7–3 Patterns in Two Voices

Student text: Page 80.

1. Notice that the model in this section is made up of two voices that move in similar and oblique motion, forming 7ths and 3rds. Sing both parts of this structure before class.
2. Your instructor will play the structure followed by embellishments of that structure.
3. Write the model's embellishments on the numbered staves provided.

To the Instructor:

1. Have the students sing each voice of the model before the early examples.
2. Play the structure and embellishments in the order printed or repeat the structure from time to time to remind students of the basis for each embellishment.

Model:

Embellishments:
1.

2.

3.

4.

5.

Harmony 6A

Chord Function Identification: I, ii, IV, V, and vi Triads

Student text: Page 81.

Each exercise consists of four block chords in four-part harmony using the following chords:

I   ii   IV   V   vi

Write the roman numeral analysis of each chord in the blanks provided.

To the Instructor:

Play the first few exercises slowly, allowing students to sing each triad in root position. Then, ask the students to sing only the roots for another few exercises. By the sixth or seventh set of progressions, the crutches may be abandoned.

Numbers 1—15 contain root-position triads only:

Numbers 16—25 contain inversions:

V I⁶ I IV   ii ii⁶ I⁶₄ V   I I I⁶ IV   V vi ii⁶ V   I vi ii ii⁶

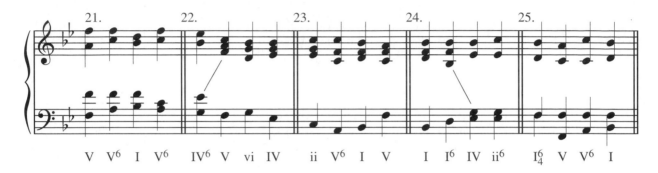

V V⁶ I V⁶   IV⁶ V vi IV   ii V⁶ I V   I I⁶ IV ii⁶   I⁶₄ V V⁶ I

Harmony 6B

Chords in Music Literature: Emphasis on ii, IV, and vi

Student text: Page 82.

1. Each exercise consists of four examples from music literature which includes a variety of harmonic rhythms and nonharmonic tones.
2. Below you see four models (A through D). Your instructor will play each of these four models. Listen carefully and try to distinguish each—one from another.

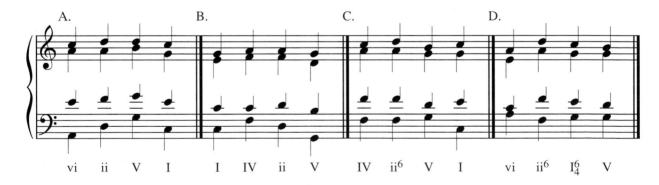

vi ii V I   I IV ii V   IV ii⁶ V I   vi ii⁶ I⁶₄ V

3. Your instructor will play an example (1 through 4) from music literature. The music literature example contains the same chords and same inversions as one of the four models above.

1. Saint-Saens: Christmas Oratorio, No. 8

Play only the chords
in the rectangle

iii | vi   ii^6 I$^6_4$ V

2. Schubert: Waltz

I   IV   ii   V

3. Anonymous: To You Jehovah

I   IV   ii   V

4. Beethoven: Trio, Op. 121A

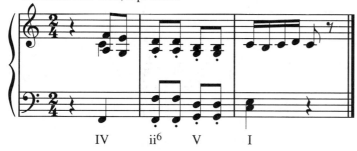

IV   ii^6 V   I

4. When you have matched the literature example with one of the four sets of chords (A through D), place the letter in the appropriate blank below, and prepare for the next example from music literature.

1. _____   2. _____   3. _____   4. _____

5. When the first four examples are completed, use the same procedure for models 5 through 8.

These (**E, F, G, H**) are the remaining four models. Pair them up with the examples from literature (**5, 6, 7, 8**).

E.				F.				G.				H.			
IV	I	ii	vi	vi	ii	V	I	I	IV	ii	vi	IV⁶	ii⁶	V	vi

5. (R) _____ 6. (R) _____ 7. (R) _____ 8. (R) _____

5. Mozart: Bastien und Bastienne, K. 46B, No. 1

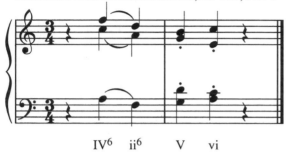

IV⁶   ii⁶   V   vi

6. Mozart: Piano Sonata, K. 545, IV

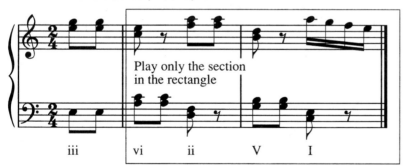

Play only the section
in the rectangle

iii   vi   ii   V   I

7. Brahms: Romance, op. 118, No. 5

IV   I   ii   vi

8. Schubert: Symphony in C

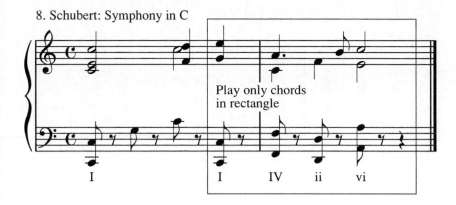

Play only chords
in rectangle

I   I   IV   ii   vi

To the Instructor:

A complete discussion of this type of exercise and suggestions for classroom use are provided in the "To the Instructor" section of Harmony 1B.

Harmony 6C

Nonharmonic Tones: Four-Voice Examples

Student text: Page 83.

Each exercise consists of two chords including a nonharmonic tone or tones.

1. Place the abbreviation indicating the nonharmonic tone in the blank provided.

UPT	=	unaccented passing tone	APP	=	appoggiatura
APT	=	accented passing tone	ET	=	escape tone
SUS	=	suspension	A	=	anticipation
NT	=	neighboring tone			

2. Exercises 1—10 consist of two chords including a nonharmonic tone.
3. Exercises 11—20 contain two nonharmonic tones. List the nonharmonic tones in the upper voice first, in the lower voice second.

To the Instructor:

Play each exercise only once or twice.

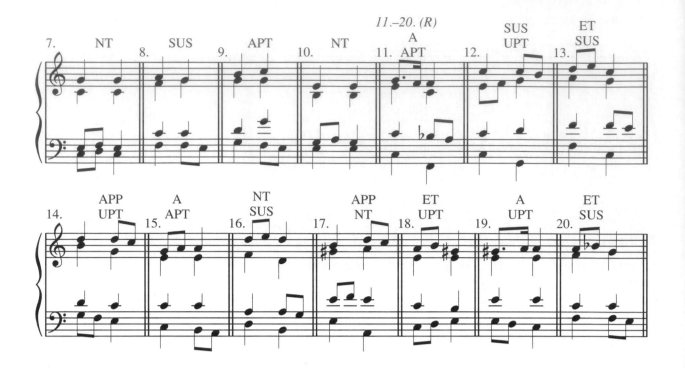

Harmony 6D

Harmonic Dictation: The I(i), ii(ii°), IV(iv), and V Triads in Chorale Phrases

Student text: Page 83.

Each exercise consists of a phrase from a **chorale.** Numbers 7—16 were harmonized by Bach. The harmonic vocabulary is as follows:

      Numbers 1—6:   All triads are in root position.
      Numbers 7—14:   Triads are in inversions as well as root position.

1.   Indicate the roman numeral analysis of each triad in the blanks provided.
2.   List any nonharmonic tones beneath the harmonic analysis.
3.   If the instructor requests it, give the melodic line of both the soprano and bass voices.
4.   If the instructor requests it, give the melodic line of both the alto and tenor voices.

To the Instructor:

For a complete discussion of this type of assignment, see Harmony 3B.

If numbers 7—14 seem too difficult for your class at this time, numbers 1—6 are intended as an introduction. All triads are in root position, and nonharmonic tones are confined to unaccented passing tones and an occasional 4—3 suspension.

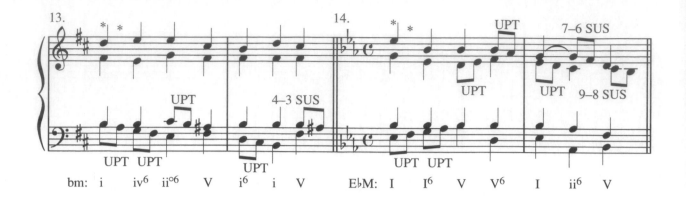

Harmony 6E

Error Detection: Triads in Four Parts

Student text: Page 85.

Each exercise consists of two triads in four parts.

1. As played by the instructor, one note in each exercise is incorrect. The bass voice contains no errors.
2. Indicate the chord (no. 1 or no. 2) containing the error.
3. Indicate which voice contains the error.

    S = soprano   A = alto   T = tenor

To the Instructor:

Play both chords, including the circled note, two or three times. The note seen by the student is placed in parentheses to the right of the circled note. If students have initial difficulty with this type of drill, roll the first few chords (bass to soprano) to get them started.

Rhythm 6A

Rhythmic Dictation: Quarter-Beat Values

Student text: Page 86.

Each exercise consists of a two-measure melody.

Complete the rhythm on a neutral pitch. The first note is given for each exercise.

To the Instructor:

Play each rhythm two or three times at a moderate tempo. These exercises provide further drill in quartuple and (in the case of compound meter) sextuple division of the beat.

Rhythm 6B

Error Detection: Triplet Figures

Student text: Page 87.

Each exercise consists of a melodic phrase. Most phrases contain triplet figures.

In one of the measures, the written rhythm will not agree with the version played.

Circle the number representing the measure with the "error."

To the Instructor:

Play each exercise two or three times and as fast as the students can absorb them.

1. Beethoven: German Dance

2.

3.

4.

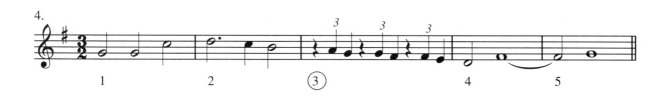

5. *(R)*

6. *(R)*

7. Mozart: Quartet, K. 499 (fourth movement) *(R)*

8. Brahms: Concerto for Violin and Orchestra, op. 77 *(R)*

1   2   3   ④   5   6

Transcription 6

Theme and Variation

Refer to instructions found in Transcription 1 (page 25).

Note: * = given material

Recorded Example 12

W. A. Mozart: "French Folk Song"

Theme

W. A. Mozart: "Variation on a French Folk Song"

Unit 7

Melody 7A

Melodic Dictation: Two-Phrase Melodies

Student text: Page 91.

Each exercise consists of a melody composed of two phrases. The second phrase begins immediately after the ‖, marked in each melody.

1. **Create an aural image of the melody.**
   After hearing each melody, immediately try to sing it in its entirety in your mind.
2. **Establish an understanding of the melody's structure.**
   After you can hear the melody in your mind, analyze the melody with solfeggio syllables or numbers.
3. Do not notate the melody until you have completed these two steps.
4. **Notate each melody on the appropriate staff below.**
   The first notes are given for the melodies in this section.

To the Instructor:

This assignment is designed to focus attention on longer sections of melody. In dictation, some instructors prefer not to break up the phrases and include the entire two phrases, even though students themselves may concentrate on the phrases separately. Others think this approach is a distraction and prefer to play phrase-by-phrase, connecting the two only as a summary on the last performance. Immediately after class members have completed their dictation, and the correct pitches and rhythms have been revealed, discuss students' errors and the reason for the errors while the thought processes are still fresh in their minds. By playing the melody again, errors in judgment can often be remedied quickly. This is also an ideal moment to discuss other essential melodic relationships. Do the two phrases form a period? If so, are the two parallel or contrasting? Is there a duplication of rhythm? Are the melodic contours of the two similar or different?

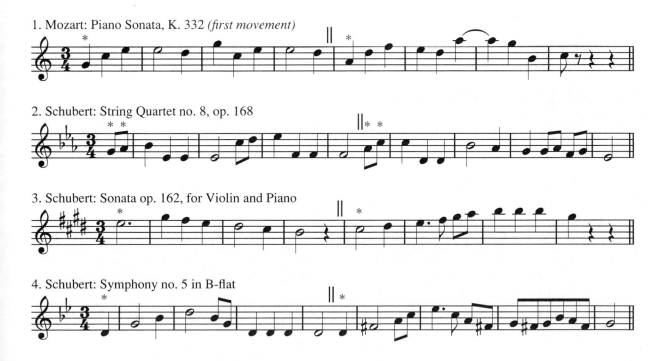

1. Mozart: Piano Sonata, K. 332 *(first movement)*

2. Schubert: String Quartet no. 8, op. 168

3. Schubert: Sonata op. 162, for Violin and Piano

4. Schubert: Symphony no. 5 in B-flat

5. Waldteufel: España Waltzes, op. 286, no. 4

6.–10. (R)*
6. Offenbach: *La Vie Parisienne*

7. Saint-Saens: *Suite Algerienne,* op. 60, for Orchestra

8. Gluck: Orpheus and Eurydice, Overture

9. Gluck: *Air de Ballet*

10. Mozart: Trio, K. 564, for Piano, Violin, and Cello

*Note or rest in workbook.
(R) means recorded.

Melody 7B

Error Detection: Handel Melodies

Student text: Page 92.

Each exercise consists of a phrase of music by Handel and contains three pitch performance errors.

Place a circle around the three numbers that represent pitches different from those played.

To the Instructor:

Give the students time to study the written melodies and imagine their sound before playing the instructor versions. Play each melody at a moderate tempo. These melodies are taken from music literature and are notated correctly in the student textbook. Errors have been added to the instructor's manual and, therefore, the students are asked to recognize errors in musical performance.

1. "Sarabande" from Suite no. 4 in D Minor for Keyboard

2. Suite no. 8 in G Major for Keyboard

3. Water Music (Bourrée)

4. Water Music (Bourrée)

5. Water Music (Bourrée)

6. Concerto Grosso in G Major, op. 6, no. 1 *(R)*

7. Concerto in F (double-wind choir plus strings) *(R)*

8. Concerto Grosso in F for String Orchestra, op. 6, no. 2 *(R)*

9. Concerto no. 4 in F for Organ and Orchestra *(R)*

1 2 3 4   5 6 7 8 9 10 11 12 13 14 15 16 17 18 19 20 21 22 ㉓ ㉔ ㉕ 26 27 28 29 30 31 32 33

10. Fireworks Music (Minuet no. 2) *(R)*

1 ② ③ 4 5 ⑥ 7 8 9 10 11 12 13 14 15 16 17 18 19 20 21 22 23

Melody 7C

Melodic Figure Identification: Melodic Devices

Student text: Page 93.

Each exercise consists of a melodic phrase.

In the blanks provided, write the type of device (below) found in each melody:

SEQUENCE   The immediate restating of a melodic figure at a higher or lower pitch so that the structure of the figure is maintained. Each unit is called a *segment*.

REPEATED MELODY   A segment of the melody is repeated with or without the same rhythm.

REPEATED RHYTHM   A rhythmic (but not melodic) figure is repeated.

Listen carefully to each melody as played and circle one of the four:

1. **SEQUENCE**   when you hear a sequence
2. **REPEATED MELODY**   when you hear a melody repeated with or without the same rhythm
3. **REPEATED RHYTHM**   when you hear a rhythm (only) repeated—no repeated melody or sequence
4. **NONE**   when you hear none of the three devices listed above

To the Instructor:

Spend enough time in class to make sure that students are well prepared for this assignment. Play all melodies at performance tempo.

1. Mahler: Symphony no. 4

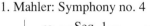

Sequence

2. Brahms: Symphony no. 4, op. 98

Repeated rhythm

3. Brahms: Symphony no. 1, op. 68

None

4. Brahms: Symphony no. 2, op. 73 *(R)*

Melody   Repeated melody   Repeated melody

5. Brahms: Symphony no. 1, op. 68 *(R)*

Sequence Seq. 1   Sequence Seq. 2   Sequence

6. Brahms: Trio in A Minor, op. 114 *(R)*

Rhythm   Repeated rhythm

7. Wagner: *Tannhäuser* (opera) *(R)*

Seq. 1   Seq. 2   Seq. 3   Sequence

8. Brahms: Symphony no. 1, op. 68 *(R)*

Rhythm   Rhythm repeated   Rhythm repeated   Repeated rhythm

Melody 7D

Intervals: All Diatonic Intervals

Student text: Page 94.

Each exercise consists of a single interval (two tones).

1. Write the name of the interval in the blank provided.
2. Write the second note of the interval on the staff in notation.

If you have difficulty identifying particular intervals, review them thoroughly before undertaking this section. For locating helpful strategy:

Unit	Type	Section	Page	Strategy for Particular Intervals					
1	Melody	D	0	m2	M2	m3	M3		
2	Melody	D	00	P5	P4				
3	Melody	D	00	m2	M2	m3	M3	P5	P4
4	Melody	D	00	m6	M6				
5	Melody	D	00	Tritone					
6	Melody	D	00	m7	M7				

To the Instructor:

This is a review for most intervals found in diatonic scales. It might be wise to assess the progress of all class members at this point, and help any who are still inaccurate in identifying the larger intervals—m6, M6, m7, M7. The table, showing the location of particular strategies, is provided to ensure an effective review.

The given note is the lower note of the interval.

11.–30. (R)

The given note is the upper note of the interval.

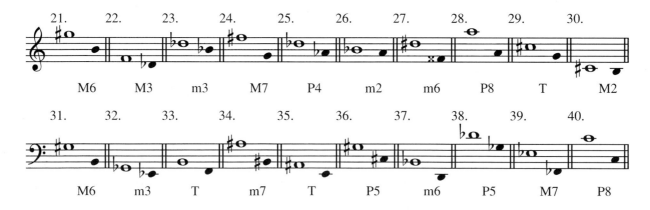

Melody 7E

Models and Embellishments: Cadence Formulas in Two Voices

Student text: Page 95.

1. The four models in this section are based on two-voice authentic cadences. Sing both parts of these structures before class.
2. Your instructor will play the structure followed by embellishments of that structure.
3. Write the model's embellishments on the numbered staves provided.

To the Instructor:

1. Have the students sing each voice of the model before the early examples.
2. Play the structure and embellishments in the order printed, or repeat the structure from time to time to remind students of the basis for each embellishment.
3. After the students have completed all exercises, choose various embellishments at random and have the students identify them by number or write them on a separate piece of paper.

Harmony 7A

Chord Function Identification: I(i), ii(ii°), iii (III, III⁺), IV(iv), V, and vi(VI) Triads

Student text: Page 96.

Each exercise consists of a series of four chords in block harmony.

In the blanks provided, write the analysis of each of the four chords.

To the Instructor:

To prepare for this set of exercises.

1. For numbers 1–10, place the following chords on the board or make an overhead transparency of this page:

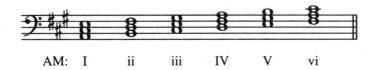

2. For numbers 11–20, place these chords on the board or make an overhead transparency of this page:

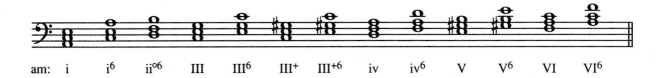

3. As you point to each symbol or chord, ask class members to sing the triad in simple position.
4. For the first three or four exercises, have class members sing the root of each chord as it is played. Then on second playing, they sing the bass tone of each chord (for the inversion).
5. At first, play each set of chords three or four times and very slowly. Then, increase the tempo slightly and decrease the number of plays.

Numbers 1–10 contain root-position triads only:

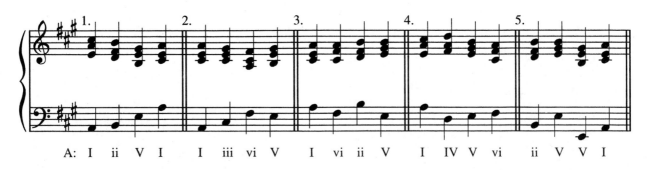

Numbers 11—20 contain inversions:

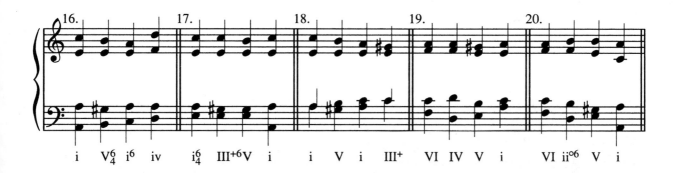

Harmony 7B

Chords in Music Literature: Emphasis on iii and vi

Student text: Page 97.

1. Each exercise consists of four examples from music literature which includes a variety of harmonic rhythms and nonharmonic tones.

2. Below you see four models (A through D). Your instructor will play each of these four models. Listen carefully and try to distinguish each—one from another.

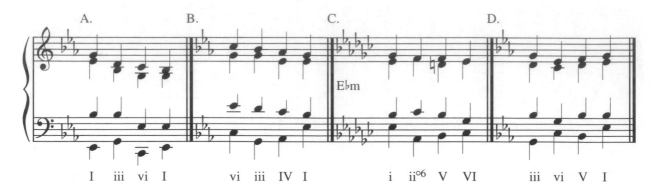

A.	B.	C.	D.
I iii vi I	vi iii IV I	i ii°⁶ V VI	iii vi V I

3. Your instructor will play an example (1 through 4) from music literature. The music literature example contains the same chords and same inversions as one of the four models above.

1. Bach: Herr Christ, der ein'ge Gott's Sohn

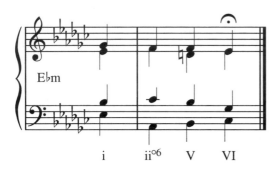

i   ii°⁶   V   VI

2. Rameau: The Temple of Glory

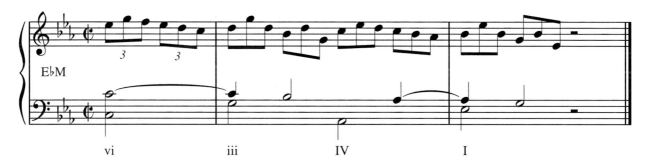

vi   iii   IV   I

3. Rachmaninoff: Nocturne, Op. 10, No. 1

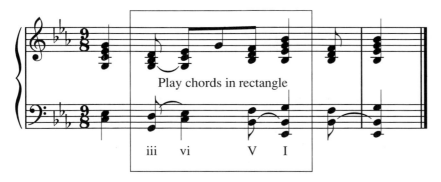

Play chords in rectangle

iii   vi   V   I

4. Brahms: Romance, Op. 118, No. 5

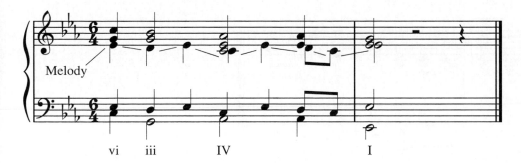

Melody

vi   iii   IV   I

4. When you have matched the literature example with one of the four sets of chords (A through D), place the letter in the appropriate blank below, and prepare for the next example from music literature.

1. _____ 2. _____ 3. _____ 4. _____

5. When the first four examples are completed, use the same procedure for models 5 through 8.

These (**E, F, G, H**) are the remaining four models. Pair them up with the examples from literature (**5, 6, 7, 8**).

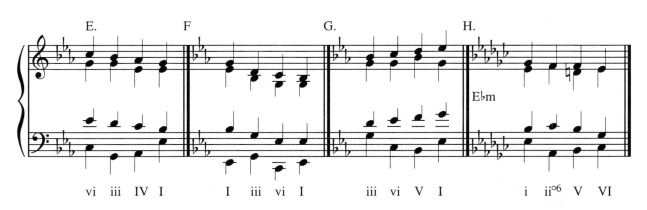

E.   F   G.   H.

E♭m

vi iii IV I   I iii vi I   iii vi V I   i ii°⁶ V VI

5. (R) _____ 6. (R) _____ 7. (R) _____ 8. (R) _____

5. Tchaikovsky: Symphony No. IV, Op. 36

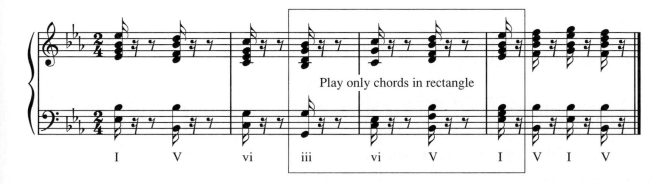

Play only chords in rectangle

I   V   vi   iii   vi   V   I   V   I   V

6. Tchaikovsky: Symphony No. IV, Op. 36

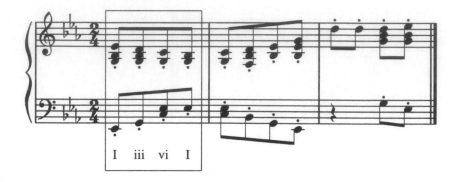

I   iii   vi   I

7. Mozart: The Marriage of Figaro, Act II, No. 10

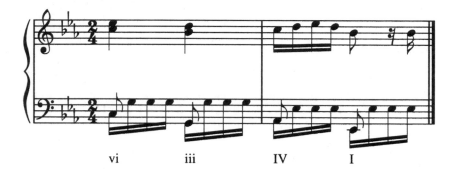

vi   iii   IV   I

8. Anonymous: Dir, dir, Jehovah, will ich singen

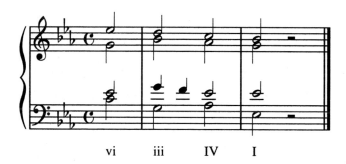

vi   iii   IV   I

To the Instructor:

A complete discussion of this type of exercise and suggestions for classroom use are provided in the "To the Instructor" section of Harmony 1B.

Harmony 7C

Harmonic Rhythm and Harmonic Analysis: I, ii, IV, V, and vi Triads

Student text: Page 98.

Each exercise consists of a phrase of music in homophonic (single-melody with chordal accompaniment) style.

1. Write the harmonic rhythm by bracketing the numbers.
2. Write the harmonic analysis above each bracket.
3. Write the melody on the staff in notation if the instructor requests you to do so.

To the Instructor:

Provide class members with the beat before beginning. You may wish to call out the numbers during the first playing. Announce in class if you wish students to take down the melody also. The first note(s) is given for each exercise.

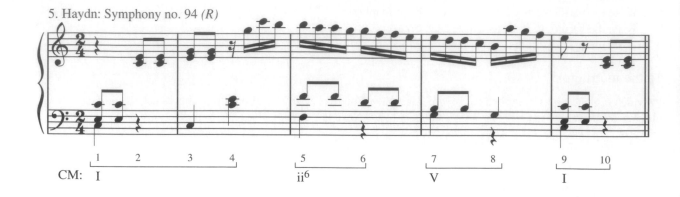

CM: I   ii⁶   V   I

Harmony 7D

Harmonic Dictation: I(i), ii(ii°), IV(iv), V, and vi(VI) Triads in Chorale Phrases

Student text: Page 99.

Each exercise consists of a chorale phrase. Numbers 7–14 are harmonizations by Bach. The harmonic vocabulary is as follows:

> Numbers 1–6:   All triads are in root position.
>
> Numbers 7–14:   Triads may be in inversions as well as root position.

1. Indicate the roman numeral analysis of each triad in the blanks provided.
2. List any nonharmonic tones beneath the harmonic analysis.
3. If the instructor requests it, give the melodic line of both the soprano and bass voices.
4. If the instructor requests it, give the melodic line of both the alto and tenor voices.

To the Instructor:

For a complete discussion of this type of assignment, see Harmony 3B.

If numbers 7–14 seem too difficult for your class at this time, numbers 1–6 are intended as an introduction. All triads are in root position, and nonharmonic tones are confined to unaccented passing tones and an occasional suspension.

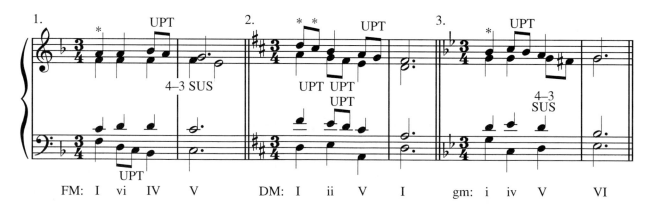

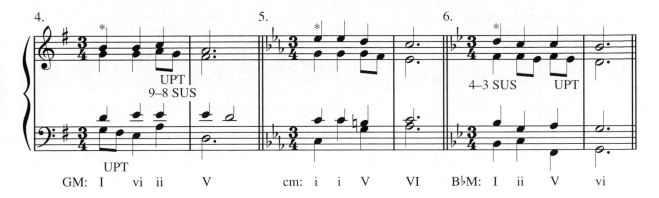

GM: I vi ii V   cm: i i V VI   B♭M: I ii V vi

7. Wie schön leuchtet der Morgenstern
(How brightly shines the morning star)

8. (Ermuntre dich, mein schwacher Geist
(Rouse thyself, my weak spirit)

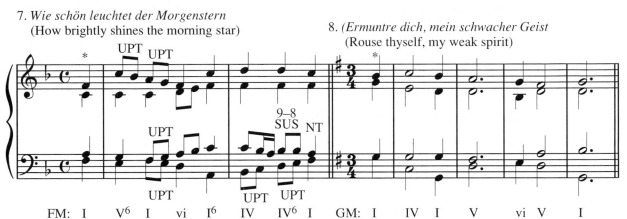

FM: I V⁶ I vi I⁶ IV IV⁶ I   GM: I IV I V vi V I

9. Alle Menschen müssen sterben
(All men must die)

10. We weiss, wie nahe mir mein Ende
(Who knows how near my end may be)

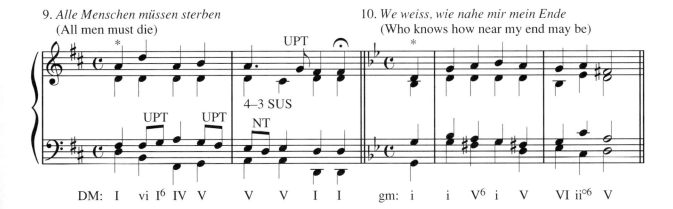

DM: I vi I⁶ IV V   V V I I   gm: i i V⁶ i V VI ii°⁶ V

11. Es ist gewisslich an der Zeit
(It is certainly time)

12. Wer nur den lieben Gott lässt walten
(He who lets only beloved God rule)

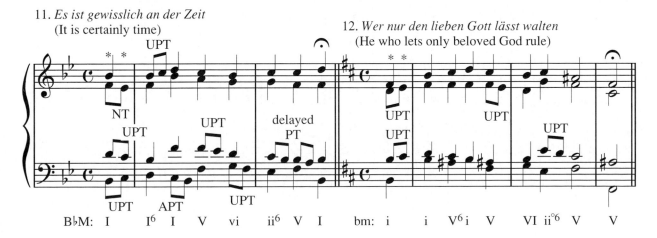

B♭M: I I⁶ I V vi ii⁶ V I   bm: i i V⁶ i V VI ii°⁶ V V

13. *Vater unser im Himmelreich*
(Our Father, Who art in heaven)

14. *Herzlich lieb hab' ich dich, O Herr*
(I love Thee dearly, O Lord)

cm: i V⁶ i iv⁶ i⁶ii°⁶ i⁶₄ V i   CM: I V vi iii I IV IV⁶ I

Harmony 7E

Error Detection: Triads in Four Parts

Student text: Page 100.

Each exercise consists of two triads in four parts.

As played by the instructor, *one* note in each exercise is incorrect. Any voice may contain an error.

1. Indicate the chord (no. 1 or no. 2) containing the error.
2. Indicate the voice containing the error:
    S = soprano   A = alto   T = tenor   B = bass

To the Instructor:

Play both chords, including the circled note, two or three times. The note seen by the student is placed in parentheses to the right of the circled note. If students have initial difficulty with this type of drill, roll the first few chords (bass to soprano) to get them started.

Chord:	2	2	2	2	1
Voice:	T	A	S	B	A

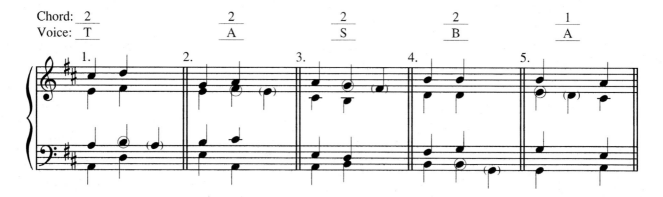

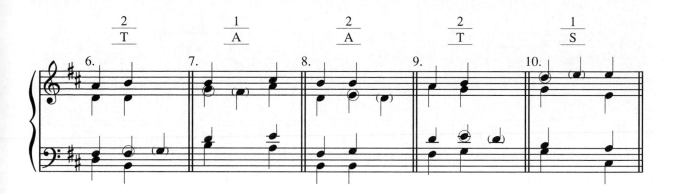

Rhythm 7A

Rhythmic Dictation: Quarter-Beat Values

Student text: Page 101.

Each exercise consists of two measures of 2/4, 3/4, 4/4, or 6/8 meter.

1. For numbers 1—10, the meter signature and first note value are given.
2. For numbers 11—20, nothing is given, but the instructor will provide the basic beat before beginning.
3. Listen for the instructor to provide the basic beat. Then, indicate:
    a. The meter signature.
    b. The rhythm on the staff using a neutral pitch.

To the Instructor:

Play the exercises at different tempi—some fast, some slow.

Three playings should suffice for most students.

Beat or say one measure before beginning each exercise.

For numbers 11—20, no meter signature or beginning note value is given.

Give a clear beat before beginning each exercise, but provide an odd number of beats to avoid giving away the meter.

Rhythm 7B

Rhythmic Dictation: Beat Units Divided into Triplets

Student text: Page 102.

Each exercise consists of a short phrase of music.

Indicate the rhythm on the staff using a neutral pitch. The value for the first note(s) is given.

To the Instructor:

Play each exercise two or three times at performance tempo.

Transcription 7

More Difficult Two-Voice Examples

Refer to instructions found in Transcription 1 (page 25).

Note: * = given material

Recorded Example 14

Arcangelo Corelli: "Largo"

Muzio Clementi: Prelude in A Minor

Unit 8

Melody 8A
Melodic Dictation: Melodies with Larger Leaps

Student text: Page 105.

Each exercise consists of a short, two-measure melody.

Complete each melody on the staff in notation. The first note of each melody is given.

To the Instructor:

Play a harmonic pattern to establish the key for each example. Ask students to recognize the key and mode as well as the scale degree of the first note. Play each melody two or three times at a moderate tempo. Ask class members to sing and analyze each melody.

*Note or rest in workbook.
(R) means recorded.

Melody 8B

Error Detection: Franck Melodies

Student text: Page 106.

Each exercise consists of a phrase of music by César Franck.

Place a circle around the three numbers that represent pitches different from those played.

To the Instructor:

Give the students time to study the written melodies and imagine their sound before playing the instructor versions. Play each melody from music literature at a moderate tempo. The instructor's manual has the melodies as they appear in their original score. The students are asked to recognize printing errors in their textbooks.

1. Franck: Symphonic Variations for Piano and Orchestra

2. Franck: Symphonic Variations for Piano and Orchestra

3. Franck: Symphony in D Minor

4. Franck: Symphony in D Minor

5. Franck: Symphony in D Minor

1 2 3   4 5 6   7 8 9   10 11 12   13 14 ⑮   ⑯ ⑰   18 19 20   21 22 23 24

6. Franck: Symphony in D Minor

1   2 3 ④   5 6   7 8 9 10 11 12 13 14 ⑮ 16 17 18 19 20 ㉑ 22 23

7. Franck: Symphony in D Minor

1 2 3 4   5 6 7   8 9 10 ⑪ 12 13   14 15 16 17 18   19 20 21 ㉒ ㉓

8. Franck: Symphony in D Minor

1 2 3 4 5 6 ⑦ 8 9   10   11 12 ⑬ 14 15 16 ⑰ 18 19

9. Franck: Prelude, Chorale, and Fugue for Piano

1   2 3   4   5 ⑥   7   8 9 10 ⑪   12 13 14 15 ⑯ 17

10. Franck: String Quartet in D

1   2   3   4   5   ⑥ 7 8 ⑨ 10 11   12   13 14 ⑮   16

Melody 8C

Harmonic Rhythm, Harmonic Analysis, Sequences, Phrase Relationships, and Cadences

Student text: Page 107.

Each exercise consists of two phrases excerpted from a Chopin mazurka.

HARMONIC RHYTHM
Place an "X" above each number where a chord change occurs. The chords found in each exercise are listed. To prepare for the exercise, play and sing each chord until it is familiar. (Review Harmony 1C, 5C, and 7C.)

HARMONIC ANALYSIS
Place the roman numeral analysis of each chord below the appropriate numbers. As you listen, keep looking at the list of possible chords and sketch the numbers where each chord occurs. Then, after a few listenings, you are ready to transfer the analysis to the requested position. (Review Harmony A Sections.)

CADENCES
Indicate the cadence types in the blanks provided. By this time you will have placed all chord analyses above the numbers and can assess the cadence type. (Review Harmony 3C.)

MELODIC SEQUENCES
Bracket the numbers where a melodic sequence is heard. This is a separate operation. All of these Chopin examples are homophonic (a single melodic line, easily distinguished) and the melody is in the *highest*-sounding voice. Listen for a melodic excerpt that is sounded more than once, but at different scale locations. (Review 5C, 6C, and 7C.)

PHRASE RELATIONSHIP
Indicate the type of phrase relationship (repeated, modified repeated, parallel, or contrasting) in the blank provided. (See below.)

		Phrase 1	Phrase 2
Repeated	If 2nd phrase repeats the 1st	A	A
Modified repeated	If 2nd phrase repeats the 1st but is slightly modified	A	A'
Parallel	If 2nd phrase is parallel to 1st	A	A' (or AP)
Contrasting	If 2nd phrase is contrasting to 1st	A	B
Melodic Dictation (optional)	Write the melody (highest voice on the blank staff).		

To the Instructor:

Review all steps above before undertaking this section. You may wish to begin with Numbers 3, 4, and 7 since they contain only root-position triads. In analyzing parallel phrases the author prefers the letters: A, AP, because the "AP" distinguishes between modified repeated and parallel construction. However, the "AP" is nonstandard, and you may wish to avoid it on that count alone. Be aware that this section is quite difficult for some students, and you may want to present only part of it—returning to it later in the semester for a more thorough study.

1. Modified repeated phrases, no sequences; Key: C major; Chords: I I$_4^6$ IV^6 V

2. Repeated phrase relationships, no sequences; Key: B major; Chords: ii^6 V I

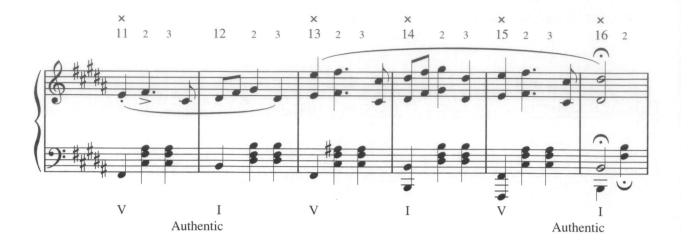

V   I   V   I   V   I

Authentic   Authentic

3.   Contrasting phrase relationship, sequence meas. 5 and 6 and 9 and 10; Key: B♭ major; Chords: I IV V V I

4. Modified repeated phrases, no sequences; Key: B♭ major; Chords: I IV V

5. Parallel phrase relationship, no sequences; Key: F major; Chords: I IV⁶₄ V

6. Parallel phrases, no sequences; Key: D major; Chords: I ii^6 V

DM: I V I V^7 Half

I ii^6 V^7 Authentic I

7. Slightly modified repeated phrases, no sequences; Key: C major; Chords: I ii V

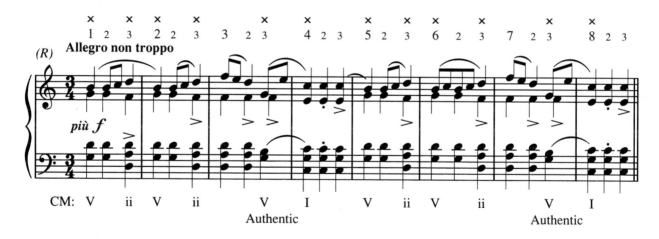

CM: V ii V ii V I V ii V ii V I

Authentic Authentic

8.   Parallel phrases, no sequences; Key: A♭ major; Chords: I I⁶₄ IV V

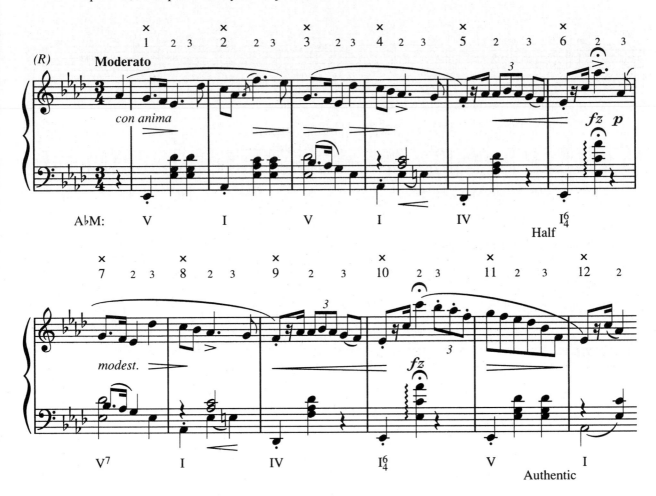

Melody 8D

Intervals: All Diatonic Intervals

Student text: Page 110.

Each exercise consists of a single melodic interval.

1.   Write the name of the interval in the blank provided.
2.   Write the remaining note of the interval on the staff.

To the Instructor:

Play the intervals melodically. Ask class members to sing each interval immediately after it is played.

The given note is the lower of the two.

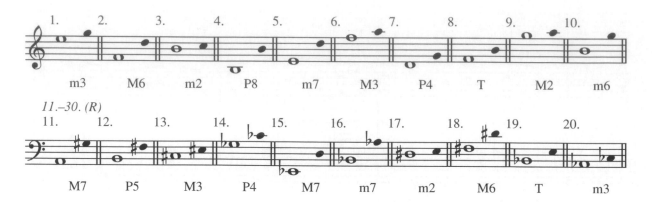

1.	2.	3.	4.	5.	6.	7.	8.	9.	10.
m3	M6	m2	P8	m7	M3	P4	T	M2	m6

11.–30. (R)

11.	12.	13.	14.	15.	16.	17.	18.	19.	20.
M7	P5	M3	P4	M7	m7	m2	M6	T	m3

The given note is the upper of the two.

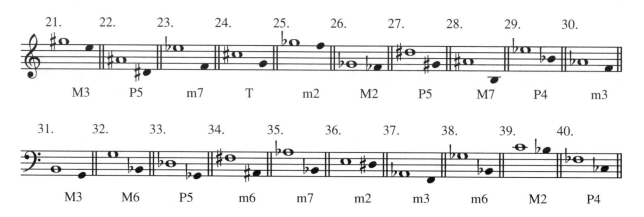

21.	22.	23.	24.	25.	26.	27.	28.	29.	30.
M3	P5	m7	T	m2	M2	P5	M7	P4	m3

31.	32.	33.	34.	35.	36.	37.	38.	39.	40.
M3	M6	P5	m6	m7	m2	m3	m6	M2	P4

Melody 8E

Models and Embellishments: 5–6 Patterns in Three Voices

Student text: Page 111.

1. The model in this section is made up of two voices that ascend in parallel thirds while a third voice ascends in oblique motion. Sing all parts of this structure before class.
2. Your instructor will play the structure followed by embellishments of that structure.
3. Write the model's embellishments on the numbered staves provided.

To the Instructor:

1. Have the students sing each voice of the model before the early examples.
2. Play the structure and embellishments in the order printed, or repeat the structure from time to time to remind students of the basis for each embellishment.
3. Students should notate all three voices of the embellishments.

Model:

Embellishments:

1.

2.

3.

4.

Harmony 8A

Chord Function Identification: Diatonic Triads (Major Mode)

Student text: Page 112.

Each exercise consists of four chords in block harmony.

Write the roman numeral analysis of each chord in the blank provided.

Numbers 1–15 use I, ii, iii, IV, V, vi in root position only:

FM: I   ii   iii   IV   V   vi

Numbers 16–25 use the following chords and their inversions:

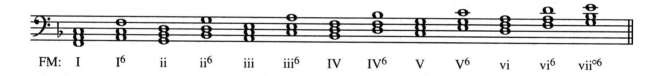

FM: I   I⁶   ii   ii⁶   iii   iii⁶   IV   IV⁶   V   V⁶   vi   vi⁶   vii°⁶

To the Instructor:

To prepare for this set of exercises:
1. Have class members sing the F major scale.
2. Place the chords found at the beginning of this section on the chalkboard. Include the analysis symbols.
3. Point to the chords one at a time, and ask class members to sing each in simple position. Improvise some of the more common progressions found in music (I, iii, vi, ii, etc.)
4. When the chord sounds are familiar and automatic, then move on to the exercises themselves.
5. For the first three or four exercises, ask class members to sing each chord (arpeggiated in simple position). From then on, the exercises should be dictated without accompanying crutches.
6. At first, play each set of chords three or four times and very slowly; then, increase the tempo slightly and decrease the number of playings.

Numbers 1–15 contain root-position chords only:

Numbers 16–25 contain inversions:

Harmony 8B

Chords in Music Literature: All Triads

Student text: Page 113.

1. Each exercise consists of four examples from music literature which includes a variety of harmonic rhythms and nonharmonic tones.
2. Below you see four models (A through D). Your instructor will play each of these four models. Listen carefully and try to distinguish each—one from another.

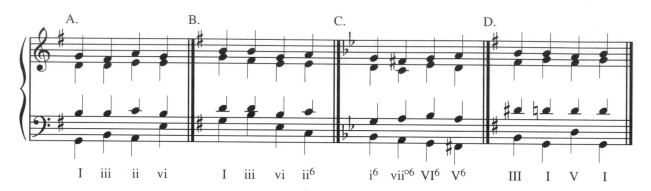

3. Your instructor will play an example (1 through 4) from music literature. The music literature example contains the same chords and same inversions as one of the four models above.

1. Schubert: Piano Sonata, D. 575, III

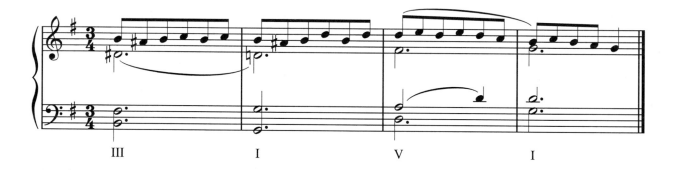

2. A. Scarlatti: O, Dolcissima Speranza

---

3. Saint-Saens: Christmas Oratorio, No. 8

        I   iii   vi   ii⁶

4. Palestrina: Victory

        I   iii   ii   vi

4. When you have matched the literature example with one of the four sets of chords (A through D), place the letter in the appropriate blank below, and prepare for the next example from music literature.

   1. _____ 2. _____ 3. _____ 4. _____

5. When the first four examples are completed, use the same procedure for models 5 through 8.

These (**E, F, G, H**) are the remaining four models. Pair them up with the examples from literature (**5, 6, 7, 8**).

  E.   F.   G.   H.

   i V⁶ i v⁶ VI   vi ii V I   III VI ii°⁶ V   I vii°⁶ vi⁶ V⁶

   5. *(R)* _____ 6. *(R)* _____ 7. *(R)* _____ 8. *(R)* _____

5. Neufville: Sarabande

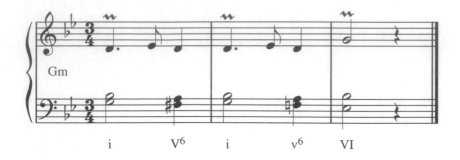

Gm

    i V^6 i v^6 VI

6. Handel: Passacaglia from Suites de Pieces, 1st Coll, No. 7

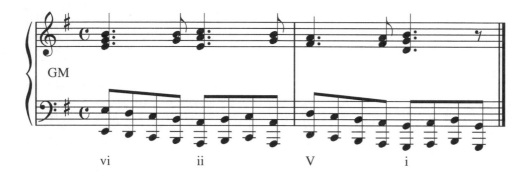

GM

    vi   ii   V   i

7. Haydn: Piano Sonata, Hob. XVI:4, II

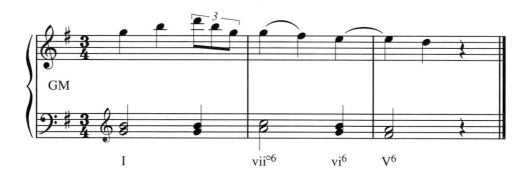

GM

    I vii^{o6} vi^6 V^6

8. Handel: Passacaglia, Suites de Pieces, 1st Collection, No. 7

Gm

    III   VI ii^{o6} V

A complete discussion of this type of exercise and suggestions for classroom use are provided in the "To the Instructor" section of Harmony 1B.

Harmony 8C

Nonharmonic Tones: Bach Chorales (1)

Student text: Page 114.

Each exercise consists of a short excerpt from a four-voice chorale by Bach.

1. The rhythm of each exercise is given on neutral pitches.
2. Nonharmonic tones are marked "X" and numbered.
3. Listen carefully to each excerpt; then write the type of each nonharmonic tone in the blank provided.

To the Instructor:

Play each exercise three or four times slowly, but do not play individual voices separately. Almost every excerpt can be analyzed in a variety of ways. Do not hesitate to alter any of the analyses to suit your preferences.

1. *Dank sei Gott in der Höhe*
   (Thanks be to God on high)

2. *Freu' dich sehr, o meine Seele* (Rejoice greatly, O my soul)

3. *Was willst du dich, o meine Seele* (What do you want, O my soul?)

1. (left column)
1. Unaccented passing tone
2. Accented passing tone
3. Accented passing tone
4. 4–3 suspension
5. Lower neighboring tone

2. (middle column)
1. Accented passing tone (or unaccented passing tone?)
2. 9–8 suspension
3. 4–3 suspension
4. Anticipation

3. (right column)
1. 4–3 suspension
2. Unaccented neighboring tone (decoration of suspension)
3. Unaccented passing tone
4. Anticipation

4. *Herr, wie du willst, so schicks mit mir (R)* (Lord, ordain what Thou wilt for me)

5. *Hilf, Herr Jesu, lass gelingen (R)* (Help, Lord Jesus, send good speed)

6. *Warum sollt' ich mich denn grämen (R)* (Why should I then grieve?)

1. Unaccented passing tone	1. 4–3 suspension	1. Anticipation
2. 4–3 suspension	2. Unaccented neighboring tone	2. Unaccented passing tone
3. Unaccented passing tone	3. Unaccented neighboring tone (decoration of suspension)	3. 4–3 suspension
		4. Unaccented passing tone
		5. Anticipation

7. *Es ist das Heil uns kommen her (R)* (Salvation has come to us) 8. *Nun lieget alles unter dir (R)* (Now all lies beneath Thee)

1. Anticipation	1. 4–3 suspension
2. Unaccented passing tone	2. Suspension decoration (nota cambiata)
3. 4–3 suspension	3. Anticipation
4. Unaccented passing tone	

Harmony 8D

Harmonic Dictation: I(i), ii, IV(iv), V, vi(VI), and vii° Triads in Chorale Phrases

Student text: Page 116.

Each exercise consists of a chorale phrase. The harmonic vocabulary is as follows:

Numbers	Harmony Included	Positions
1–6	All listed above	Root position exclusively
7–10	All listed above, except vi (VI) An occasional vii	Root position and inversions

1. Indicate the roman numeral analysis of each triad in the blanks provided.
2. List any nonharmonic tones beneath the harmonic analysis.
3. If the instructor requests it, give the melodic line of both the soprano and bass voices.
4. If the instructor requests it, give the melodic line of both the alto and tenor voices.

To the Instructor:

For a complete discussion of this type of assignment, see Harmony 3B.

If numbers 7–12 seem too difficult for your class at this time, numbers 1–6 are intended as an introduction. There, all triads are in root position, and nonharmonic tones are confined to unaccented passing tones and an occasional suspension.

Harmony 8E

Error Detection: Triads in Four Parts

Student text: Page 117.

Each exercise consists of two chords. In the second chord, one of the four tones is not played as written.

Indicate the error in the second chord by circling the note.

Play both chords slowly, but do not "roll" them.

The note seen by the student is in parentheses to the right of the circled note.

Rhythm 8A

Rhythmic Dictation: Quarter-Beat Values

Student text: Page 118.

Each exercise consists of a two-measure melody.

Complete each rhythm on a neutral pitch.

To the Instructor:

Play each exercise two or three times, after which class members should repeat the rhythm by clapping before writing. Exercises in compound meter contain sextuple division of the beat; the rest contain quartuple (quarter-beat) division.

Rhythm 8B

Error Detection: Quarter-Beat Values

Student text: Page 119.

Each exercise consists of a melodic phrase from music literature in which one rhythmic error exists.

Circle the number that indicates the measure of the error.

To the Instructor:

Play each exercise two or three times at performance tempo.

1. Verdi: Nabucodonosor Overture

2. Tchaikovsky: Symphony no. 5 in E Minor, op. 64 (fourth movement)

3. Respighi: "Near a Catacomb" from The Pines of Rome

4. Rameau: Suite in E Minor for Harpsichord

5. Pachelbel: Ciaconna in F Minor for Organ

6. Nicolai: The Merry Wives of Windsor (Overture) *(R)*

7. Mozart: *Phantasie no. 1 mit Fugue,* K. 394 *(R)*

8. Mozart: Piano Sonata, K. 576 *(R)*

9. Mozart: Piano Sonata, K. 576 *(R)*

10. Mozart: *Divertimento* in F, K. 138 *(R)*

Transcription 8

Challenging Examples with Two and Three Voices

Refer to instructions found in Transcription 1 (page25).

Note: * = given material

Recorded Example 16

Muzio Clementi: Sonata, op. 36

Un poco Adagio

Cornelius Gurlitt: *Allegretto*

Unit 9

Melody 9A

Melodic Dictation: Short Melodies from Music Literature

Student text: Page 123.

Each exercise consists of a short melodic excerpt from music literature.

Complete each melody on the staff in notation.

To the Instructor:

Play each melody two or three times at a moderate tempo. Ask class members to sing (in any register) and analyze each melody after it is played.

14. *(R)*

*Note or rest in workbook.
(R) means recorded.

Melody 9B

Error Detection: Bach Melodies

Student text: Page 124.

Each exercise consists of a phrase of music by Bach.

Place a circle around the three numbers that represent pitches different from those played.

To the Instructor:

Give the students time to study the written melodies and imagine their sound before playing the instructor versions. Play each melody at a moderate tempo. These melodies are taken from music literature and are notated correctly in the student textbook. Errors have been added to the instructor's manual and, therefore, the students are asked to recognize errors in musical performance.

1. English Suite no. 1

2. English Suite no. 2

3. English Suite no. 2

4. English Suite no. 3

5. English Suite no. 4

1   2   3   4   5   6   7   ⑧   ⑨   10   11   12   13   ⑭

6. English Suite no. 4

1   2   3   4   5   6   ⑦   8   ⑨   10   11   12   13   14   ⑮   16   17

7. French Suite no. 3

1   ②   3   4   5   6   ⑦   8   9   10   11   12   ⑬   14   15   16   17   18   19   20

8. French Suite no. 1

1   2   3   4   ⑤   6   ⑦   8   9   10   11   ⑫   13   14   15   16

9. French Suite no. 2

1   2   ③   4   5   6   7   8   9   10   11   12   13   ⑭   15   16   17   18   19   20   21   22   ㉓   24

10. English Suite no. 6

1   2   3   4 5 6   7   8   9   10   11   12 13 14   15   16 ⑰   ⑱   ⑲

Melody 9C

Melodic Dictation: Two-Part Dictation

Student text: Page 125.

Each exercise consists of a short, two voice melodic composition.

Complete the missing tones on the staff in notation.

To the Instructor:

Dictate slowly enough to ensure proper understanding, but do not play either voice separately. Encourage class members to think of each voice in relation to the other.

Melody 9D

Intervals: Harmonic Intervals of the m3, Tritone, P5, m6, M6, and m7

Student text: Page 127.

Each exercise consists of a single interval.

1. Immediately after hearing the interval, sing both pitches: lower to upper for numbers 1—30, and upper to lower for numbers 31—60.
2. Harmonic intervals (both pitches sound together) are considered more difficult than melodic (one note, then the other) because the two tend to fuse into a single homogenized effect.
3. Separating the two into distinct pitches helps considerably in recognizing and identifying the interval, but remember that this procedure is temporary.
4. Gradually you must learn to identify intervals directly—without going through the intermediary step. Use the crutch for a while, and at the same time keep trying to graduate to the next level.
5. Write the remaining note of the interval on the staff.
6. Write the name of the interval in the blank provided.

To the Instructor:

Play both tones of the interval simultaneously. Ask class members to sing the tones immediately after they are played.

The given note is the lower of the two.

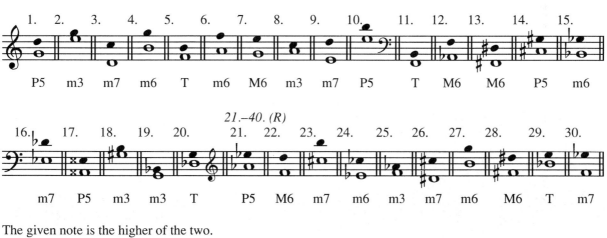

The given note is the higher of the two.

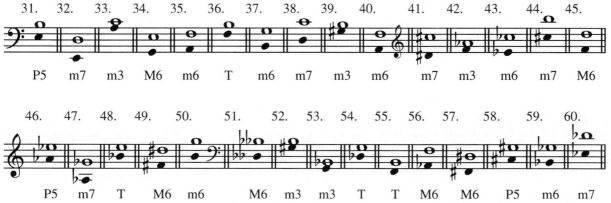

Melody 9E

Models and Embellishments: Descending First-Inversion Triads

Student text: Page 128.

1. The model in this section is made up of descending first-inversion triads (three voices). Sing all parts of this structure before class.
2. Your instructor will play the structure followed by embellishments of that structure.
3. Write the model's embellishments on the numbered staves provided.

To the Instructor:

1. Have the students sing each voice of the model before the early examples.
2. Play the structure and embellishments in the order printed, or repeat the structure from time to time to remind students of the basis for each embellishment.
3. Students should notate all three voices of the embellishments.

Harmony 9A

Chord Function Identification: Six-Four Chord

Student text: Page 129.

Each exercise consists of a series of four chords in block harmony.

Indicate:

1. The analysis of each of the four chords in the blanks provided.
2. If requested by your instructor, show the embellishing nature of these chords using brackets as shown below.
3. The type of $^6_4$ chord:

CADENTIAL   The tonic $^6_4$ chord resolves to the V chord at the cadence.

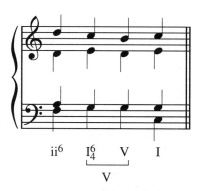

PASSING BASS   The lowest tone (usually bass) acts as a passing tone between two triads, often between a triad and its inversion or vice versa.

NEIGHBORING TONE, or
STATIONARY BASS

The bass tone is preceded and followed by the same tone, and is interposed between two root positions of the same triad.

ARPEGGIATED BASS

The bass participates in an arpeggiation of a chord.

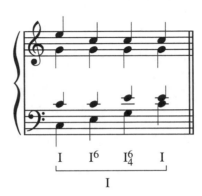

The following illustration indicates the correct procedure:

Instructor plays

Response:

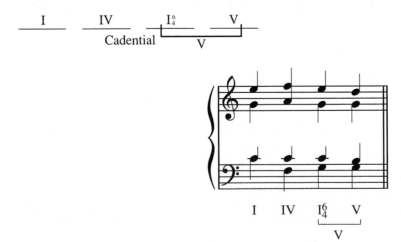

To the Instructor:

To prepare the student for this set of exercises:

1. Have the students sing the C-major scale (for exercises 11—20, the C-minor scale).
2. Place the following chord symbols on the chalkboard:

I	ii	IV	V	vi
I^6	ii^6	IV^6	V^6	vi^6
I^6_4		IV^6_4	V^6_4	

3. As you point to each symbol on the chalkboard, ask the students to sing the triad. Drill the root positions first until they are thoroughly familiar. Then move to the first inversions, having students sing from the bass (lowest tone) up. Then, work with the $^6_4$ inversions, still singing up from the bass tone. When these are thoroughly familiar, progress to the exercises.
4. For the first three or four exercises, have students sing the root of each chord as it is played. Then, on second playing, they sing the *bass note* of each chord (to determine the inversion).
5. After the first three or four exercises, the chord should be identified without the crutches.

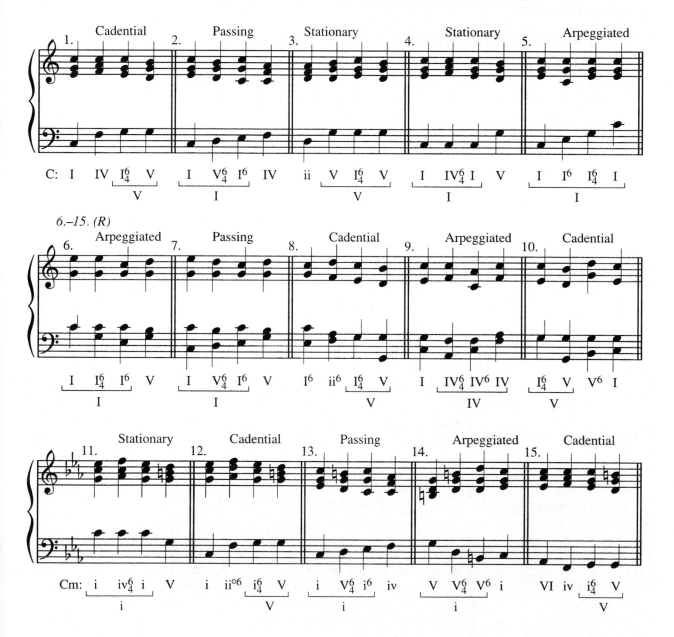

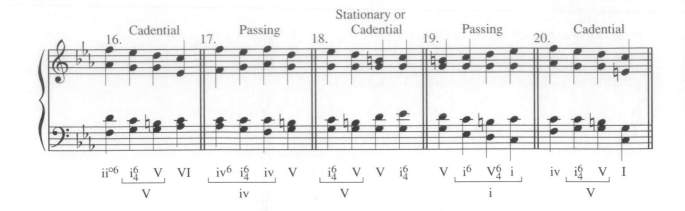

Harmony 9B

Chords in Music Literature: Six-Four Chords

Student text: Page 131.

1. Each exercise consists of four examples from music literature which includes a variety of harmonic rhythms and nonharmonic tones.
2. Below you see four models (A through D). Your instructor will play each of these four models. Listen carefully and try to distinguish each—one from another.

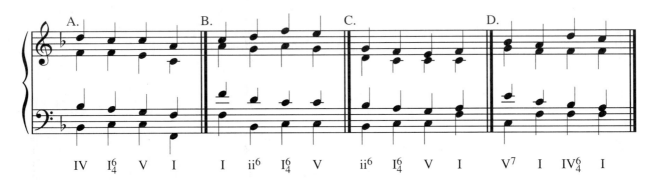

3. Your instructor will play an example (1 through 4) from music literature. The music literature example contains the same chords and same inversions as one of the four models above.

1. Haydn: Piano Sonata, Hob. XVI/12, III

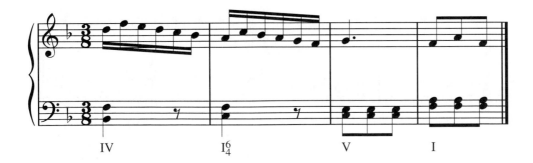

2. Haydn: Piano Sonata, Hob. XVI/3, III

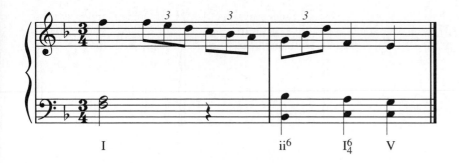

I   ii⁶   I⁶₄   V

3. Haydn: Piano Sonata, Hob. deest. III

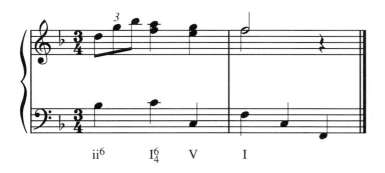

ii⁶   I⁶₄   V   I

4. Mozart: Piano Sonata, K 570, III

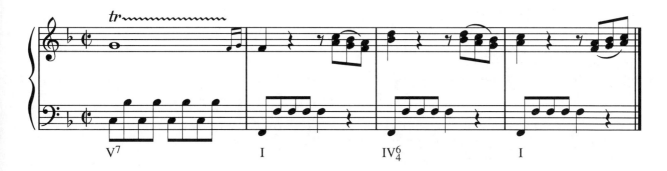

V⁷   I   IV⁶₄   I

4. When you have matched the literature example with one of the four sets of chords (A through D), place the letter in the appropriate blank below, and prepare for the next example from music literature.

    1. _____ 2. _____ 3. _____ 4. _____

5. When the first four examples are completed, use the same procedure for models 5 through 8.

These (**E, F, G, H**) are the remaining four models. Pair them up with the examples from literature (**5, 6, 7, 8**).

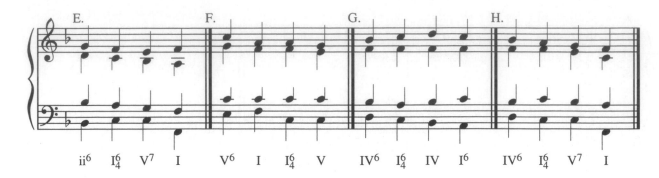

E.				F.				G.				H.			
ii^6	I$^6_4$	V^7	I	V^6	I	I$^6_4$	V	IV^6	I$^6_4$	IV	I^6	IV^6	I$^6_4$	V^7	I

5. (R) _____ 6. (R) _____ 7. (R) _____ 8. (R) _____

5. Mozart: Fantasy, K 397

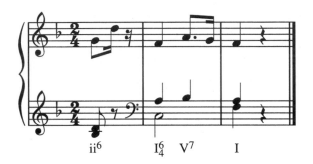

ii^6 I$^6_4$ V^7 I

6. Beethoven: Piano Sonata, Op. 2, No. 1

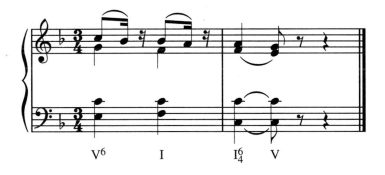

V^6 I   I$^6_4$ V

7. Mozart: Piano Sonata, K 330

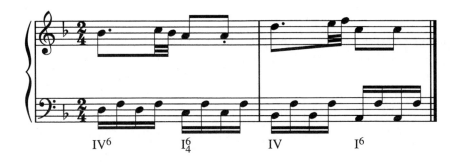

IV^6 I$^6_4$ IV   I^6

8. Schubert: Drei Klavierstücke, No. 1, II Series 11. No. 13.

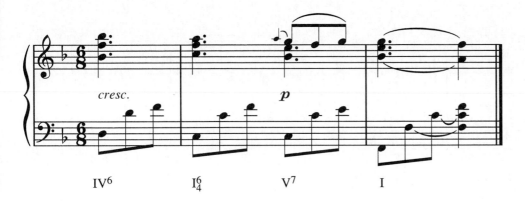

IV⁶   I⁶₄   V⁷   I

To the Instructor:

A complete discussion of this type of exercise and suggestions for classroom use are provided in the "To the Instructor" section of Harmony 1B.

Harmony 9C

Harmonic Rhythm and Harmonic Analysis of Familiar Melodies

Student text: Page 132.

Each exercise consists of a phrase in four-part harmony from a familiar melody. The first melody note is given for each exercise. Recognize when a harmony is used longer than a single beat.

1. Write the melody on the staff in notation.
2. Bracket the melody tones that are supported by a harmony that continues longer than one beat.
3. Indicate the harmonic analysis of each bracketed area above the bracket. (If more than one position of a chord occurs within a bracket, indicate the one with the *lowest*-sounding tone.)
4. Circle and name any nonharmonic tones contained in the melody. Use abbreviations.

To the Instructor:

Play each four-part phrase at performance tempo.

1. Spilman: "Flow Gently, Sweet Afton"

AM: V⁶   I   I⁶   V   I   I   I⁶   IV   IV⁶   IV   I

2. Harrison: "In the Gloaming"

FM: I   IV I   I   V   IV⁶ IV⁶ I   ii   ii   I   I   V⁶ V   I

3. Bayley: "Long, Long Ago"

FM: I   I⁶ V⁶ I vi   I⁶ IV V I   I⁶ IV V   IV V   I

4. Folk Song: "All Through the Night" *(R)*

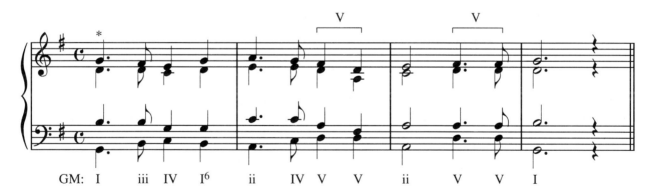

GM: I   iii IV I⁶   ii   IV V   V   ii   V   V   I

5. Spiritual: "Deep River" *(R)*

FM: I   V I   ii⁶ IV   I   I   vi IV   IV   I   I

6.   Foster: "Old Folks at Home" *(R)*

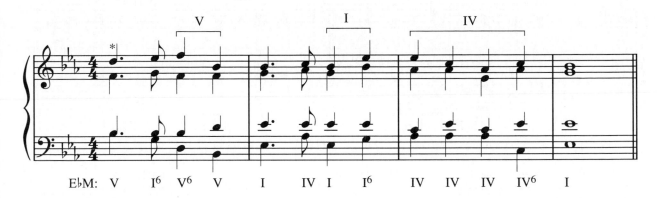

EbM: V   I⁶   V⁶   V   │   I   IV   I   I⁶   │   IV   IV   IV   IV⁶   │   I

Harmony 9D

Harmonic Dictation: All Diatonic Triads in Chorale Phrases

Student text: Page 133.

Each exercise consists of a chorale phrase.

1.   Phrases 1–3—contain only four root-position triads each. Nonharmonic tones are limited to unaccented passing tones and an occasional suspension.
2.   Phrases 4–9—contain seven triads each in any position. Nonharmonic tones are: UPT, APT, ET, and 4–3 suspensions.
3.   Indicate the roman numeral analysis of each triad in the blanks provided.
4.   List any nonharmonic tones beneath the harmonic analysis.
5.   If the instructor requests it, give the melodic line of both the soprano and bass voices.
6.   If the instructor requests it, give the melodic line of both the alto and tenor voices.

To the Instructor:

For a complete discussion of this type of assignment, see Harmony 3B.

If your students have completed this type of assignment in all previous units, they should be well prepared for any of these phrases. If you require four-voice dictation, and class members have difficulty with the alto and tenor voices, play the soprano and bass voices staccato, and the alto and tenor legato once or twice.

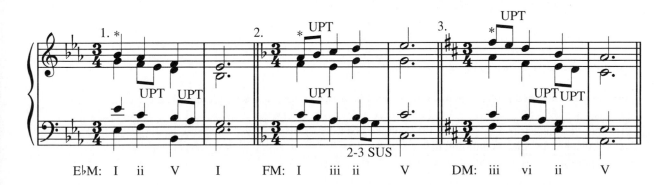

EbM: I   ii   V   I   │   FM: I   iii   ii   V   │   DM: iii   vi   ii   V

Harmony 9E

Error Detection: Triads in Four Parts

Student text: Page 134.

Each exercise consists of two triads in four parts.

As played by the instructor, *one* note in each exercise is incorrect. Any voice may contain an error.

1. Indicate the chord (no. 1 or no. 2) containing the error.
2. Also indicate the voice containing the error:
   S = soprano   A = alto   T = tenor   B = bass

To the Instructor:

Play both chords, including the circled note, two or three times. The note seen by the student is placed in parentheses to the right of the circled note. If students have initial difficulty with this type of drill, roll the first few chords (bass to soprano) to get them started.

Rhythm 9A

Rhythmic Dictation: Compound Meters with Quarter-Beat Values

Student text: Page 135.

Each exercise consists of a short, two-measure melodic excerpt. The meter signature and beginning durational value are given.

Complete each rhythm on a neutral pitch.

To the Instructor:

Play each rhythmic exercise two or three times at the fastest tempo the class can assimilate. Suggest that students tap the meter on the desk with one hand and say the rhythmic syllables simultaneously. If students are not accustomed to rhythmic syllables, then ask them to tap the rhythm with the other hand.

Transcription 9

Three-Voice Examples

Refer to instructions found in Transcription 1 (page 25).

Note: * = given material

Recorded Example 18

Cornelius Gurlitt: Etude in D Minor

Allegro non troppo

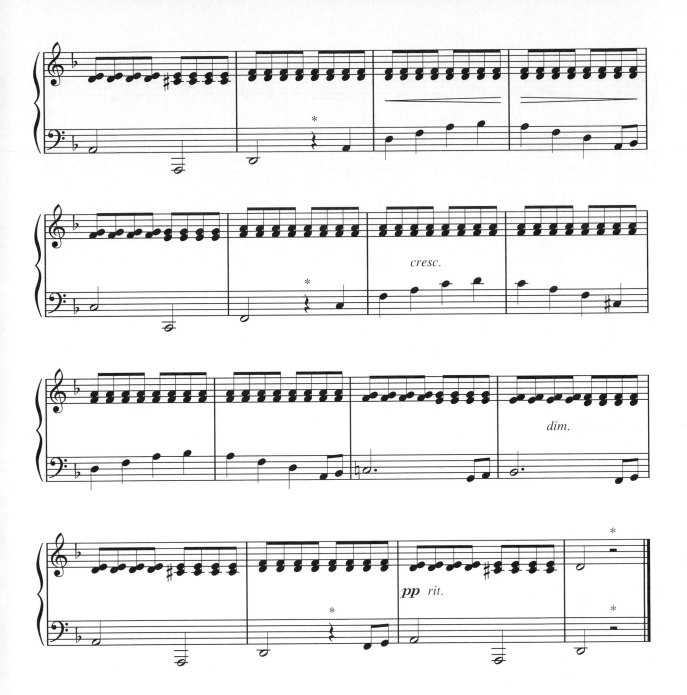

Recorded Example 19

L. van Beethoven, arr.: "Austrian Air"

Unit 10

Melody 10A

Melodic Dictation: Sequences

Student text: Page 139.

Each exercise consists of eight notes, four of which are given.

Write the remaining four notes on the staff in notation.

To the Instructor:

Play the sequences two or three times slowly.

Diatonic sequences with no accidentals:

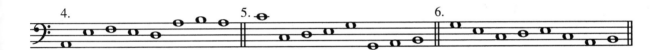

Diatonic sequences:

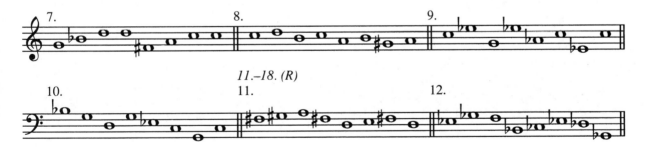

Nondiatonic sequences:

Melody 10B
Error Detection: Themes from Music Literature Lacking Accidentals

Student text: Page 140.

Each exercise consists of a short melodic excerpt from music literature.

1. The following themes are excerpted from the interior of longer compositions, and the actual key of the melody is in conflict with the key signature.
2. In the student's printed version, the accidentals that would help to determine the actual key of the excerpts have been removed.

The instructor plays the excerpt exactly as written by the composer.

3. Write the missing accidentals on the staff in notation.
4. Write the key of the melody in the blank provided.

To the Instructor:

Play each melody two or three times at performance tempo. Discuss each melody thoroughly after class members have completed their answers. In a few instances, alternate answers are possible.

The notes of each melody are numbered for convenience in class discussions.

1. Beethoven: Piano Sonata, op. 31, no. 1

2. Beethoven: String Quartet in A, op. 18, no. 5

3. Beethoven: Symphony no. 8 in F, op. 93

4. Beethoven: Symphony no. 7 in A, op. 92

5. Beethoven: Symphony no. 7 in A, op. 92

6. Beethoven: Piano Sonata, op. 31, no. 1 *(R)*

BM

1 2 3 4 5 6 7 8 9 10 11 12 13 14 15 16

7. Mozart: *Il Re Pastore* Overture, K. 208 *(R)*

GM

1 2 3 4 5 6 7 8 9 10 11 12 13 14 15 16 17 18 19 20 21 22 23 24 25 26 27

8. Mozart: *Cosi Fan Tutti* Overtre, K. 588 *(R)*

Gm

1 2 3 4 5 6 7 8 9 10 11 12 13 14 15 16 17 18

9. Schumann: String Quartet in A, op. 41, no. 3 *(R)*

Fm or A♭M

1 2 3 4 5 6 7 8 9 10 11 12 13

10. Schubert: Symphony no. 7 in C, (Great) *(R)*

GM

1 2 3 4 5 6 7 8 9 10 11 12 13 14 14¹/₂ 15 16 17 18 19 20

(R) means recorded.

Melody 10C

Two-Voice Dictation

Student text: Page 141.

Each exercise consists of a short excerpt of music in two voices.

Numbers 1—7: Write the numbers indicating the harmonic intervals occurring between the two voices. It is not necessary to give the quality of the interval. Thus, instead of P8, M3, A4, M7, and so on, simply state 8, 3, 4, 7, and so on.

Numbers 8—11: Complete the two-voice compositions as dictated. The first note in each voice is given.

To the Instructor:

The first ten exercises are designed to make the student more aware of the relationship between two melodies. At first, play the exercises slowly enough for the students to experience the harmonic intervals as separate entities. Little by little the tempo of dictation may be increased, and the student will be able to memorize several intervals sounded in rapid succession.

For exercises 11—16, dictate both voices at the same time; try to give equal emphasis to each voice.

Melody 10D

Intervals: All Intervals Played Harmonically

Student text: Page 143.

Each exercise consists of a single interval

1.   Indicate the name of the interval in the blank provided.
2.   Write the remaining note of the interval on the staff.

To the Instructor:

Make sure all class members can sing both pitches of each interval. As students become more adept, check occasionally to make sure that they are picking up the interval directly—without the crutch.

The given note is the lower of the two:

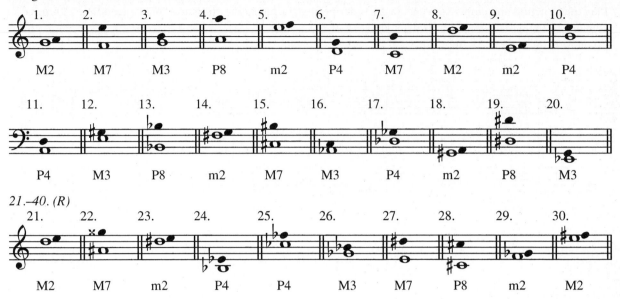

1.	2.	3.	4.	5.	6.	7.	8.	9.	10.
M2	M7	M3	P8	m2	P4	M7	M2	m2	P4

11.	12.	13.	14.	15.	16.	17.	18.	19.	20.
P4	M3	P8	m2	M7	M3	P4	m2	P8	M3

21.–40. (R)

21.	22.	23.	24.	25.	26.	27.	28.	29.	30.
M2	M7	m2	P4	P4	M3	M7	P8	m2	M2

The given note is the higher of the two:

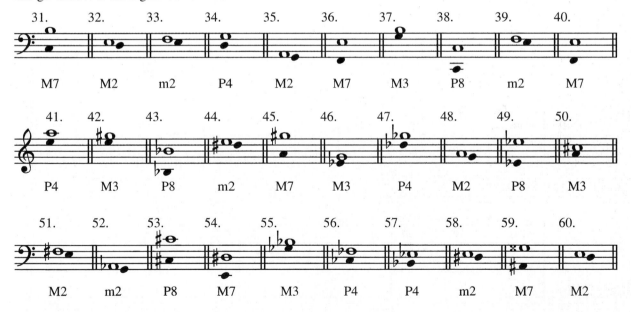

31.	32.	33.	34.	35.	36.	37.	38.	39.	40.
M7	M2	m2	P4	M2	M7	M3	P8	m2	M7

41.	42.	43.	44.	45.	46.	47.	48.	49.	50.
P4	M3	P8	m2	M7	M3	P4	M2	P8	M3

51.	52.	53.	54.	55.	56.	57.	58.	59.	60.
M2	m2	P8	M7	M3	P4	P4	m2	M7	M2

Melody 10E

Models and Embellishments: 7th-Chord Patterns in Three Voices

Student text: Page 144.

1. The model in this section is made up of three voices performing a circle progression or series of ascending fourth root progressions. Sing all parts of this structure before class.

2. Your instructor will play the structure followed by embellishments of that structure.
3. Write the model's embellishments on the numbered staves provided.

To the Instructor:

1. Have the students sing each voice of the model before the early examples.
2. Play the structure and embellishments in the order printed, or repeat the structure from time to time to remind students of the basis for each embellishment.
3. Students should notate all three voices of the embellishments.

Model:

Embellishments:
1.

2.

3.

4.

5.

Harmony 10A

Chord Function Identification: Dominant 7th Chords

Student text: Page 145.

Each exercise consists of a series of four chords in block harmony.

1. Analyze each of the four chords in the blanks provided.
2. The V^7 is the only new chord introduced in this unit. It is analyzed as follows:

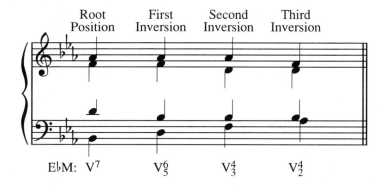

	Root Position	First Inversion	Second Inversion	Third Inversion
E♭M:	V^7	V$^6_5$	V$^4_3$	V$^4_2$

3. Write the analysis in the blanks provided.

To the Instructor:

To prepare the student for this set of exercises:

1. Have the students sing the E-flat major scale.
2. For numbers 1—15 place the following chord symbols on the board:

I	ii	IV	V	V^7	vi

For numbers 16—25, the following:

I	ii	IV	V	V^7	vi
I^6	ii^6	IV^6	V^6	V$^6_5$	vi^6
I$^6_4$				V$^4_3$	
				V$^4_2$	

3. As you point to each symbol on the board, ask the students to sing the triad or 7th chord in simple position, from lowest to highest tone. Drill the root positions first until they are thoroughly familiar. Then practice the inversions, stressing the inversions of the V⁷. When these have been mastered, progress to the exercises.
4. For the first three or four exercises, have students sing the root of each chord as it is played. Then on second playing, have them sing the bass tone of each chord (to determine the inversion).
5. After the first three or four exercises, the chords should be identified without such artificial aids.
6. Clear examples of passing $^6_4$ chords are enclosed in brackets to show their embellishing nature. Discuss these chords with the class. You may wish to discuss other inversions of the V⁷ and their embellishing nature in these short examples.

Numbers 1—15 contain root-position chords only:

Numbers 16—25 contain inversions:

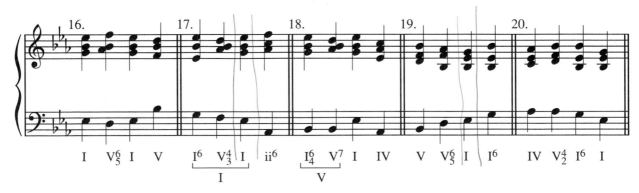

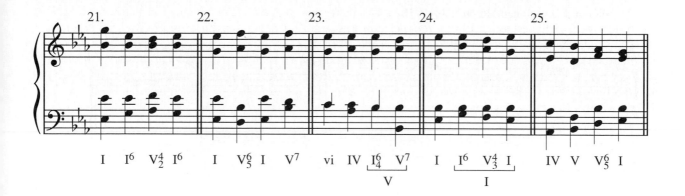

$$\text{I} \quad \text{I}^6 \quad \text{V}^4_2 \quad \text{I}^6 \qquad \text{I} \quad \text{V}^6_5 \quad \text{I} \quad \text{V}^7 \qquad \text{vi} \quad \text{IV} \quad \underset{\text{V}}{\underline{\text{I}^6_4 \quad \text{V}^7}} \qquad \text{I} \quad \underset{\text{I}}{\underline{\text{I}^6 \quad \text{V}^4_3 \quad \text{I}}} \qquad \text{IV} \quad \text{V} \quad \text{V}^6_5 \quad \text{I}$$

Harmony 10B

Chords in Music Literature: Dominant 7th Chords (All Inversions)

Student text: Page 146.

1. Each exercise consists of four examples from music literature which includes a variety of harmonic rhythms and nonharmonic tones.
2. Below you see four models (A through D). Your instructor will play each of these four models. Listen carefully and try to distinguish each—one from another.

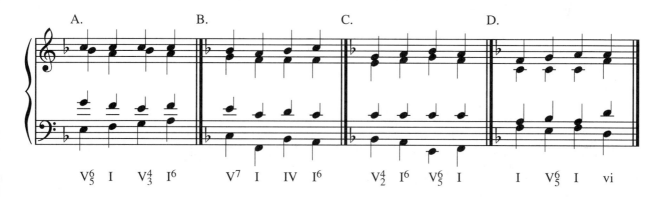

$$\underset{\text{A.}}{\text{V}^6_5 \quad \text{I} \quad \text{V}^4_3 \quad \text{I}^6} \qquad \underset{\text{B.}}{\text{V}^7 \quad \text{I} \quad \text{IV} \quad \text{I}^6} \qquad \underset{\text{C.}}{\text{V}^4_2 \quad \text{I}^6 \quad \text{V}^6_5 \quad \text{I}} \qquad \underset{\text{D.}}{\text{I} \quad \text{V}^6_5 \quad \text{I} \quad \text{vi}}$$

3. Your instructor will play an example (1 through 4) from music literature. The music literature example contains the same chords and same inversions as one of the four models above.

   1. Haydn: Piano Sonata, Hob. XVI/2, I

$$\text{V}^7 \qquad \text{I} \qquad \text{IV} \qquad \text{I}^6$$

2. Haydn: Piano Sonata, Hob. XVI/12, III

$$\text{I} \qquad \text{V}^6_5 \qquad \text{I} \qquad \text{vi}$$

3. Haydn: Piano Sonata, Hob. XVI/2, I

$$\text{V}^6_5 \qquad \text{I} \qquad \text{V}^4_3 \qquad \text{I}^6$$

4. Haydn: Piano Sonata, Hob. XVI/1, I

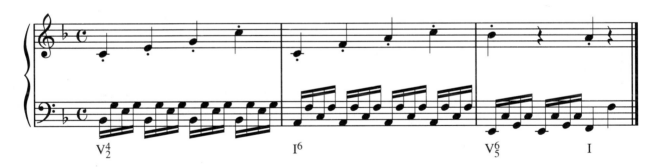

$$\text{V}^4_2 \qquad \text{I}^6 \qquad \text{V}^6_5 \qquad \text{I}$$

4. When you have matched the literature example with one of the four sets of chords (A through D), place the letter in the appropriate blank below, and prepare for the next example from music literature.

1. _____ 2. _____ 3. _____ 4. _____

5. When the first four examples are completed, use the same procedure for models 5 through 8.

These (**E, F, G, H**) are the remaining four models. Pair them up with the examples from literature (**5, 6, 7, 8**).

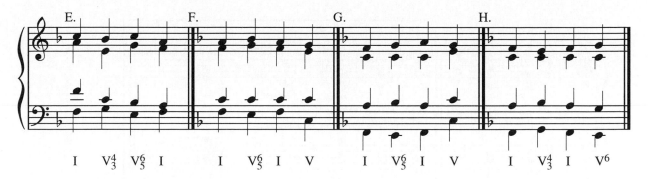

E.   I   V$_3^4$ V$_5^6$ I   F.   I   V$_5^6$ I   V   G.   I   V$_5^6$ I   V   H.   I   V$_3^4$ I   V^6

5. *(R)* _____   6. *(R)* _____   7. *(R)* _____   8. *(R)* _____

5. Mozart: The Magic Flute, Act II, No. 20

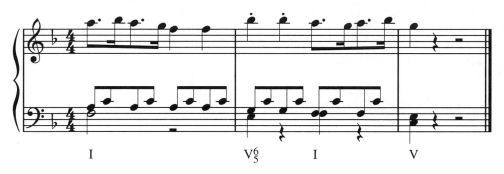

I   V$_5^6$ I   V

6. Beethoven: Rondo, Op. 51, No. 1

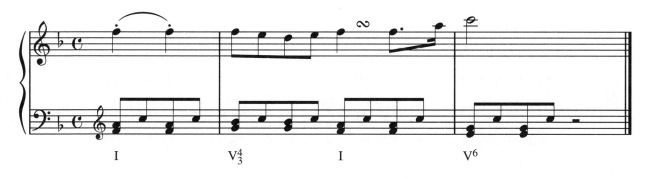

I   V$_3^4$ I   V^6

7. Mozart: Piano Sonata, K. 283, I

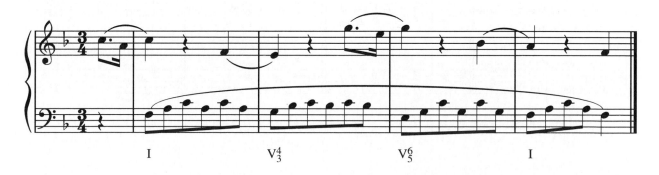

I   V$_3^4$ V$_5^6$ I

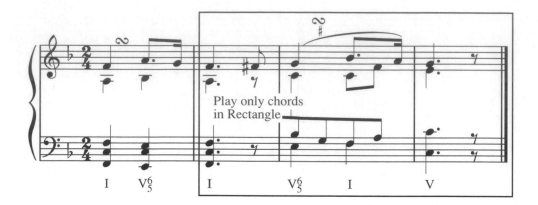

Play only chords
in Rectangle

I   V$^6_5$ I   V$^6_5$ I   V

To the Instructor:

A complete discussion of this type of exercise and suggestions for classroom use are provided in the "To the Instructor" section of Harmony 1B.

Harmony 10C

Nonharmonic Tones: Bach Chorales (2)

Student text: Page 147.

Each exercise consists of a short excerpt in four-part harmony from a Bach chorale.

Each exercise contains two, three, or four nonharmonic tones. The rhythm (only) is given.

Circle the nonharmonic tones, and write the abbreviations representing the types in the blanks provided. Keep the order the same as in the excerpt. Each exercise is numbered for greater ease in class discussions.

To the Instructor:

Play each exercise at performance tempo two or three times. If necessary, emphasize the nonharmonic tones.

UPT	=	unaccented passing tone	APP	=	appoggiatura
APT	=	accented passing tone	SUS	=	suspension
NT	=	neighboring tone	A	=	anticipation
ET	=	escape tone			

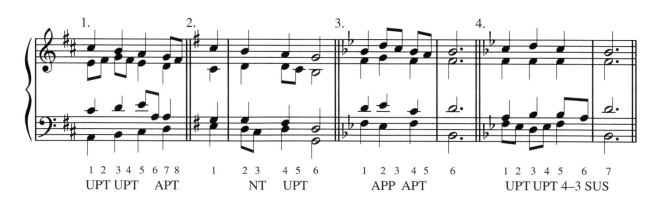

1 2 3 4 5 6 7 8   1   2 3   4 5 6   1 2 3 4 5   6   1 2 3 4 5   6   7
UPT UPT   APT   NT   UPT   APP APT   UPT UPT 4–3 SUS

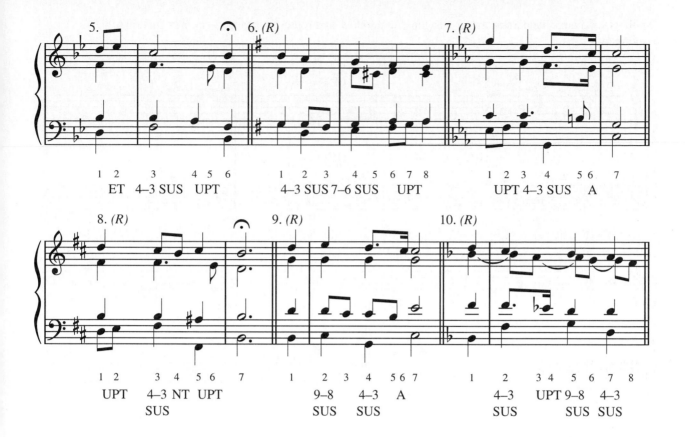

Harmony 10D

Harmonic Dictation: The Dominant 7th Chord in Chorale Phrases

Student text: Page 148.

Each exercise consists of a chorale phrase.

Numbers	No. of Chords	Position
1–3	4	All in root position
4–9	7	Root position and inversions

1. Indicate the roman numeral analysis of each triad in the blanks provided.
2. List any nonharmonic tones beneath the harmonic analysis.
3. If the instructor requests it, give the melodic line of both the soprano and bass voices.
4. If the instructor requests it, give the melodic line of both the alto and tenor voices.

To the Instructor:

For a complete discussion of this type of assignment, see Harmony 4D.

Numbers 1—3 are considerably easier than those that follow, and represent an excellent introduction to the assignment.

*Note or rest in workbook.

Harmony 10E

Error Detection: Triads or Dominant 7th Chords

Student text: Page 149.

Each exercise consists of two chords.

As played by the instructor, one note in each exercise is incorrect. Any voice may contain an error.

1. Indicate the chord (no. 1 or no. 2) containing the error.
2. Also indicate the voice where the error occurs:
    S = soprano   A = alto   T = tenor   B = bass

To the Instructor:

Play both chords, including the circled note, two or three times. The note seen by the student is placed in parentheses to the right of the circled note. If students have initial difficulty with this type of drill, roll the first few chords (bass to soprano) to get them started.

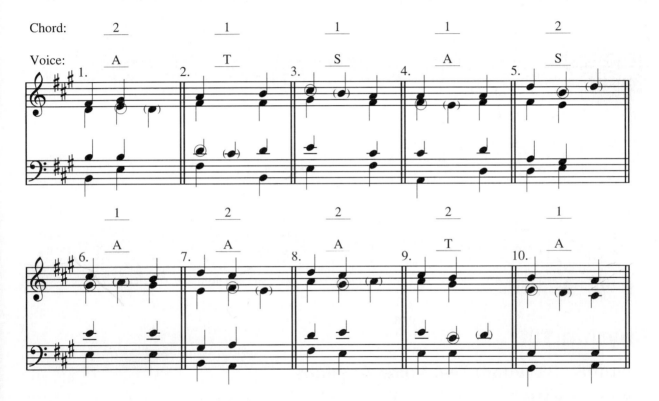

Rhythm 10A

Rhythmic Dictation: Triple and Triplet Subdivisions

Student text: Page 150.

Each exercise consists of a short melodic excerpt of music. Most, but not all of these exercises contain triple or triplet subdivision of the beat.

Complete the rhythm of each excerpt on a neutral pitch.

To the Instructor:

Play each exercise two or three times at performance tempo. Ask class members to clap the complete rhythm before beginning to write. Most, but not all of these exercises contain triple or triplet subdivision of the beat.

Review of Previous Material

Rhythm 10B

Rhythmic Dictation: Two-Voice Rhythms

Student text: Page 151.

Each exercise consists of a two-voice excerpt.

Complete the rhythmic values for both voices on a neutral pitch.

To the Instructor:

Play both voices at equal intensity two or three times.

Transcription 10

Two Chorale Melodies with Bass

Refer to instructions found in Transcription 1 (page 25).

Note: * = given material

Recorded Example 20

J. S. Bach: "I Stand by Your Manger"

Recorded Example 21

J. S. Bach: "Jesus, Our Comfort and Life"

Unit 11

Melody 11A

Melodic Dictation: Short Melodies That Modulate to Closely Related Keys

Student text: Page 153.

Each exercise consists of a melody that modulates to a closely related key.

Notate each melody on the appropriate staff below. The first notes are given for the melodies in this section.

To the Instructor:

Play each melody once or twice. Ask class members to sing the tonic that prevails at the beginning of the melody and the tonic that is in effect at the end. After the relationship of tonics is well in mind, ask students to write the melody on the appropriate staff. An additional two or three playings will probably be necessary for students to check their final results.

* Note or rest in workbook
(R) means recorded.

Melody 11B

Error Detection: Excerpts from Music Literature

Student text: Page 154.

Each exercise consists of a short melodic excerpt from music literature.

1. In each exercise, the notes are on the proper lines or spaces, but either lack proper accidentals or contain accidentals that should be removed. The first note of each exercise is correct.
2. Add or delete accidentals to make the printed copy conform to that played by the instructor. Do not change the letter names of the notes.
3. The notes in each exercise are numbered for convenience in class discussions.

To the Instructor:

Play each exercise three or four times at performance tempo. Ask class members to sing along with the last playing. Do not play sections of an excerpt separately unless students have considerable difficulty.

1. Mozart: *Divertimento* in B-flat, K. 287

2. Mozart: Minuet in D, K. 355

1   2   3   (4)   5   6   7   (8)   9   10   (11)   12   13   14

3. Mozart: *Deutscher Tanz* no. 1 for Orchestra, K. 600

1   2   3   4   5   6   7   (8)   9   10   (11)   12   13   14   15   16   17   18   19   20   (21)   22

4. Mozart: Concerto in C Minor for Piano and Orchestra, K. 491

1   2   3   4   (5)   6   (7)   8   9   10   11   12   13   (14)   15   16   17

5. Mozart: Concerto in F Major for Piano and Orchestra, K. 459

1   2 3 4 5   6 7 8   (9) 10 11   12 13 14   15 16 (17) 18   (19) 20 21 (22)   23 24 25 26   27 28

6. Brahms: Concerto no. 1 in D Minor for Piano and Orchestra, op. 15 *(R)*

1   2   3   4   5   6   7   8   9   10   (11)   12   13   (14)   15   (16)   17   18   (19)   20

7. Brahms: Concerto no. 2 in B-flat for Piano and Orchestra, op. 83 *(R)*

1   2   3   (4)   5   6   7   (8)   9   10   11   12   13   14   (15)   16   17

8. Mendelssohn: Songs Without Words, op. 53, no. 2 *(R)*

1   2   (3)   4   5   6   (7)   8   9   10   (11)   12   13   14   15   16   17   18

9. Beethoven: Symphony no. 9 in D Minor, op. 125, *(R)*

   1   2   3   4   5   6 ⑦ 8   9 10 11 ⑫ 13 14 15 ⑯ 17

10. Berlioz: Beatrice and Benedict (Overture) *(R)*

   1   ②   3   4   ⑤   6   7   8   ⑨   ⑩

Melody 11C

Phrase Relationships and Cadences

Student text: Page 155.

Each exercise consists of a number of phrases of homophonic music.

1. Identify the number of phrases in each excerpt.
2. Identify the relationship of the phrases to each other (using letters). Use "**P**" after a letter to indicate a parallel relationship.
3. Identify the types of cadences at the end of each phrase.
4. Optional: Write the first phrase on the staff in notation.

To the Instructor:

Play each exercise two or three times at performance tempo.

Ask a piano major class member to play the exercises. Assign the music a week in advance to give the performer an opportunity to practice. If a live performance cannot be arranged, use the tapes that accompany this text.

It is hoped that these exercises will trigger spontaneous class discussion of style, form, and analysis. The instructor might also ask students to include an analysis of harmonic rhythm and chord progressions, as well as identification of compositional devices such as sequence.

   1. Clementi: Sonatina, op. 37, no. 1 (second movement)

6	A A' BA A' B' (Answer)	
	A A B A A BP* (Alternate)	A: Auth A': Auth B: Half A: Auth A': Auth B': Auth
No. of phrases	Phrase relationships	Type of cadence at the end of each phrase (in order of appearance)

2. Clementi: Sonatina, op. 36, no. 3 (second movement) Students may hear this example as two-bar phrases.

4	A B A' BP or B'	A: Auth B: Half A': Auth BP or B': Auth
No. of phrases	Phrase relationships	Type of cadence at the end of each phrase (in order of appearance)

3. Clementi: Sonatina, op. 36, no. 3 (third movement)

5	A B A B' C	A: Auth B: Auth A: Auth B': Auth C: Auth
No. of phrases	Phrase relationships	Type of cadence at the end of each phrase (in order of appearance)

4.   Clementi: Sonatina, op. 36, no. 4 (first movement)

4	A B A' C or B'	A: Auth (melodic) B: Half A': Auth (melodic) C: Auth (C major)
No. of phrases	Phrase relationships	Type of cadence at the end of each phrase (in order of appearance)

5. Clementi: Sonatina, op. 36, no. 5 (third movement) (R)*

4	A B or AP A' B or AP'	A: Half B' or AP: Auth A': Half B' or AP': Auth
No. of phrases	Phrase relationships	Type of cadence at the end of each phrase (in order of appearance)

6. Clementi: Sonatina, op. 36, no. 6 (second movement) *(R)*

4	A AP A' AP'	A: Half AP: Auth A': Half AP': Auth
No. of phrases	Phrase relationships	Type of cadence at the end of each phrase (in order of appearance)

7.   Clementi: Sonatina, op. 37, no. 1 (first movement) *(R)*

4	A B A BP	A: Auth B: Half A: Auth BP: Auth
No. of phrases	Phrase relationships	Type of cadence at the end of each phrase (in order of appearance)

8.   Clementi: Sonatina, op. 36, no. 2 (third movement) *(R)*

4	A B A BP or B'	A: Half B: Half A: Half BP or B': Auth
or: 8	: A A' B C A A' B' D	or: A: Half A': Half B: Plagal C: Half A: Half A': Half B: Plagal or Auth D: Auth
No. of phrases	Phrase relationships	Type of cadence at the end of each phrase (in order of appearance)

Melody 11D

Intervals: All Intervals Played Harmonically

Student text: Page 157.

Each exercise consists of a single interval played harmonically.

1. Write the name of the interval in the blank provided.
2. Write the remaining note on the staff.

To the Instructor:

Play both tones of the interval simultaneously. Ask class members to sing the tones (lowest tone first) immediately. Repeat the procedure if necessary; then students should complete the directions above.

The given note is the lower of the two:

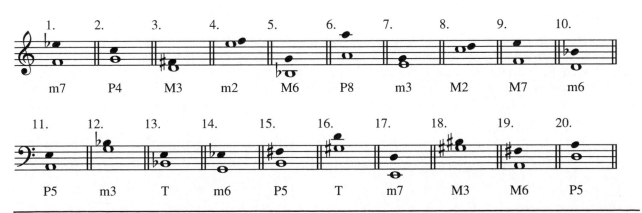

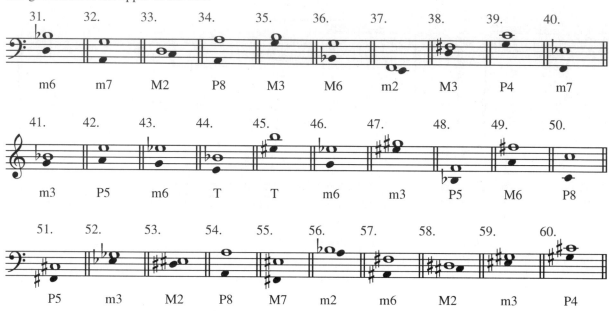

The given note is the upper of the two:

Melody 11E

Models and Embellishments: Chord Progression with Melodic Embellishments

Student text: Page 158.

1. The model in this section is made up of a famous chord progression with melodic and textural embellishments. You will probably recognize it as the progression of the Pachelbel "Canon." Sing all parts of this structure before class.
2. Your instructor will play the structure followed by embellishments of that structure.
3. Write the model's embellishments on the numbered staves provided.

To the Instructor:

1. Have the students sing each voice of the model before the early examples.
2. Play the structure and embellishments in the order printed, or repeat the structure from time to time to remind students of the basis for each embellishment.
3. Students should notate all four voices of the embellishments.
4. In many of the Models and Embellishments exercises, you may choose to play the embellishments in a different order than printed.

Model:

Embellishments:

1.

2.

3.

4.

5.

Harmony 11A

Chord Function Identification: vii°⁷ (Diminished 7th Chord)

Student text: Page 159.

Each exercise consists of a series of four chords in block harmony.

Indicate the analysis of each of the four chords in the blank provided.

The new chord:

Em: vii°⁷

To the Instructor:

To prepare for this set of exercises:

1. Have the class sing the E harmonic-minor scale.
2. For numbers 1—15, place the following chord symbols on the blackboard:
   E minor: i   iv   V⁷   VI   vii°⁷
   For numbers 16—25:
   E minor: i   i⁶   i$^6_4$ ii°⁶   V   V$^6_5$ VI⁶   vii°⁷   vii°$^6_5$ vii°$^4_3$
3. As you point to each symbol on the board, ask students to sing the triad or 7th chord (in simple position, from lowest to highest).

Numbers 1—15 contain root-position chords only:

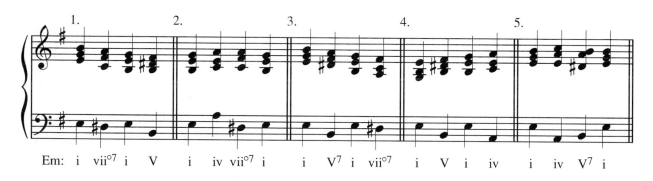

Em: i vii°⁷ i V   i iv vii°⁷ i   i V⁷ i vii°⁷   i V i iv   i iv V⁷ i

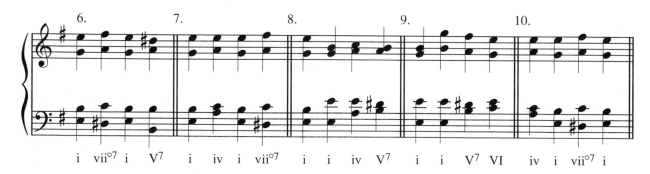

i vii°⁷ i V⁷   i iv i vii°⁷   i i iv V⁷   i i V⁷ VI   iv i vii°⁷ i

i   i   vii°⁷ i   V⁷ i   iv V   i   iv i   vii°⁷ i   vii°⁷ i   VI   iv iv V⁷ i

Numbers 16—25 contain inversions:

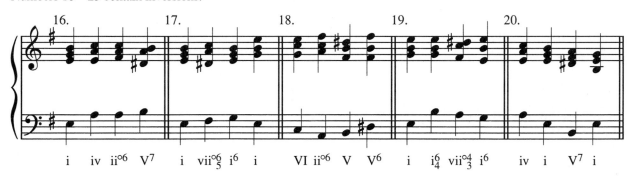

i   iv ii°⁶ V⁷   i   vii°⁶₅ i⁶ i   VI ii°⁶ V   V⁶   i   i⁶₄ vii°⁴₃ i⁶   iv i   V⁷ i

i   vii°⁶₅ vii°⁷ i   iv i⁶ vii°⁷ i   V⁶ V⁷ i   i   i   V⁶ i   vii°⁷ i   iv iv⁶ i

Harmony 11B

Chords in Music Literature: vii°⁷ (Diminished 7th Chord)

Student text: Page 160.

1. Each exercise consists of four examples from music literature which includes a variety of harmonic rhythms and nonharmonic tones.
2. Below you see four models (A through D). Your instructor will play each of these four models. Listen carefully and try to distinguish each—one from another.

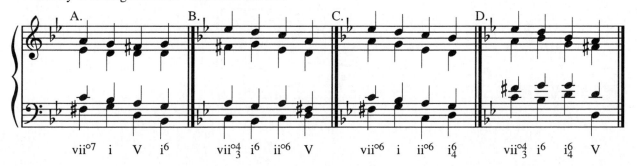

vii°⁷ i   V   i⁶   vii°⁴₃ i⁶ ii°⁶ V   vii°⁶ i   ii°⁶ i⁶₄   vii°⁴₃ i⁶ i⁶₄ V

3. Your instructor will play an example (1 through 4) from music literature. The music literature example contains the same chords and same inversions as one of the four models above.

1. Haydn: Piano Sonata, Hob. XVI/11, III

vii°7   i   ii°6 i⁶₄

2. Haydn: Piano Sonata, Hob. XVI/11, I

vii°⁴₃   i⁶   ii°6 V

3. Haydn: Piano Sonata, Hob. XVI/11, I

vii°⁴₃   i⁶ i⁶₄ V

4. Legrenzi: Che Fiero Costume

vii°7   i   V   i⁶

4. When you have matched the literature example with one of the four sets of chords (A through D), place the letter in the appropriate blank below, and prepare for the next example from music literature.

1. _____ 2. _____ 3. _____ 4. _____

5. When the first four examples are completed, use the same procedure for models 5 through 8.

These (**E, F, G, H**) are the remaining four models. Pair them up with the examples from literature (**5, 6, 7, 8**).

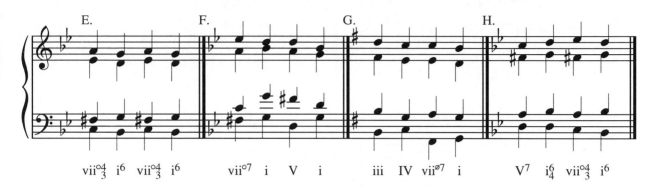

5. *(R)* _____ 6. *(R)* _____ 7. *(R)* _____ 8. *(R)* _____

5. Strauss: Ach lieb, ich muss nun scheiden

6. Haydn: Piano Sonata, Hob. XVI/14, III

7. Handel: Prelude and Lesson in A Minor (G18 & 19)

vii°7   i   V   i

8. Handel: Suite in E Minor (G163—167), III

V⁷   i⁶₄   vii°⁴₃   i⁶

To the Instructor:

A complete discussion of this type of exercise and suggestions for classroom use are provided in the "To the Instructor" section of Harmony 1B.

Harmony 11C

Aural Analysis: Aspects of Two-Phrase Excerpts

Student text: Page 161.

The complete questions appearing in the student workbook are reprinted here for the instructor's convenience.

Each exercise consists of two phrases from a Haydn piano sonata containing parallel phrases, contrasting phrases, or Alberti bass.

If circumstances prevent these from being played live in class, use the tapes that accompany this text.

To the Instructor:

The following questions should trigger spontaneous class discussions of style, form, and analysis. Encourage these discussions and always permit alternative analyses when they are based on logic.

1. Listen carefully three or four times to each excerpt and then circle the letter of all true statements.

The instructor now plays no. 1. (R)

Haydn: Piano Sonata, Hob. XVI/49 (first movement) *(R)*

    ⓐ   The first phrase begins with tonic harmony while the second begins with dominant harmony.
    b.   The two phrases are contrasting type.
    ⓒ   A five-tone rhythmic motive is heard twice in each phrase.
    d.   The two phrases are in modified parallel construction.
    e.   Both phrases contain imitation.
    f.   Both phrases contain only tonic and dominant harmony.
    ⓖ   Both phrases are homophonic.
    ⓗ   The first phrase has a prominent 7—6 suspension.
    i.   The second phrase has a prominent 4—3 suspension.
    ⓙ   The last phrase ends with tonic harmony.
    k.   Both phrases have the same cadence types.
    ⓛ   Both phrases have the same rhythm.
    m.   The second phrase is a repetition of the first with the mode changed.
    ⓝ   The second phrase contains a sequence.
    o.   The second phrase contains an extension.

The instructor now plays no. 2.

Haydn: Piano sonata, Hob. XVI/8 (finale)

2. Circle the letter of all true statements.

   a. The basic harmony is tonic and dominant only.
   b. The basic harmony is tonic, supertonic, and dominant only.
   c. The basic harmony is subdominant and dominant only.
   d. The basic harmony is tonic and subdominant only.
   e. The basic harmony is tonic, supertonic, subdominant, and dominant only.
   f. The texture is polyphonic.
   g. The excerpt contains a change of mode.
   h. The excerpt contains an Alberti bass figure.
   i. The second phrase contains an extension.
   j. The most prominent nonharmonic device is the suspension.

3. Circle the letter (a—e) that indicates the correct harmonic rhythm. Each "X" indicates the beginning of a different harmony (the rhythm of the melody is reproduced for convenience).

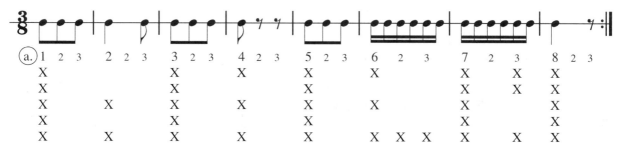

The instructor now plays no. 3. (R)

Haydn: Piano Sonata, Hob XVI/13 (finale) *(R)*

4. Circle the letter of all true statements. The basic harmony in this excerpt is:

   a. Tonic and subdominant only.
   b. Tonic, subdominant, and dominant only.
   c. Tonic, supertonic, and dominant only.
   d. Tonic and dominant only.
   e. Tonic, supertonic, subdominant, and dominant only.

5. Circle the true statements regarding the excerpt (assuming two phrases):

   a. The most prominent nonharmonic tone is the suspension.
   b. The texture is polyphonic.
   c. The second phrase contains an extension.
   d. The first phrase is a sequence made up of two legs.
   e. The excerpt contains a change of mode.
   f. The harmonic rhythm is fast, consisting of at least ten changes per phrase.
   g. The phrases are in modified repeated relationship.
   h. The first phrase emphasizes tonic harmony while the second contrasts both subdominant and dominant harmony.
   i. The same type of cadence punctuates both phrases.
   j. A prominent false sequence appears in both phrases.

The instructor now plays no. 4 (R)

Haydn: Piano Sonata Scherzo, Hob. XVI/9 (last movement) *(R)*

6. Circle the letter of all true statements. The basic chords in this excerpt are:

   a. Tonic, subdominant, and dominant only.
   b. Tonic and subdominant only.
   c. Tonic, supertonic, and dominant only.
   ⓓ Tonic and dominant only.
   e. Tonic, submediant, and dominant only.

7. Assuming two phrases, the two cadences are (in order of appearance):

   a. Half and authentic.
   ⓑ Authentic and authentic.
   c. Authentic and half.
   d. Half and half.
   e. Plagal and authentic.

8. Assuming two phrases, the relationship between the two could be construed logically in two ways:

   ⓐ Either modified repeated or parallel.
   b. Either contrasting or parallel.
   c. Either exact repeated or parallel.
   d. Either exact or modified repeated.
   e. Either contrasting or modified repeated.

Harmony 11D

Harmonic Dictation: Chorale Phrases That Modulate

Student text: Page 163.

Each exercise consists of a chorale phrase.

Numbers	No. of Chords	Position	Nonharmonic Tones
1–9	5	Root position only	Occasional passing tone
10–13	7–9	Root position and inversions	Several—any type

For numbers 1–9 (practice outside of class):

1. Identifying modulations is not easy and requires some long-range thinking. Numbers 1–9 afford an ideal introduction because in each phrase:

Chord No.	Function
1	Is always tonic in the original key
1–3	Always establishes the original key
5	Is always tonic in the new key
4–5	Always forms a cadence in the new key

   This narrows the possibilities and gives you an opportunity to concentrate on the modulation itself. The following procedure is recommended:

2. Practice recognition of inversions in numbers 10–13.
3. Listen to all five chords. Compare the first and last chords. Remember that both are tonic chords—original and new.

---

4. Sing only the roots of the two chords—first, then second. You can tell the relationship of the two by the interval formed.
5. When you have figured out the new key, analyzing the five chords is considerably simplified.
6. Indicate the roman numeral analysis of each triad. Because all phrases modulate, the blanks have been omitted throughout.
7. List any nonharmonic tones beneath the harmonic analysis.
8. If the instructor requests it, give the melodic line of both the soprano and bass voices.
9. If the instructor requests it, give the melodic line of both the alto and tenor voices.

To the Instructor:

This introductory procedure works equally well in class and may be used there to advantage. Drill numbers 1—9 thoroughly before tackling 10—13, which are by Bach, and are obviously more difficult. Unless all members of your class are unusually talented, some may need extra time to breach the difficult gap between the first nine phrases and the remainder of the assignment. In numbers 1—9 a more graphic analysis is shown only in this Instructor's Manual. The authors find that students prefer this design, but whether to introduce it to your students or not is your own choice.

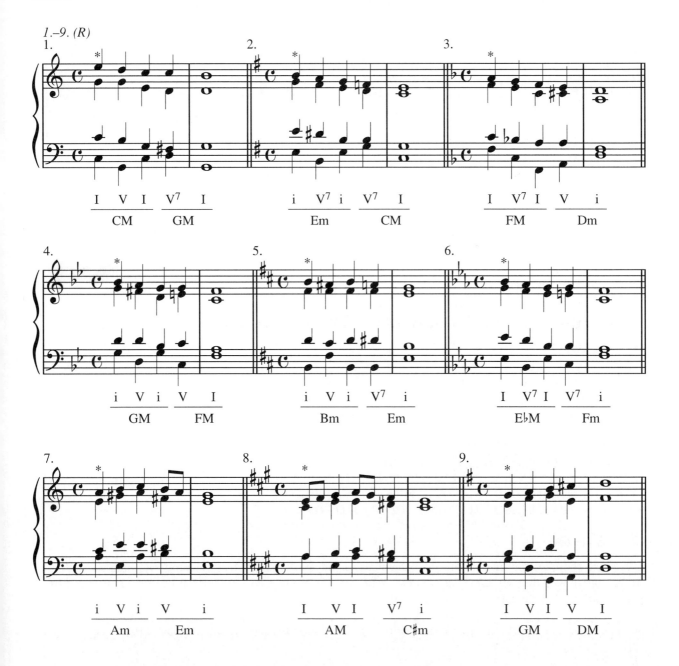

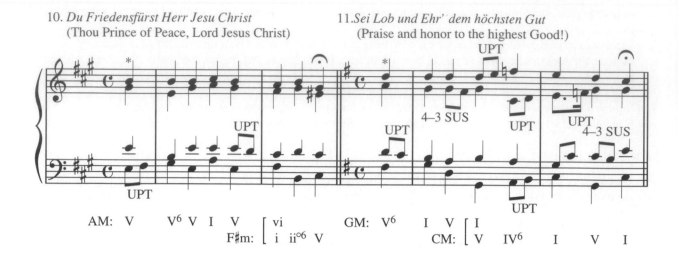

10. *Du Friedensfürst Herr Jesu Christ*
(Thou Prince of Peace, Lord Jesus Christ)

11. *Sei Lob und Ehr' dem höchsten Gut*
(Praise and honor to the highest Good!)

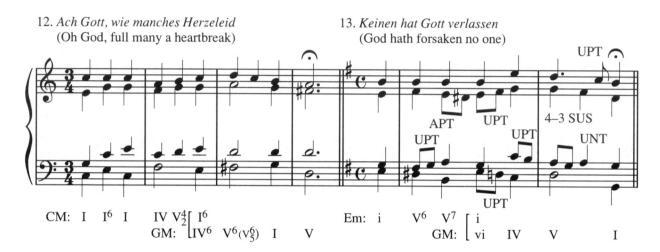

12. *Ach Gott, wie manches Herzeleid*
(Oh God, full many a heartbreak)

13. *Keinen hat Gott verlassen*
(God hath forsaken no one)

Harmony 11E

Chord Quality Identification: MM, Mm, mm, dm, and dd 7th Chords

Student text: Page 164.

Each exercise consists of a single 7th chord.

In the blanks, write the abbreviation for the type of 7th chord played.

MM = MAJOR TRIAD AND MAJOR 7TH
Mm = MAJOR TRIAD AND MINOR 7TH
mm = MINOR TRIAD AND MINOR 7TH
dm = DIMINISHED TRIAD AND MINOR 7TH
dd = DIMINISHED TRIAD AND DIMINISHED 7TH

To the Instructor:

Play each 7th chord two or three times without emphasis on any one factor. Ask class members to sing each 7th chord beginning with the root immediately after it is played. If students have particular difficulty, ask them to first sing the triad and then the interval from root to 7th.

In numbers 1—20, all 7th chords are in root position and the 7th is in the soprano (highest sounding) voice.

In numbers 21—30, the 7th chords are all in root position, but the 7th may be in any voice (except the bass, of course).

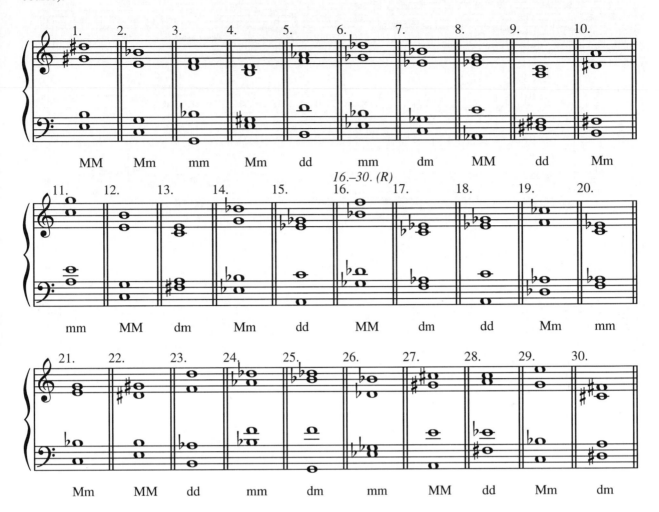

Rhythm 11A

Rhythmic Dictation: The Quartolet

Student text: Page 165.

Each exercise consists of a short rhythmic excerpt. Many, but not all of these exercises contain **quartolets,** rhythmic groupings of four normally given to groupings of three.

Complete the rhythm on a neutral pitch.

To the Instructor:

After playing the exercise two or three times, ask class members to clap the same rhythm. If the excerpt is too long, divide it into sections. Play the exercises again once or twice for students to check their answers. Only half of these exercises contain quartolets.

Rhythm 11B

Error Detection: More Difficult Rhythmic Errors

Student text: Page 166.

Each exercise consists of a short melody with one rhythm error.

Circle the number indicating the beat that differs rhythmically from what is written.

To the Instructor:

Although these exercises are notated to be played in a melodic fashion, they may be tapped, rapped, or played on a neutral pitch if the instructor desires.

Transcription 11
Three-Voice Examples

Refer to instructions found in Transcription 1 (page 25).

Note: * = given material

Recorded Example 22

W. A. Mozart: From "Two Small Pieces"

Recorded Example 23

Joseph Haydn: Piano Sonata in G Major

Unit 12

Melody 12A

Melodic Dictation: Modulations to Closely Related Keys

Student text: Page 169.

Each exercise consists of a melodic excerpt that modulates to a closely related key.

Complete the melody on the staff in notation.

To the Instructor:

Play each melody once or twice. Ask class members to sing the tonic that prevails at the beginning of the melody and the tonic that is in effect at the end. After the relationship of tonics is well in mind, ask students to write the melody on the appropriate staff. An additional two or three playings will probably be necessary for students to check their final results.

7. (R)

8. (R)

9. (R)

10. (R)

(R) means recorded.
*Note or rest in workbook.

Melody 12B

Error Detection: Two-Voice Compositions

Student text: Page 170.

Each exercise consists of a short excerpt from compositions by Baroque period composers, J. S. Bach and G. P. Telemann.

1. Each excerpt contains *three* printing pitch errors.
2. The notes of each composition are numbered.
3. Circle the numbers representing incorrect pitches (as played).
4. The first note of each voice in all exercises is correct.

To the Instructor:

Play each excerpt at least three times at performance tempo or slightly slower.

1. J. S. Bach: Goldberg Variations no. 12

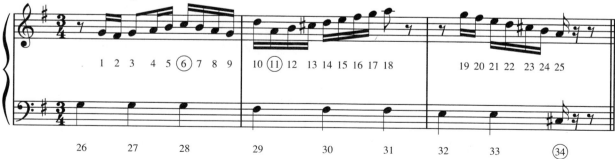

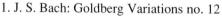

2. J. S. Bach: Goldberg Variations no. 11

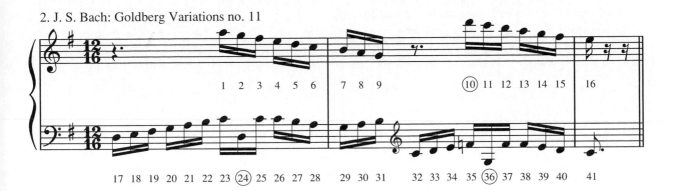

3. Telemann: *Christ lag in Todesbanden,* Chorale Prelude

4. J. S. Bach: Goldberg Variations no. 7

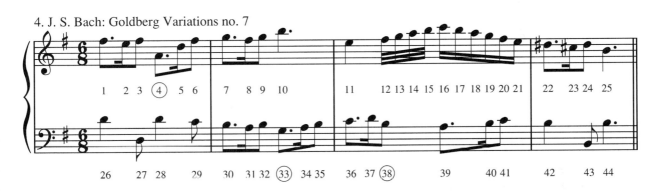

5. J. S. Bach: Goldberg Variations no. 9

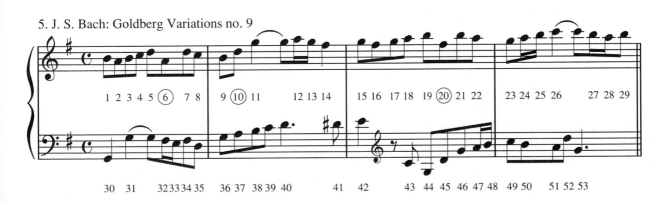

6. Telemann: *Christ lag in Todesbanden*, Chorale Prelude

Melody 12C

Binary, Rounded Binary, and Three-Part Form

Student text: Page 172.

Each exercise consists of a complete composition in **binary, rounded binary,** or **three-part form.** Rounded binary lacks a truly distinct and independent B section and thus is distinguished from three-part form.

The measure numbers for each composition are given. The instructor will provide the beat duration so that you can follow the composition from the given numbers.

Indicate:

1. the phrases by bracketing the numbers (The first phrase of each composition is correctly bracketed for you.)
2. the phrase relationships:

    A   =   the first phrase of each composition or any other like it

    A' =   any other phrase that is a modified repetition of "A"

    AP =   a phrase that stands in parallel relationship to "A"

    B   =   a contrasting phrase to "A"

    B' =   any other phrase that is a modified repetition of "B"

3. the type of cadence at the end of each phrase
4. the key of each cadence
5. any melodic sequences or repetitions (These are also given for the first phrase of each composition.)
6. the overall form of the composition

To the Instructor:

This section can be used in a variety of ways. The instructor may elect any of the following approaches:

For overall analysis only

Class members are responsible only for identifying the overall form—binary, rounded binary, or three-part form. Details such as recognition of the phrases, cadences, sequences, and repetitions are omitted.

The advantage of this procedure lies in the simplicity of the goal. Less time will be consumed, fewer playings necessary, and the class members can concentrate on the overall form.

For overall analysis and phrase structure only

Class members are responsible only for identifying the phrase structure and the overall form. The details of phrase relationships, cadence types, and melodic idioms are omitted.

This involves class members more than the first approach, but does not require the refinement of the following approach.

For analysis of overall form, phrase structure, phrase relationships, cadences, and compositional practices such as sequence and repetition

This means total involvement, requires more playings, and demands more concentration on the part of class members. The advantage to this approach is that it is a greater challenge and requires the most disciplined listening.

Regardless of the information desired, the following procedures are advised:

1. Count out loud the meter beats, at least two measures before beginning to play. This will orient class members to the measure numbers given.
2. Play each composition at performance tempo or slightly slower. It is advantageous for a piano major class member to play these compositions. If it is convenient, assign the compositions at least a week before the class meeting. As a last resort, play the recordings that accompany this book.
3. Some repeat signs have been removed from compositions 1 and 3 to conserve class time. In no instance is the basic form changed. For those who prefer the unexpurgated versions, the repeat signs may be replaced. The measure numbers in the text should also be revised.

1. Mozart Piano Sonata (Alla Turca), K. 331 *(R)*

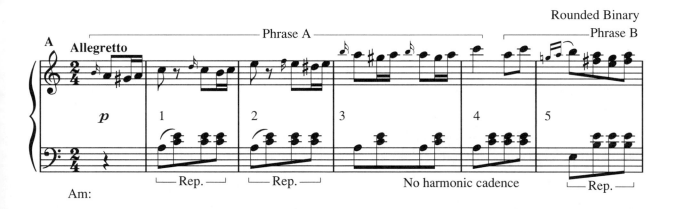

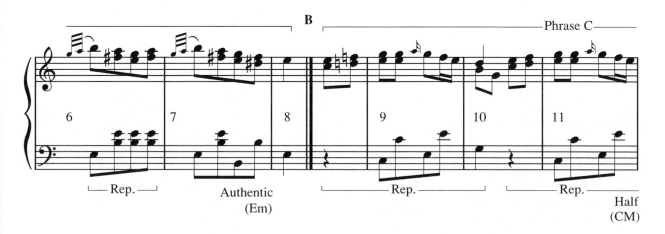

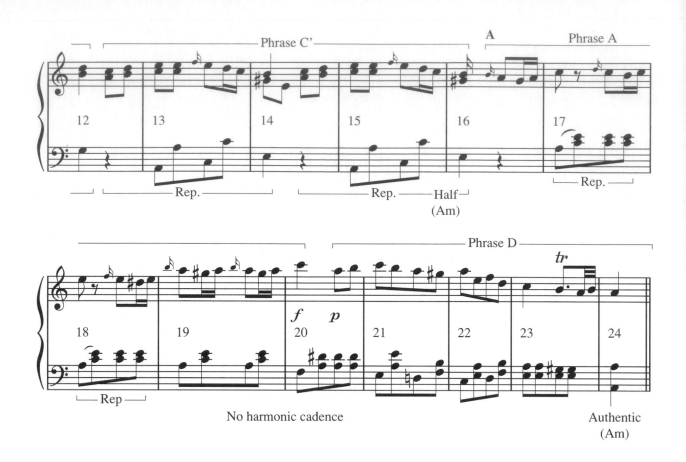

2. Schumann: *Trällerliedchen* (Humming Song) from Album for the Young, op. 68 *(R)*

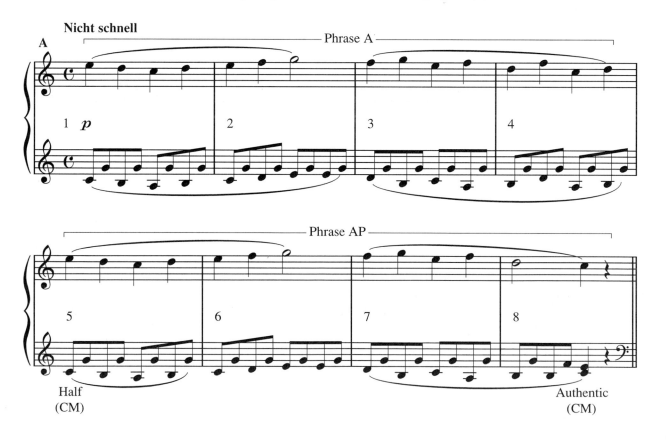

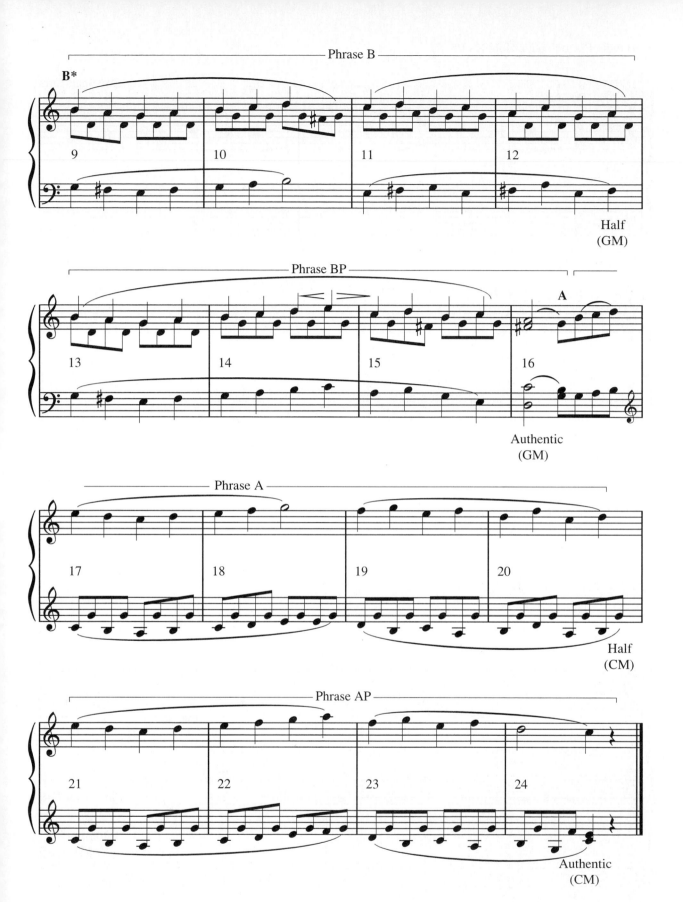

*Note that B is largely a transposition of A to the dominant, and hence might also be designated as A'.

3. Haydn: Piano Sonata, Hob. XVI/5 *(R)*

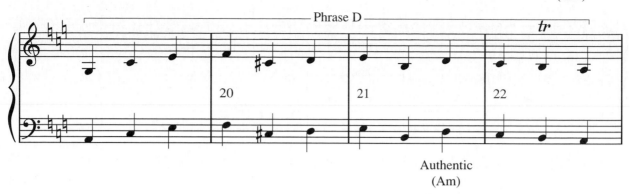

Phrase D

20　21　22

Authentic
(Am)

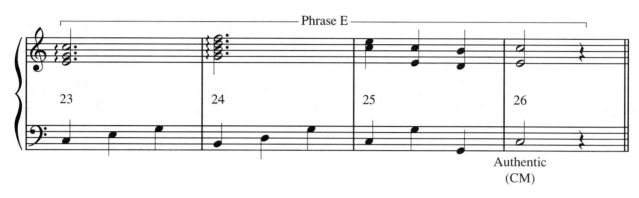

Phrase E

23　24　25　26

Authentic
(CM)

Phrase D'

27　28　29　30

Authentic
(dm)

Phrase D''

31　32　33　34

Authentic
(CM)

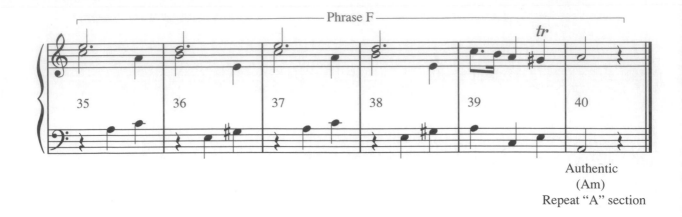

Authentic
(Am)
Repeat "A" section

4. Clementi: Sonatina, op. 36, no. 2 *(R)*

Rounded Binary

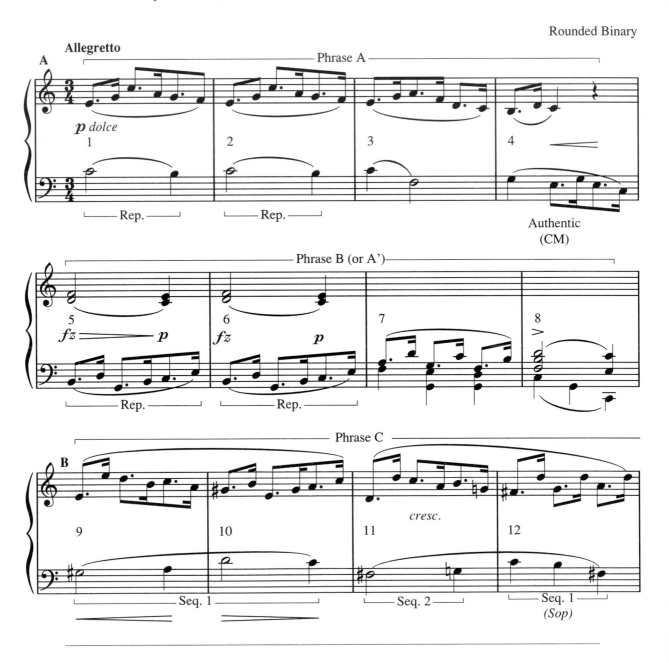

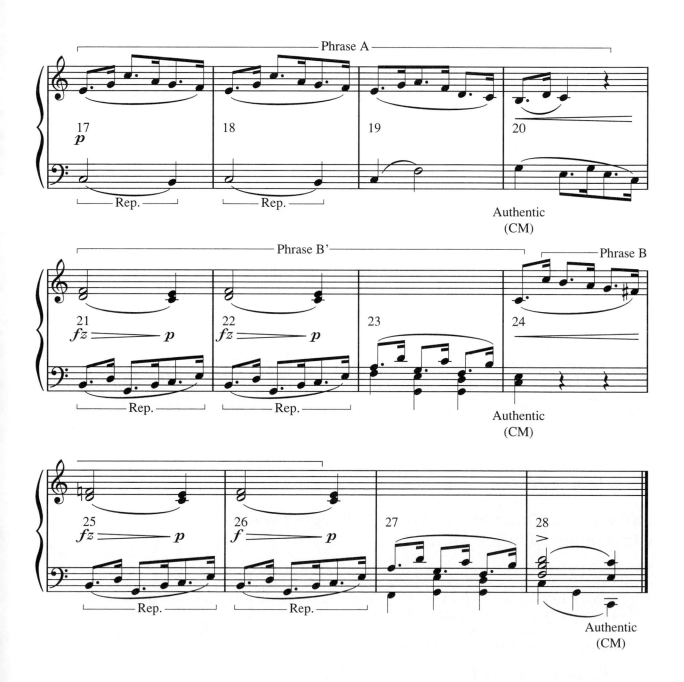

Melody 12D

Interval Dictation: Two Intervals in Succession

Student text: Page 173.

Each exercise consists of three tones played melodically without relating them to a scale or key center.

The first note is given. Write the two remaining notes on the staff.

To the Instructor:

Play the three tones slowly two or three times. As in added class activity, ask students to name the intervals formed.

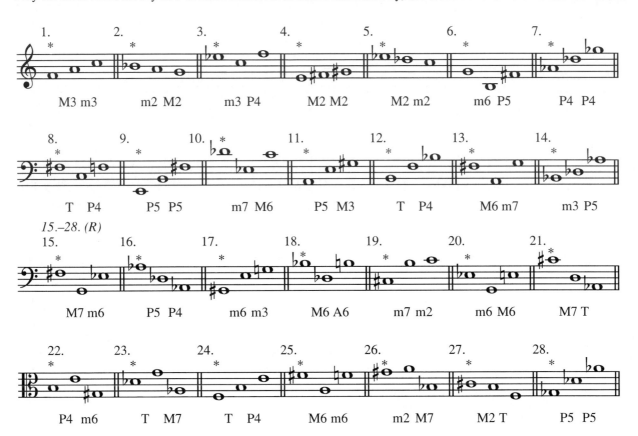

1.	2.	3.	4.	5.	6.	7.
M3 m3	m2 M2	m3 P4	M2 M2	M2 m2	m6 P5	P4 P4

8.	9.	10.	11.	12.	13.	14.
T P4	P5 P5	m7 M6	P5 M3	T P4	M6 m7	m3 P5

15.–28. (R)

15.	16.	17.	18.	19.	20.	21.
M7 m6	P5 P4	m6 m3	M6 A6	m7 m2	m6 M6	M7 T

22.	23.	24.	25.	26.	27.	28.
P4 m6	T M7	T P4	M6 m6	m2 M7	M2 T	P5 P5

Melody 12E

Models and Embellishments: I-V-I Progression with Melodic Embellishments

Student text: Page 174.

1. The model in this section is a I-V-I progression using four voices. The upper three voices are always in close position. Sing all parts of this structure before class.
2. Your instructor will play the structure followed by embellishments of that structure.
3. Write the model's embellishments on the numbered staves provided.

1. Have the students sing each voice of the model before the early examples.
2. Play the structure and embellishments in the order printed, or repeat the structure from time to time to remind students of the basis for each embellishment.
3. Students should notate all four voices of the embellishments.

Harmony 12A

Chord Function Identification: Nondominant 7th Chords

Student text: Page 175.

Each exercise consists of a series of four chords in block harmony.

Indicate the analysis of the four chords in the blanks provided.

Numbers 1—15 are in root position only:

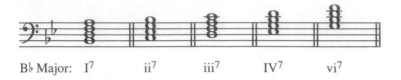

B♭ Major: I⁷   ii⁷   iii⁷   IV⁷   vi⁷

Numbers 16—25 contain inversions:

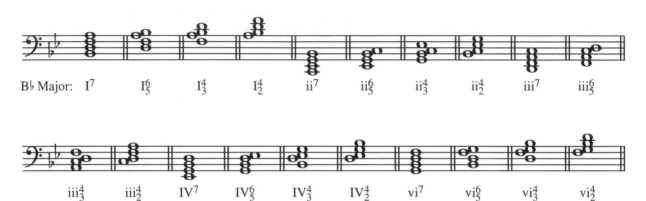

B♭ Major: I⁷   I$^6_5$ I$^4_3$ I$^4_2$ ii⁷   ii$^6_5$ ii$^4_3$ ii$^4_2$ iii⁷   iii$^6_5$

iii$^4_3$ iii$^4_2$ IV⁷   IV$^6_5$ IV$^4_3$ IV$^4_2$ vi⁷   vi$^6_5$ vi$^4_3$ vi$^4_2$

To the Instructor:

To prepare for this set of exercises, ask students to sing the B-flat major scale. Then, drill all chords, asking students to sing notes in root position and the inversions.

In dictating these chords, ask students to sing the root of each. After the first six or seven exercises, the practice may be discontinued.

Numbers 1—10 contain root-position chords only.

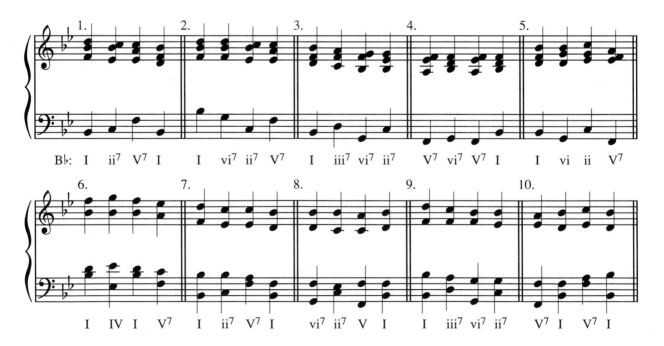

B♭:   I   ii⁷   V⁷   I   I   vi⁷   ii⁷   V⁷   I   iii⁷   vi⁷   ii⁷   V⁷   vi⁷   V⁷   I   I   vi   ii   V⁷

I   IV   I   V⁷   I   ii⁷   V⁷   I   vi⁷   ii⁷   V   I   I   iii⁷   vi⁷   ii⁷   V⁷   I   V⁷   I

Numbers 16—25 contain inversions:

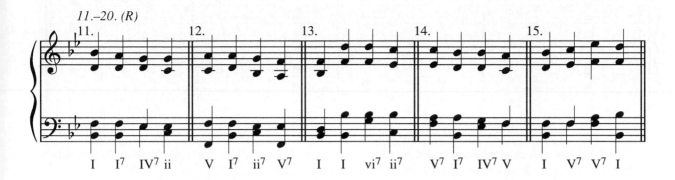

11.–20. (R)

11. 12. 13. 14. 15.

I I⁷ IV⁷ ii   V I⁷ ii⁷ V⁷   I I vi⁷ ii⁷   V⁷ I⁷ IV⁷ V   I V⁷ V⁷ I

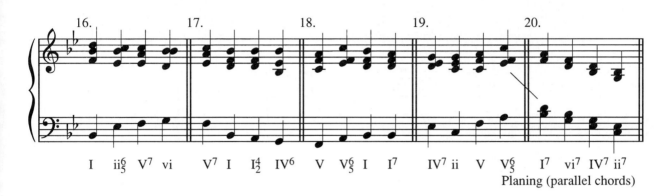

16. 17. 18. 19. 20.

I ii⁶₅ V⁷ vi   V⁷ I I⁴₂ IV⁶   V V⁶₅ I I⁷   IV⁷ ii V V⁶₅   I⁷ vi⁷ IV⁷ ii⁷

Planing (parallel chords)

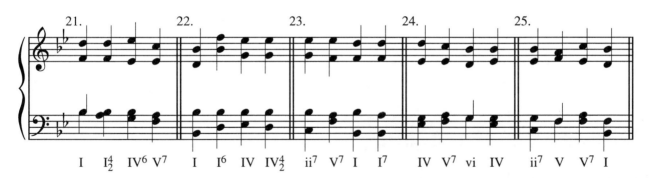

21. 22. 23. 24. 25.

I I⁴₂ IV⁶ V⁷   I I⁶ IV IV⁴₂   ii⁷ V⁷ I I⁷   IV V⁷ vi IV   ii⁷ V V⁷ I

Harmony 12B

Chords in Music Literature: Nondominant 7th Chords

Student text: Page 176.

1. Each exercise consists of four examples from music literature which includes a variety of harmonic rhythms and nonharmonic tones.
2. Below you see four models (A through D). Your instructor will play each of these four models. Listen carefully and try to distinguish each—one from another.

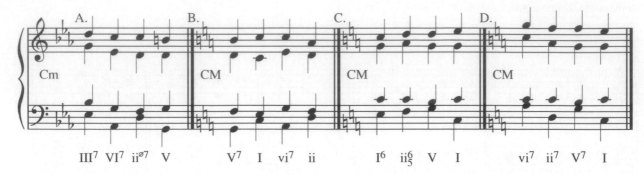

Cm — III⁷ VI⁷ ii°⁷ V

CM — V⁷ I vi⁷ ii

CM — I⁶ ii⁶₅ V I

CM — vi⁷ ii⁷ V⁷ I

3. Your instructor will play an example (1 through 4) from music literature. The music literature example contains the same chords and same inversions as one of the four models above.

1. Verdi: Requiem and Kyrie

Play only the chords in the rectangle

iii⁷ | vi⁷   ii⁷   V⁷   I

2. Porpora: Et Misericordia

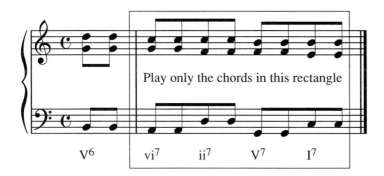

Play only the chords in this rectangle

V⁶   vi⁷   ii⁷   V⁷   I⁷

3. Schubert: Der Alpenjäger

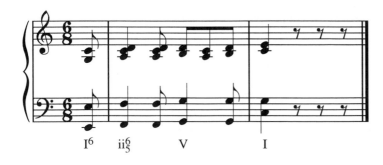

I⁶   ii⁶₅   V   I

4. Mozart: Piano Sonata, K 494

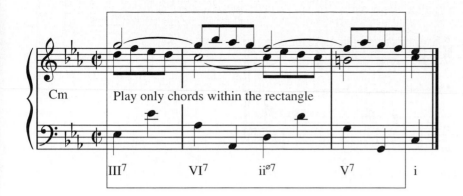

Cm

Play only chords within the rectangle

III⁷   VI⁷   ii⁰⁷   V⁷   i

4. When you have matched the literature example with one of the four sets of chords (A through D), place the letter in the appropriate blank below, and prepare for the next example from music literature.

1. _____   2. _____   3. _____   4. _____

5. When the first four examples are completed, use the same procedure for models 5 through 8.

These (**E, F, G, H**) are the remaining four models. Pair them up with the examples from literature (**5, 6, 7, 8**).

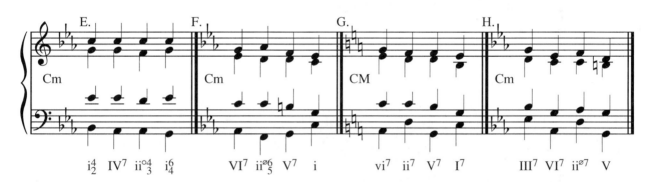

E.

Cm

i⁴₂   IV⁷   ii⁰⁴₃   i⁶₄

F.

Cm

VI⁷   ii⁰⁶₅   V⁷   i

G.

CM

vi⁷   ii⁷   V⁷   I⁷

H.

Cm

III⁷   VI⁷   ii⁰⁷   V

5. (R) _____   6. (R) _____   7. (R) _____   8. (R) _____

5. Pergolesi: Se Tu M'ami, se sospiri

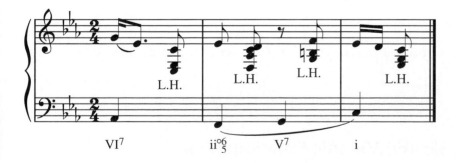

L.H.   L.H.   L.H.   L.H.

VI⁷   ii⁰⁶₅   V⁷   i

6. Brahms: Ballade, Op. 118, No. 3

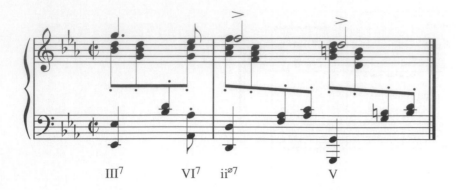

$$\text{III}^7 \qquad \text{VI}^7 \qquad \text{ii}^{\varnothing 7} \qquad \text{V}$$

7. Medtner: Novelette, Op. 17, No. 1

$$\text{vi}^7 \qquad \text{ii}^7 \qquad \text{V}^7 \qquad \text{I}^7$$

8. Puccini: La Boheme, Act IV

$$\text{i}^4_2 \qquad\qquad \text{VI}^7 \qquad \text{ii}^{\circ 4}_3 \qquad \text{i}^6_4$$

To the Instructor:

A complete discussion of this type of exercise and suggestions for classroom use are provided in the "To the Instructor" section of Harmony 1B.

Harmony 12C

Aural Analysis: Harmonic and Melodic Relationships in Musical Periods from Haydn Sonatas

Student text: Page 179.

Each exercise consists of a period (two phrases) extracted from a Haydn piano sonata.

Using the measure and beat numbers provided, complete the following:

1. Bracket the harmonic rhythm beneath the numbers.
2. Under each bracket indicate the chord analysis. The instructor will indicate which of the following is preferred:
   a. Write only the basic chords—it is not necessary to show inversions.
   b. Write the basic chords and include the proper inversion. Use the lowest-sounding tone within each bracket in determining the position of the chord.
3. Bracket the phrases above the numbers.
4. At the end of each phrase bracket, indicate the type of cadence.

To the Instructor:

Play each period two or three times at performance tempo.

1. Haydn: Piano Sonata in D Major, Hob. XVI/33 (second movement)

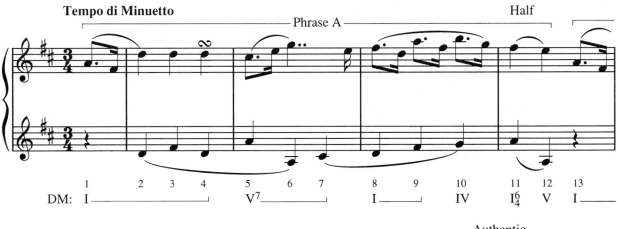

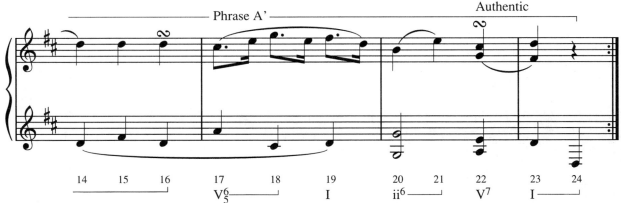

2. Haydn: Piano Sonata in C Major, Hob. XVI/21 (third movement)

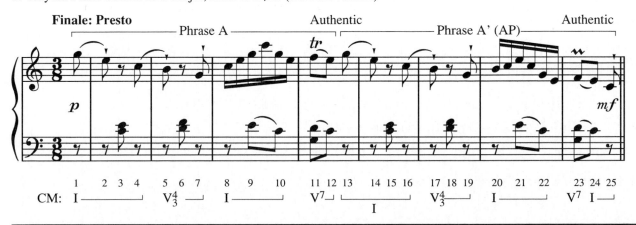

3. Haydn: Piano Sonata in C Major, Hob. XVI/35 (R) (third movement)

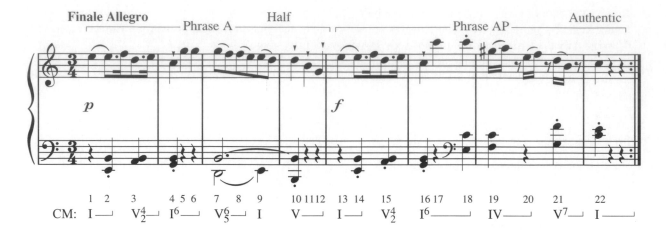

4. Haydn: Piano Sonata in C Major, Hob. XVI/35 (R) (first movement)

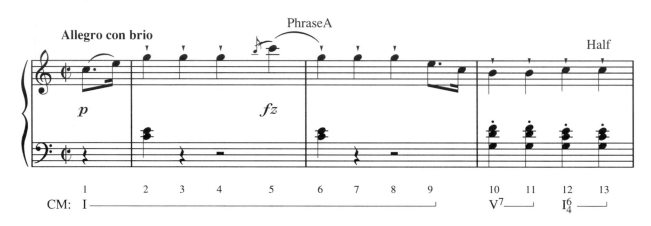

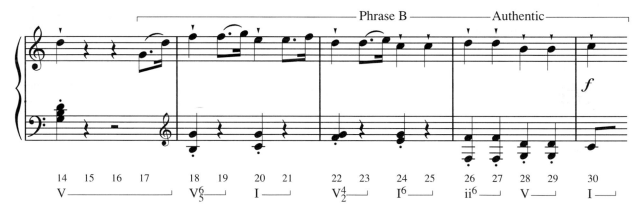

5. Haydn: Piano Sonata in E Minor, Hob. XVI/34 *(R)* (third movement)

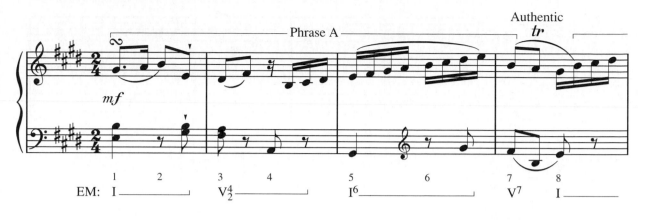

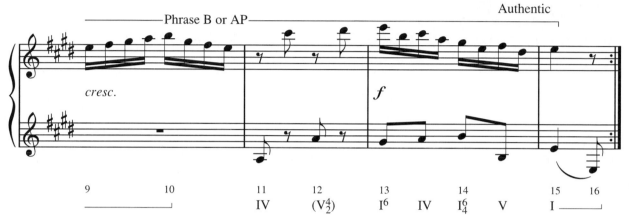

6. Haydn: Piano Sonata in E Major, Hob. XVI/13 (third movement) *(R)*

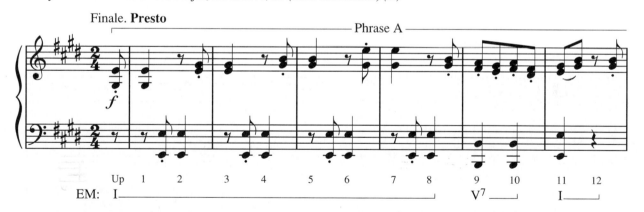

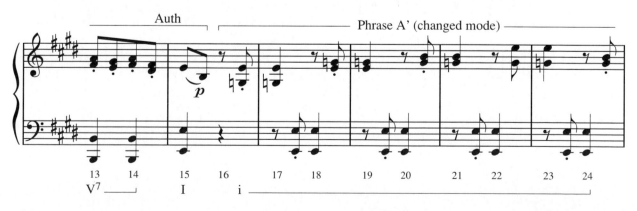

25	26	27	28	29	30	31	32	33	34	35
V^7		i_4^6	V		i_4^6	V^7		i_4^6	V	
								i_4^6	V^7	i_4^6 V

Harmony 12D

Harmonic Dictation: Modulations to Closely Related Keys

Student text: Page178.

Each exercise consists of a phrase from a Bach chorale that modulates. The first chord and its analysis are given for each exercise.

1. Indicate the analysis of each chord beneath the lower staff.
2. List any nonharmonic tones beneath the harmonic analysis.
3. Write the melodic line of both the soprano and bass voices.
4. Write the melodic line of both the alto and tenor voices.

To the Instructor:

This set of chorale phrases may be used for any or all of the following purposes:

1. For students to indicate the harmonic analysis only.
2. To indicate nonharmonic tones in addition to the harmonic analysis.
3. As a vehicle for four-part dictation.

1. *Freu' dich sehr, o meine Seele*
   (Rejoice, O my soul)

2. *Gelobet seist du, Jesu Christ*
   (Praised be Thou, Jesus Christ)

3. *Keinen hat Gott verlassen*
(God has forsaken no one)

4. *Jesu, nun sei gepreiset*
(Jesus, now be praised)

5. *Jesu, meine Zuversicht*
(Jesus, my confidence)

6. *Es ist das Heil uns kommen her*
(Salvation has come to us)

7.–8. *(R)*

7. *Uns ist ein Kindlein heut' gebor'n*
(To us this day a Child is born)

8. *Jesu, deine tiefen Wunden*
(Jesus, Thy deep wounds)

Harmony 12E

Chord Quality Identification: MM, Mm, mm, dm, and dd 7th Chords

Student text: Page 180.

Each exercise consists of a single 7th chord played in four-part harmony.

Only MM, Mm, mm, dm, and dd 7th chords are used.

In the blanks, indicate the type of 7th chord played.

To the Instructor:

Put an example of each 7th-chord type on the board, and ask class members to sing it. For the first few exercises, ask students to sing the chord immediately after it is played. Then they should silently employ the same procedure.

In numbers 1—10, all chords are in root position and the 7th is in the soprano voice.

In numbers 11—20, all chords are in root position, but the 7th may be in any voice except the bass.

In numbers 21—30, the chords may be in any position and the 7th in any voice.

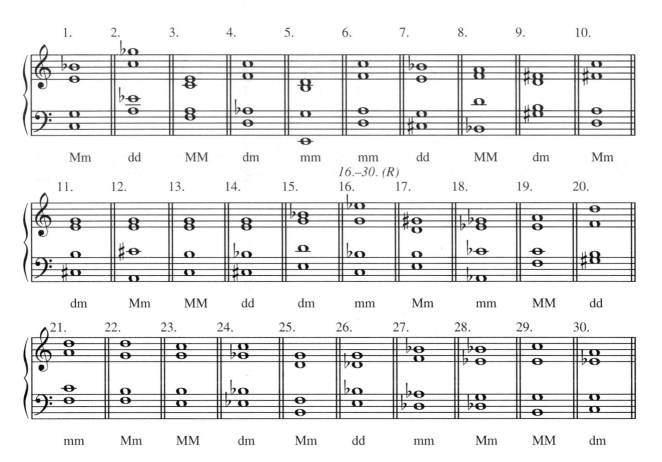

Rhythm 12A

Rhythmic Dictation: Eighth-Beat Values

Student text: Page 180.

Each exercise consists of a short melodic excerpt.

Complete the rhythm on a neutral pitch.

To the Instructor:

Press these exercises to the fastest possible tempo, at which class members can maintain comprehension. Play each melody at least three or four times.

1. Mozart: Fantasy in D Minor, K. 397

2. Mozart: Rondo in D, K. 485

3. Tchaikovsky: 1812 Festival Overture, op. 49

4. Wagner: *Tristan und Isolde*

5. Wagner: *Gotterdammerung (R)*

6. Mascagni: *Cavalleria Rusticana (R)*

7. Schubert: Three Military Marches, op. 51, no. 2 *(R)*

8. Schrecker: *Kleine Suite (R)*

9. Rimski-Korsakov: *Le Coq-d'Or* (Suite) *(R)*

10. Moussorgsky: A Night on Bald Mountain *(R)*

Rhythm 12B
Error Detection: Eighth-Beat Values
Student text: Page 182.

Each exercise consists of a short melodic excerpt containing a single rhythmic error.

Circle the number indicating the point at which the printed version does not agree with that played.

To the Instructor:

Since the problem involved in this set of exercises is a matter of selection rather than dictation, the tempos may be increased. Play each excerpt three or four times. These exercises contain octupel divisions of the beat, except for the three in compound meter, which contain triple or sextuple beat divisions.

Transcription 12

Keyboard Music with Two and Three Voices

Refer to instructions found in Transcription 1 (page25).

Note: * = given material

Recorded Example 24

J. S. Bach: *Menuett*

Muzio Clementi: Sonatina, op. 36 in C Major

Fine

D.C.

Unit 13

Melody 13A

Melodic Dictation: Modulation in Two-Phrase Periods

Student text: Page 185.

Each exercise consists of a melody composed of two phrases. The second phrase begins immediately after the ‖, marked in each melody, and ends with a modulation.

Notate each melody on the appropriate staff below.

To the Instructor:

For a complete discussion of two-phrase melodies, see Melody 7A. Immediately after class members have completed their dictation and the correct pitches and rhythms have been revealed, discuss students' errors (and the reason for the errors) while the thought processes are still fresh in their minds. This is also the ideal moment to discuss other essential melodic relationships. Do the two phrases form a period? If so, are the two parallel or contrasting? Is there a duplication of rhythm? Are the melodic contours of the two similar or different?

1. Beethoven: Sonata for Violin and Piano, op. 12, no. 2

2. Beethoven: Sonata for Violin and Piano, op. 23

3. Beethoven: Sonata for Violin and Piano, op. 24

4. Schubert: Sonata for Piano, op. 42

5. Schubert: Sonata for Piano, op. 122

6.–10. (R)
6. Chopin: Mazurka, op. 67, no. 4

7. Chopin: Mazurka, op. 50, no. 2

8. Chopin: Mazurka, op. 50, no. 2

9. Beethoven: Sonata for Violin and Piano, op. 12, no. 1

10. Schubert: Sonata for Piano, op. 42

CM

GM

* Note or rest in workbook.
(R) means recorded.

Melody 13B

Error Detection: Brahms Melodies

Student text: Page 186.

Each exercise consists of a short melodic excerpt from compositions by Brahms containing three pitches that are played differently from those printed.

Circle the three numbers representing the pitches that differ from those played.

To the Instructor:

Play each melody two or three times at performance tempo or slightly slower. Numbers beneath the pitches are given for classroom convenience.

1. Symphony no. 4

1   2   3   ④   5   6   ⑦   8   9   10   ⑪   12   13   14   15   16

2. Symphony no. 4

1   2   ③   4 5   6   7   8   9   10 11   12 13   14   15   ⑯   17   18   19   ⑳ 21

3. Symphony no. 4

1 2 3 ④ 5 6 7 8 9 10 11 12 13 14 ⑮ 16 17 ⑱ 19 20

4. Symphony no. 3

1 2 3 ④ 5 6 7 8 9 10 11 12 ⑬ 14 15 16 17 18 ⑲ 20

5. Symphony no. 1

1 2 3 4 ⑤ 6 7 8 9 10 11 12 13 14 15 16 ⑰ 18 19 20 21 ㉒ 23 24 25

6. Symphony no. 1

1 2 3 ④ 5 6 7 8 9 10 11 ⑫ 13 14 15 ⑯ 17 18

7. Symphony no. 1

1 2 3 4 5 6 7 8 9 10 ⑪ 12 13 ⑭ 15 16 17 18 ⑲ 20 21

8. Symphony no. 2

1 2 3 ④ 5 6 7 8 9 10 11 12 13 14 15 ⑯ 17 ⑱ 19 20 21

9. Symphony no. 2

1 2 ③ 4 5 6 7 8 9 ⑩ 11 12 ⑬ 14

10. Symphony no. 4

1 2 ③ ④ 5   6 7 8   9 10 11   12 ⑬ 14   15 16 17   18

Melody 13C

Binary, Rounded Binary, and Three-Part Form

Student text: Page 188.

Each exercise consists of a complete composition in binary, rounded binary (incipient three-part), or three-part form.

Listen to composition no. 1 two or three times, then answer the following questions. Listen again to the composition to check your answers. *(R)*

To the Instructor:

Play the compositions at performance tempo. A live performance is preferred, but the tapes accompanying this text may be used to advantage.

Repeat signs have been removed from composition number 1 for economy of class time. If preferred, the sections within each double bar may be repeated. Only the answer to question 3 will be affected, and in this instance, double all the numbers (2 becomes 4, 6 becomes 12, etc.).

*(R) means recorded.

1. Mozart: Piano Sonata, K. 331 *(R)*

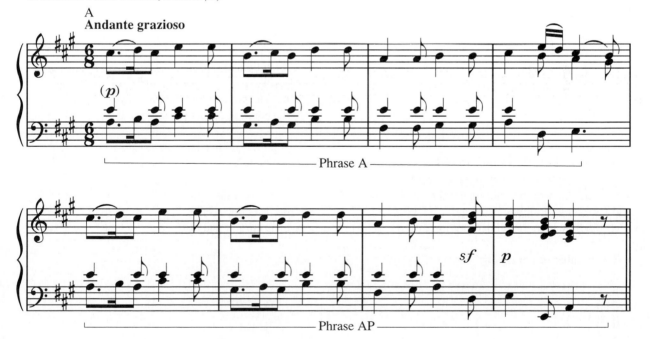

Phrase B

Phrase AP'

Phrase extension

1. The form is:
   a. three-part
   (b.) rounded binary
   c. rounded three-part
   d. incipient two-part
   e. two-part

2. This composition:
   a. modulates to the dominant and subdominant
   b. modulates to the dominant and relative minor
   c. modulates to the dominant only
   (d.) does not modulate
   e. modulates to the relative minor only

3. The number of phrases is:
   a. 2
   b. 6
   (c.) 4
   d. 3
   e. 7

4. Cadences represented are:
   a. plagal and authentic only
   b. authentic only
   c. deceptive, half, and authentic
   d. deceptive and authentic only
   (e.) half and authentic only

5. A phrase with a cadential extension is:
   (a.) the last
   b. the first
   c. the second
   d. does not occur
   e. both first and last

Repeat signs in measures 17 and 32 of composition number 2 have been removed for economy of class time. Also, an eight-measure transition between measures 32 and 33 has been deleted. For those who prefer it, the unexpurgated version may be used without a change in any of the answers.

2. Chopin: Mazurka No. 43, op. 67, no. 2 *(R)*

Listen to composition no. 2 and answer the following questions: *(R)*

6. The form is:
    a. three-part
    b. rounded binary
    c. rounded three-part
    d. incipient two-part
    e. two-part

7. This composition:
    a. modulates to the dominant only
    b. modulates to the relative major only
    c. does not modulate
    d. modulates to the relative major and the dominant
    e. modulates to the relative major and subdominant

8. The cadence at the end of the first phrase is:
    a. authentic in the relative major
    b. authentic in the original key
    c. half in the original key
    d. plagal in the dominant key
    e. half in the relative major

The instructor will play an excerpt from composition no. 2.

To the Instructor:

Play measures 21 through 24 separately.

9. This excerpt is an example of:
    1. repetition
    2. a series of escape tones
    3. sequence
    4. a succession of Mm7th chords
    5. circle-of-5ths progressions

    a. 1, 2, 3, and 4
    b. 3 and 4 only
    c. 1, 3, and 4 only
    d. 2, 3, 4, and 5
    e. 3, 4, and 5 only

10. This is an example of music from the:
    a. Baroque period
    b. Classical period
    c. Romantic period
    d. Renaissance period
    e. Post-Romantic period

Repeat signs have been removed from composition number 3 for economy of class time. If preferred, both the "A" and "B" sections may be repeated. None of the answers will be affected.

3. Handel: "Sarabande" from Suite no. 15 for Keyboard *(R)*

Listen to composition no. 3 and answer the following questions. (Note: The first phrase and some of the other phrases contain strong, interior cadence-like figures.) *(R)*

11. The form is:
    a. three-part
    b. rounded binary
    c. rounded three-part
    d. incipient two-part
    e. two-part

12. The second phrase ends with a:
    a. deceptive cadence
    b. Phrygian cadence (iv⁶/V)
    c. plagal cadence
    d. imperfect authentic cadence
    e. perfect authentic cadence

13. This composition basically contains:
    a. a through-composed melody
    b. phrases of uneven length
    c. parallel phrases combining to form periods
    d. sequences of phrase length
    e. an ostinato

14. Cadence types are:
    a. authentic, half, and plagal
    b. authentic only
    c. authentic, half, Phrygian, and deceptive
    d. authentic and plagal only
    e. authentic and Phrygian only

15. This is an example of music from the:
   a. Baroque period
   b. Classical period
   c. Romantic period
   d. Renaissance period
   e. Post-Romantic period

Melody 13D

Interval Dictation: Two and Three Intervals in Succession

Student text: Page 190.

Each exercise consists of two intervals (three tones) for exercises 1—10 and three intervals (four tones) for exercises 11—20. These short melodic segments are played without relating them to a scale or key center.

1. Indicate the tones played in each exercise. (The first note is given.)
2. Indicate the intervals produced in the blanks provided.

Example 1 illustrates the correct procedure.

To the Instructor:

Play each exercise two or three times slowly. For the first few exercises, ask class members to sing the tones (after they are played).

1. (Example)	2.	3.	4.	5.
M2 M3	P5 m3	M3 M3	m3 M2	M6 M2

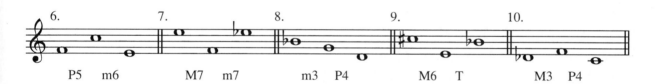

6.	7.	8.	9.	10.
P5 m6	M7 m7	m3 P4	M6 T	M3 P4

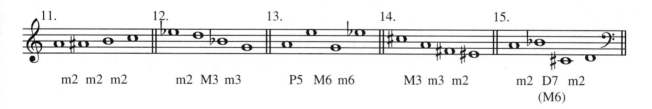

11.	12.	13.	14.	15.
m2 m2 m2	m2 M3 m3	P5 M6 m6	M3 m3 m2	m2 D7 m2
				(M6)

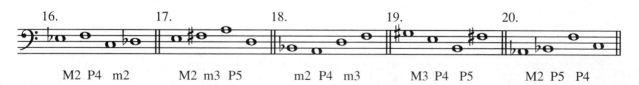

16.	17.	18.	19.	20.
M2 P4 m2	M2 m3 P5	m2 P4 m3	M3 P4 P5	M2 P5 P4

Melody 13E

Models and Embellishments: I-V-I Progression with Diatonic Melodic Embellishments

Student text: Page 190.

1. The model in this section is a I-V-I progression using four voices. The upper three voices are always in open position. Sing all parts of this structure before class.
2. Your instructor will play the structure followed by embellishments of that structure.
3. Write the model's embellishments on the numbered staves provided.

To the Instructor:

1. Have the students sing each voice of the model before the early examples.
2. Play the structure and embellishments in the order printed, or repeat the structure from time to time to remind students of the basis for each embellishment.
3. Students should notate all four voices of the embellishments.

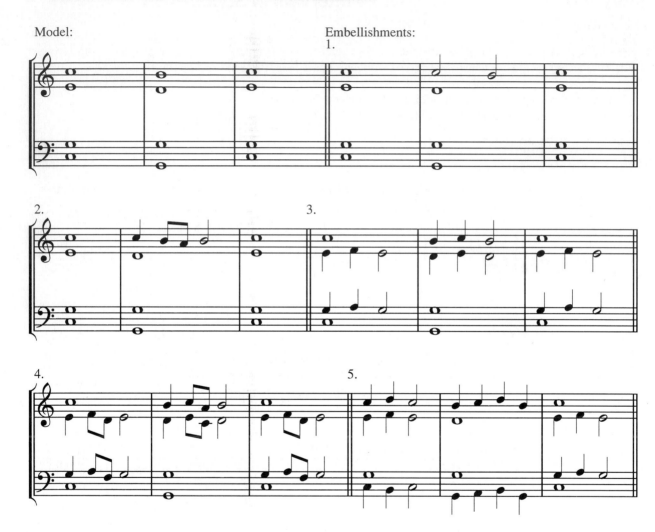

Model: Embellishments:
                                              1.

2.   3.

4.   5.

Two five-measure examples based on the same model.

6.

Harmony 13A

Chord Function Identification: Secondary Dominants of V and ii

Student text: Page 192.

Each exercise consists of a series of four chords in block harmony.

Analyze each of the four chords in the blanks provided.

New chords:

CM: V/V   V⁷/V   vii°⁷/V   V/ii   V⁷/ii   vii°⁷/ii

To the Instructor:

After singing the C-major scale, students should drill each of the secondary dominant forms.

For the first three or four exercises, have the students sing the root of each chord and observe the quality of the chord. Point out the difference in chord quality between diatonic and secondary dominant functions.

Gradually eliminate the drill, and encourage students to internalize the sounds of the chords.

Numbers 1—15 contain chords in root position only.

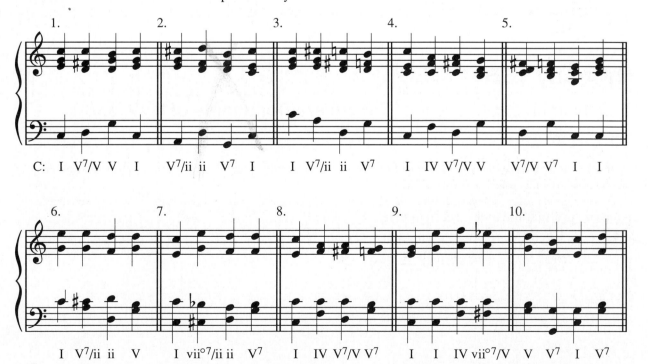

11.–20. (R)

11. I vii°⁷/V V I   12. I vii°⁷/ii V⁷/V V⁷   13. I IV IV vii°⁷/V V   14. I V⁷/V V⁷   15. I V/ii ii V

Numbers 16—25 contain inversions.

16. I V⁶/ii V/V V   17. I I⁶ vii°⁷/ii ii   18. V⁷/V V⁶₅/V V V   19. I I⁶ IV V⁷/V   20. V vii°⁷/V V I

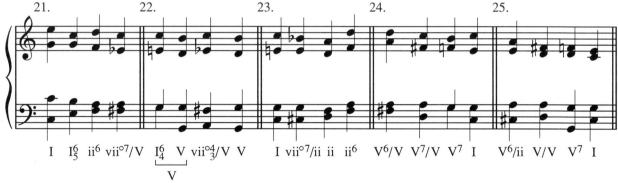

21. I I⁶₅ ii⁶ vii°⁷/V   22. I⁶₄ V vii°⁴₃/V V / V   23. I vii°⁷/ii ii ii⁶   24. V⁶/V V⁷/V V⁷ I   25. V⁶/ii V/V V⁷ I

Harmony 13B

Chords in Music Literature: Secondary Dominants of ii, IV, and V

Student text: Page 192.

1. Each exercise consists of four examples from music literature which includes a variety of harmonic rhythms and nonharmonic tones.
2. Below you see four models (A through D). Your instructor will play each of these four models. Listen carefully and try to distinguish each—one from another.

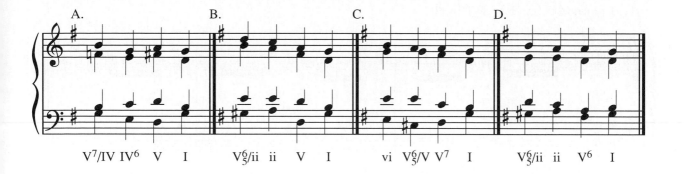

A. B. C. D.

V^7/IV IV^6 V I V^6_5/ii ii V I   vi V^6_5/V V^7 I V^6_5/ii ii V^6 I

3. Your instructor will play an example (1 through 4) from music literature. The music literature example contains the same chords and same inversions as one of the four models above.

1. Beethoven: Piano Concerto No. 4, II

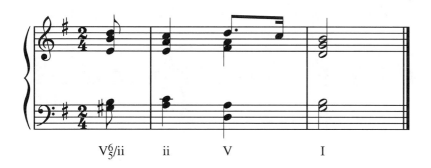

V^6_5/ii ii   V   I

2. Beethoven: Ohne Liebe Lebe, Op. 52/6

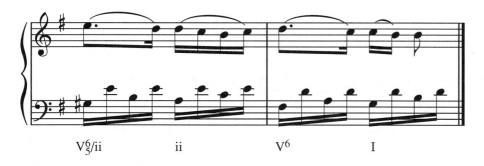

V^6_5/ii ii V^6 I

3. Bach: Courante, BWV 838

V^7/IV IV^6 V   I

4. Haydn: Piano Sonata, Hob. XVI/14, III

vi   V⁶₅/V   V⁷   I

4. When you have matched the literature example with one of the four sets of chords (A through D), place the letter in the appropriate blank below, and prepare for the next example from music literature.

1. _____ 2. _____ 3. _____ 4. _____

5. When the first four examples are completed, use the same procedure for models 5 through 8.

These (**E, F, G, H**) are the remaining four models. Pair them up with the examples from literature (**5, 6, 7, 8**).

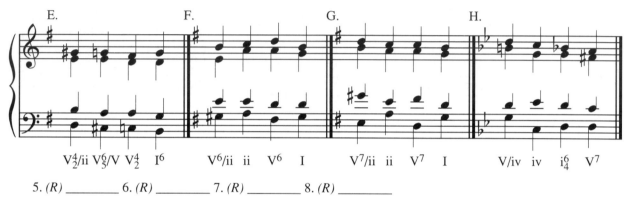

V⁴₂/ii V⁶₅/V V⁴₂ I⁶   V⁶/ii ii V⁶ I   V⁷/ii ii V⁷ I   V/iv iv i⁶₄ V⁷

5. (R) _____ 6. (R) _____ 7. (R) _____ 8. (R) _____

5. Haydn: Piano Sonata, Hob. XVI/6, II

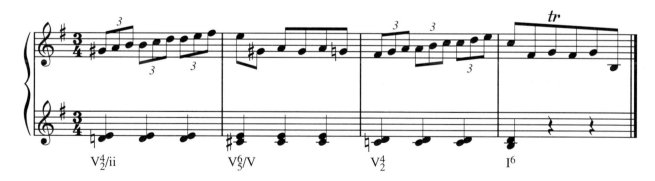

V⁴₂/ii   V⁶₅/V   V⁴₂   I⁶

6. Schubert: Danksagung an den Bach, D. 795/4

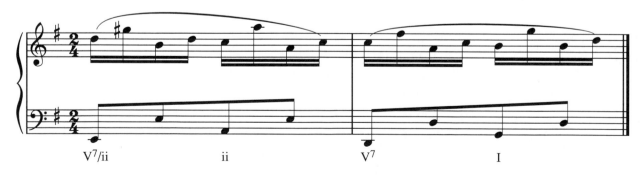

V⁷/ii   ii   V⁷   I

---

7. Schubert: Die schöne Müllerin, D. 795/4

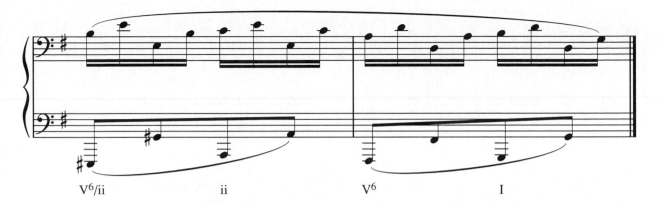

V⁶/ii   ii   V⁶   I

8. Zelter: Schäfers Klagelied (song)

V/iv   iv   i⁶₄   V⁷

To the Instructor:

A complete discussion of this type of exercise and suggestions for classroom use are provided in the "To the Instructor" section of Harmony 1B.

Harmony 13C

Aural Analysis: Key, Phrase, and Cadence Relationships in Musical Excerpts

Student text: Page 193.

Each exercise consists of four phrases of music by Baroque-period composers.

Listen carefully three or four times to each excerpt and then answer the multiple-choice questions. Each question has only one correct answer. Circle the letter indicating the correct answer.

To the Instructor:

It is ideal for these excerpts to be played live and at performance tempo in class. If your pianistic ability does not permit, ask a piano-major member of the class to prepare them for presentation in class. All else failing, use the tapes that accompany the text.

The more objective aspects of the excerpts are presented here. Use your own questions to lead students to discuss other relationships of a more subjective nature.

The instructor now plays no. 1. (R)

Answer the questions relating to this excerpt.

The complete questions appearing in the student text are reprinted here for your convenience.

Assume that this excerpt contains four phrases. It begins in B-flat major.

1. Keys expressed in this excerpt are:
    a. B♭M, FM, and E♭M
    b. B♭M, cm, and FM
    c. B♭M, E♭M, only
    d. B♭M, E♭M, and FM
    e. B♭M, FM, only

2. The relationship of the four phrases in this excerpt is:
    a. A   A'   A   B
    b. A   B   A   C
    c. A   B   A'   C
    d. A   B   A   B
    e. A   A'   A   A

3. The cadences punctuating the four phrases of this excerpt (in order of appearance):
    a. authentic, half authentic, half
    b. half, authentic, half, authentic
    c. all are authentic
    d. authentic, authentic, half, authentic
    e. deceptive, authentic, half, authentic

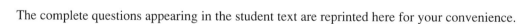

4. Harmony in the first phrase (in order of appearance) is:
   (a.) tonic to dominant to tonic
   b. tonic to subdominant to dominant to tonic
   c. tonic to dominant
   d. tonic to supertonic to dominant to tonic
   e. tonic to subdominant to dominant

The instructor now plays no. 2. (R)

Answer the questions (5, 6, and 7) relating to this excerpt.

2. Thomas Arne: Sonata no. IV *(Siciliano) (R)*

Assume that this excerpt contains four phrases. The composition begins in G minor.

5. The cadences at the end of the second and fourth phrases are (in order of appearance):
   a. authentic, authentic
   b. authentic, half
   c. half, authentic
   d. plagal, half
   e. half, half,

6. The phrase relationships are:
   a. A B B' C
   b. A B A' C
   c. A B A B
   d. A A' B C
   e. A A' A' B

7. The excerpt begins in G minor and ends in:
   a. B-flat minor
   b. E-flat minor
   c. C minor
   d. D minor
   e. A minor

The instructor now plays no. 3. (R)

Answer the questions (8, 9, and 10) relating to this excerpt.

Assume that this excerpt contains four phrases. It begins in F major.

3. Thomas Arne: Sonata no. IV *(Siciliano) (R)*

8. The keys in order of their appearance are:
   - a. FM   B♭M   CM   FM
   - b. FM   GM   B♭M   FM
   - c. FM   CM   GM   FM
   - d. FM   DM   CM   FM
   - ⓔ. FM   CM   B♭M   FM

9. The phrase relationships are:
   - a.   A   A'   A'   C
   - b.   A   A'   B   A
   - ⓒ.   A   B   A   B'
   - d.   A   B   A'   C
   - e.   A   B   B   C

10. The cadences (punctuating the phrases) in order of appearance are:
    - a. half, authentic, half, authentic
    - ⓑ. all are authentic cadences
    - c. plagal, authentic, plagal, authentic
    - d. half, half, half, authentic
    - e. authentic, half, half, authentic

Harmony 13D

Harmonic Dictation: Chorale Phrases Containing 7th Chords

Student text: Page 195.

Each exercise consists of a chorale phrase.

Numbers	No. of Chords	Position	Nonharmonic Tones
1–6	4	Root position only	Occasional passing tone
7–12	7–8	Root position and inversions	Several—any type

Suggested procedure for numbers 1–6 (outside of class):

1. As you listen to each chord try to match the pitch of the root (bass pitch)—by *thinking* it rather than *singing* it.
2. Immediately recall the complete succession of chord roots.
3. Associate the root pitches with solfeggio syllables or numbers and write them down.
4. Convert the syllables or numbers to actual pitches and write out the bass notes on the staves provided.

5. If you wish, you can also add the basic analysis symbols, but watch out for the presence of 7th chords, included in this assignment.
6. If your instructor requests, in successive listenings, pick out the soprano, alto, and tenor parts. Relate each to syllables or scale numbers.
7. Convert the syllables or numbers to actual pitches and add the notes to the staves.
8. When you have completed the phrase, listen one more time to check your answers.

To the Instructor:

This introductory procedure works equally well in class and may be used there to advantage. Numbers 1—6 should be well within the grasp of even the marginal students. Drill thoroughly on these phrases before embarking on 7—12, which are by Bach, and are obviously more difficult. Unless all members of your class are unusually talented, some may need extra time to breach the difficulty gap between the first six phrases and the remainder of the assignment.

9. *Was mein Gott will, das g' scheh'*
(May what my God wills come to pass)

10. *Jesu, meine Freude*
(Jesus, my joy)

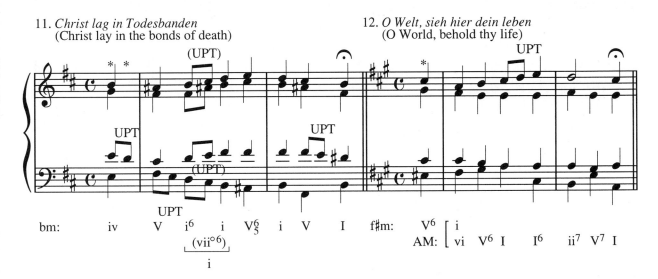

11. *Christ lag in Todesbanden*
(Christ lay in the bonds of death)

12. *O Welt, sieh hier dein leben*
(O World, behold thy life)

Harmony 13E

Error Detection: Triads and 7th Chords

Student text: Page 197.

Each exercise consists of two chords in four parts.

1. As played by the instructor, *one* note in each exercise is incorrect. Any voice may contain an error.
2. Indicate the chord (no. 1 or no. 2) containing the error.
3. Also indicate the voice where the error occurs:
   S = soprano   A = alto   T = tenor   B = bass

To the Instructor:

Play both chords, including the circled note, two or three times. The note seen by the student is placed in parentheses to the right of the circled note.

Rhythm 13A

Rhythmic Dictation: Introduction to the Supertriplet

Student text: Page 198.

Each exercise consists of a short melodic excerpt.

Complete the rhythm on a neutral pitch. A **supertriplet** is a triplet that exceeds the length of a single beat.

To the Instructor:

After playing each exercise once or twice, ask class members to tap or clap the rhythm exactly as played. Repeat the procedure until students can accurately repeat the rhythm. Then, allow time for notation. All but the last exercise contain supertriplets.

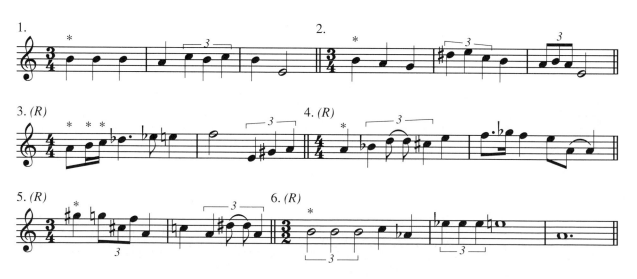

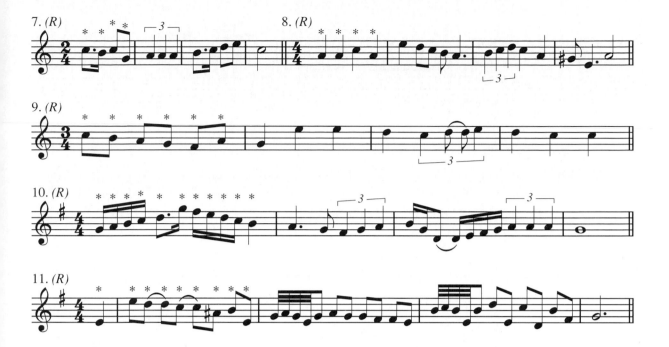

Rhythm 13B

Error Detection: Eighth-Beat Values

Student text: Page 198.

Each exercise consists of a melodic excerpt containing *one* error in rhythm.

Circle the number indicating the beat that is *not* played as notated.

To the Instructor:

Play each exercise two or three times at a moderate tempo.

4.

1 2 3 4 ⑤ 6 7 8

5. *(R)*

1 2 3 ④ 5 6 7 8 9

6. *(R)*

1 2 3 4 ⑤ 6 7 8

7. *(R)*

1 2 3 4 5 6 7 ⑧

8. *(R)*

1 2 3 4 5 ⑥ 7 8 9

Transcription 13

Keyboard Music with Two and Three Voices

Refer to instructions found in Transcription 1 (page 25).

Note: * = given material

Recorded Example 26

Joseph Haydn: Piano Sonata in C Major

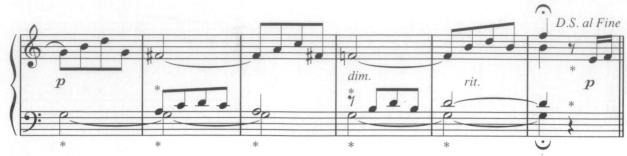

Recorded Example 27

W. A. Mozart: "Forgiving for Spring"

Unit 14

Melody 14A

Melodic Dictation: Modulation in Two-Phrase Melodies

Student text: Page 203.

Each exercise consists of a melody composed of two phrases. The second phrase begins immediately after the ‖, marked in each melody. A variety of phrase, key, and cadential relationships exists in these examples from music literature.

Notate each melody on the appropriate staff below.

To the Instructor:

For complete information concerning two-phrase melodies, see Melody 7A. The two-phrase melodies in this section represent a variety of phrase and key relationships and melodic cadences. This is an excellent opportunity to review and solidify previously presented material. Some contain modulations and others do not, some form periods while others are open-ended, and a broad difficulty level exists between the easiest and most complex.

1. Haydn: Piano Sonata no. 21 in F Major

2. Haydn: Symphony no. 97 in C Major

3. Haydn: Piano Sonata no. 23 in A Major

4. Haydn: Piano Sonata no. 23 in A Major

5. Haydn: Piano Sonata no. 20 in D Major

6.–10. (R)

6. Haydn: Piano Sonata no. 17 in G Major

7. Haydn: Piano Sonata no. 12 in G Major
8. Haydn: Piano Sonata no. 12 in G Major
9. Haydn: Piano Sonata no. 60 in C Major
10. Haydn: Piano Sonata no. 53 in E Minor

*Note or rest in workbook.

(R) means recorded.

Melody 14B

Error Detection: Excerpts from Music Literature

Student text: Page 204.

Each exercise consists of a short melodic excerpt from music literature containing three pitches that are played differently from those printed.

Circle the numbers representing the pitches that are different from those played. There are *three* printing errors in each melody.

To the Instructor:

Play each melody two or three times at performance tempo or slightly slower. Numbers beneath the pitches are given for classroom convenience.

1. Schumann: Symphony no. 4, op. 120

1 2 ③ 4 5 6 7 8 9 10 11 12 13 14 15 16 17 ⑱ 19 20 21 22 ㉓ 24

2. Smetana: *The Bartered Bride* (Opera)

1 2 3 4 5 6 ⑦ 8 9 ⑩ ⑪ 12 13 14 15 16 17

3. Johann Strauss, II: Voices of Spring Waltz, op. 410

1 2   3 4   5 6 7 8   9 10 11 12 ⑬ 14   15   16 17   18 19   ⑳ 21   ㉒ 23

4. Richard Strauss: Alpine Symphony, op. 64

1 ② 3 4 5   6 7 8 9 10   11 12 13 14 15   16 17 ⑱ 19 20   ㉑

5. R. Strauss: Thus Spake Zarathustra, op. 30

1   2   3   4   ⑤ 6 7 ⑧ 9 10 11   12 13 14 ⑮ 16

6. R. Strauss: *Aus Italien* (From Italy), op. 16 *(R)*

1   2   3   4 5 6 7 8   ⑨ 10 ⑪ 12   13   14 15 16 ⑰

7. R. Strauss: *Aus Italien* (From Italy), op. 16 *(R)*

1 2 3 4   5 6 ⑦ 8   9   10 11 12 13 14   15 16 ⑰ 18 19   20 21 22 ㉓ 24   25

8. Rossini-Respighi: *La Boutique Fantastique* (Ballet) *(R)*

1 2 3   4 5 6 7 ⑧ 9   10 11 ⑫ 13 14 15   16 17 18 19 20 21   22 ㉓ 24

9. Rossini: *La Cenerentola* (Overture) *(R)*

1   2   3   4   5   6   7 ⑧ 9   ⑩ 11 ⑫ 13 14 15 16 17   18

10. Rossini-Respighi: *La Boutique Fantastique* (Ballet) *(R)*

1 ②3 4 5 6 7 8 9 10 11 12 ⑬ 14 15 16 17 18 19 20 ㉑ 22 23 24

*(R) means recorded.

Melody 14C

Mode Identification: Dorian, Phrygian, Lydian, and Mixolydian Modes

Student text: Page 205.

Each exercise consists of the Dorian, Phrygian, Lydian, or Mixolydian scale.

DORIAN MODE is the same as the natural minor scale with a raised 6th. Listen for a natural minor scale with a *raised 6th degree*.

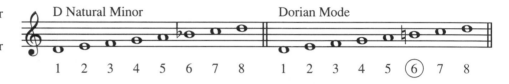

PHRYGIAN MODE is the same as the natural minor scale except for a lowered 2nd. Listen for a natural minor scale with a *lowered 2nd degree*.

LYDIAN MODE is the same as the major scale except for a raised 4th. Listen for a major scale with a *raised 4th degree*.

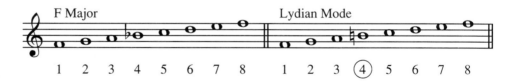

MIXOLYDIAN MODE is the same as the major scale except for a lowered 7th. Listen for a major scale with a *lowered 7th degree*.

In the blanks provided, name the mode you hear.

To the Instructor:

Explain very carefully the ways in which modal scales differ from their major and minor counterparts. In every case, only one tone is different.

Play each mode two or three times at a moderate tempo. Ask class members to sing each mode immediately after it is played.

1. Dorian   2. Lydian   3. Mixolydian

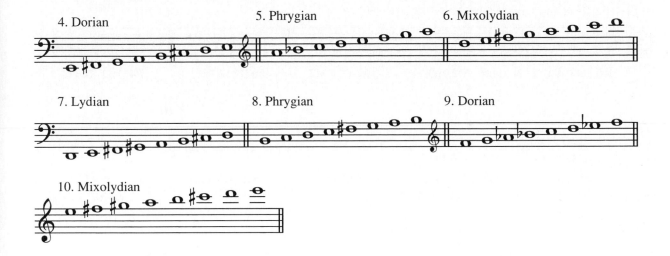

In numbers 11—20, the modal scales will be played in reverse order—from the highest tone to the lowest.

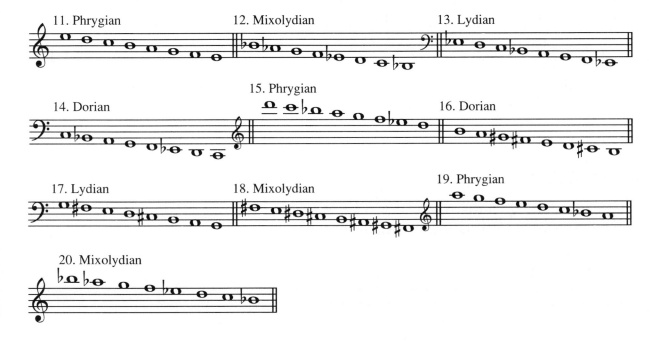

Melody 14D
Interval Dictation: Three Intervals in Succession

Student text: Page 206.

Each exercise consists of three intervals played in succession.

The first note is given. Write the remaining notes on the staff in notation.

To the Instructor:

Play each exercise two or three times at a slow tempo. For additional drill, ask class members to name the intervals formed.

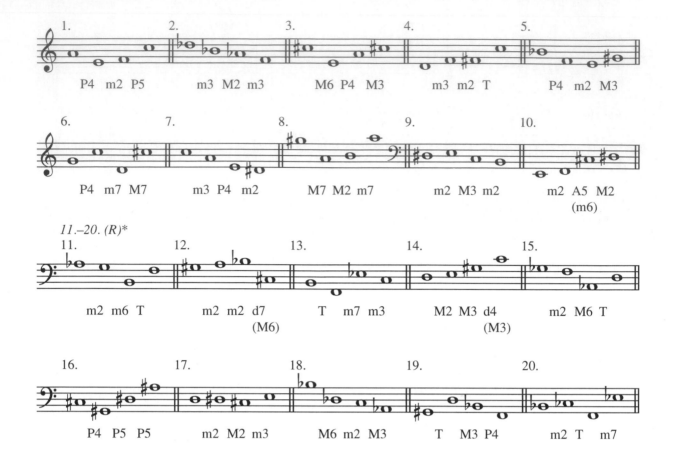

1. P4 m2 P5   2. m3 M2 m3   3. M6 P4 M3   4. m3 m2 T   5. P4 m2 M3

6. P4 m7 M7   7. m3 P4 m2   8. M7 M2 m7   9. m2 M3 m2   10. m2 A5 M2 (m6)

11.–20. (R)*

11. m2 m6 T   12. m2 m2 d7 (M6)   13. T m7 m3   14. M2 M3 d4 (M3)   15. m2 M6 T

16. P4 P5 P5   17. m2 M2 m3   18. M6 m2 M3   19. T M3 P4   20. m2 T m7

Melody 14E

Models and Embellishments: I-V-I Progression with Chromatic Melodic Embellishments

Student text: Page 207.

1. The model in this section is a I-V-I progression using four voices and containing chromatic embellishment. The upper three voices are always in open position. Sing all parts of this structure before class.
2. Your instructor will play the structure followed by embellishments of that structure.
3. Write the model's embellishments on the numbered staves provided.

To the Instructor:

1. Have the students sing each voice of the model before the early examples.
2. Play the structure and embellishments in the order printed, or repeat the structure from time to time to remind students of the basis for each embellishment.
3. Students should notate all four voices of the embellishments.

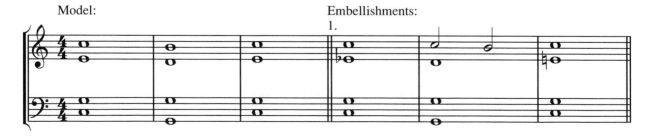

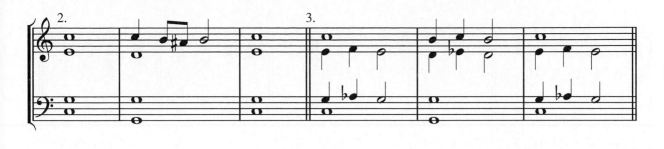

Harmony 14A

Chord Function Identification: Secondary Dominants of IV(iv) and vi(VI)

Student text: Page 208

Each exercise consists of a series of four chords in block harmony.

Indicate the analysis of each of the four chords in the blank provided.

New chords:

G Minor: V^7/iv vii°⁷/iv V/VI V^7/VI vii°⁷/VI

To the Instructor:
This set of exercises concentrates on V^7 and vii°⁷ of both iv and VI.

To prepare for this set of exercises, ask students to sing the G-harmonic minor scale. Then, drill all chords, asking students to sing each in root position and inversions.

When playing these chords for dictation, ask students to sing the root of each. After the first six or seven exercises, the practice may be discontinued.

Numbers 1—15 contain root-position chords only:

Numbers 16—25 contain inversions:

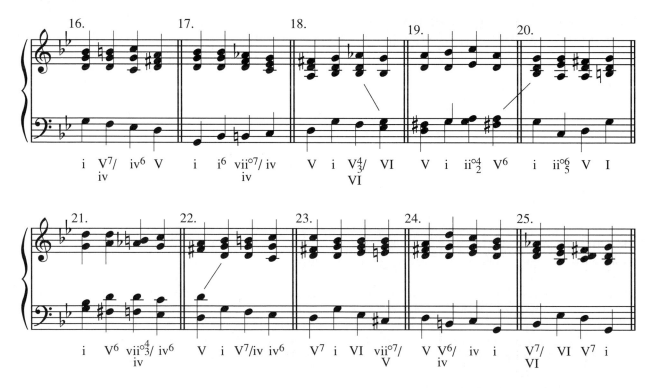

Harmony 14B

Chords in Music Literature: Secondary Dominants and Leading Tone Chords of iii and IV

Student text: Page209.

1. Each exercise consists of four examples from music literature which includes a variety of harmonic rhythms and nonharmonic tones.
2. Below you see four models (A through D). Your instructor will play each of these four models. Listen carefully and try to distinguish each—one from another.

A.	B.	C.	D.
VI V$_3^4$/iv iv V	V$_5^6$/IV IV V^7 I	V^7/iii iii V$_3^4$ I	vii^{o7}/V i$_4^6$ V^7 i

3. Your instructor will play an example (1 through 4) from music literature. The music literature example contains the same chords and same inversions as one of the four models above.

1. Beethoven: Piano Sonata, Op. 14, No. 2, II

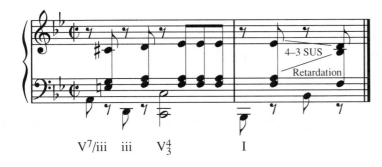

V^7/iii   iii   V$_3^4$ I

2. Beethoven: Piano Sonata, Op. 13, IV

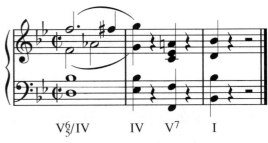

V$_5^6$/IV   IV   V^7 I

3. Beethoven: Op. 13, II

vii^{o7}/V   i$_4^6$ V^7 i

4.Beethoven: Op. 13, IV

VI V_3^4/iv iv V i V i V i

4.   When you have matched the literature example with one of the four sets of chords (A through D), place the letter in the appropriate blank below, and prepare for the next example from music literature.

1. _____ 2. _____ 3. _____ 4. _____

5.   When the first four examples are completed, use the same procedure for models 5 through 8.

These (**E, F, G, H**) are the remaining four models. Pair them up with the examples from literature (**5, 6, 7, 8**).

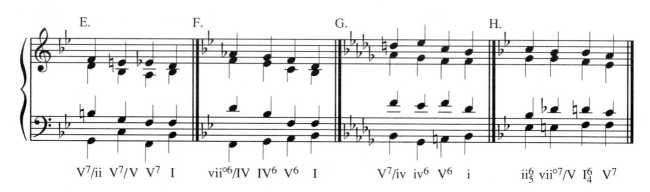

E.   F.   G.   H.

V^7/ii V^7/V V^7 I   vii°⁶/IV IV⁶ V⁶ I V^7/iv iv⁶ V⁶ i   ii$_5^6$ vii°⁷/V I$_4^6$ V^7

5. (R) _____ 6. (R) _____ 7. (R) _____ 8. (R) _____

5. Beethoven: Piano Sonata, Op. 14, No. 2

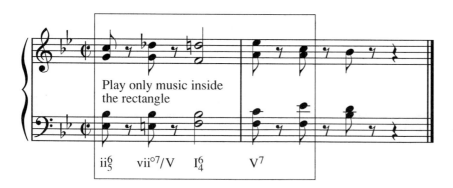

Play only music inside the rectangle

ii$_5^6$ vii°⁷/V   I$_4^6$ V^7

6. Beethoven: Piano Sonata, Op. 2, No. 2, III

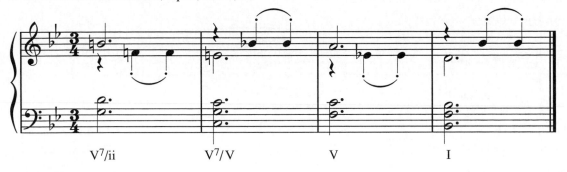

V⁷/ii   V⁷/V   V   I

7. Beethoven: Piano Sonata, Op. 2, No. 3, III   8. Beethoven: Piano Sonata, Op. 2, No. 3, III6

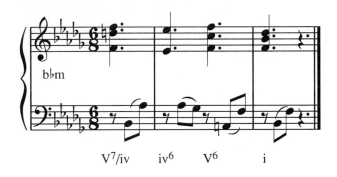

bbm

V⁷/iv   iv⁶   V⁶   i

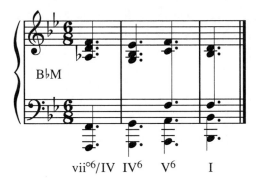

BbM

vii°⁶/IV   IV⁶   V⁶   I

To the Instructor:

A complete discussion of this type of exercise and suggestions for classroom use are provided in the "To the Instructor" section of Harmony 1B.

Harmony 14C

Aural Analysis: Four-Phrase Excerpt from a Beethoven Piano Sonata

Student text: Page 209.

This section consists of a single four-phrase excerpt from a Beethoven piano sonata.

1. Listen to the excerpt four to six times.
2. Become familiar with the statements that follow.
3. Circle the numbers representing *true* statements regarding the excerpt. The questions are grouped according to category.

To the Instructor:

Give class members at least two or three minutes to read the statements, then play the excerpt two or three times. Allow sufficient time for students to discover the true statements. Finally, play the excerpt an additional two or three times (pausing between playings) for students to check their answers.

If you are not a pianist, assign the excerpt at least a week in advance to a class member who is a piano major. If all else fails, use the recording that accompanies this text.

Beethoven: Piano Sonata, op. 10, no. 1 (second movement) *(R)*

Phrase Relationships and Construction

1. The first and third phrases are in modified repeated relationship (consider all voices).
2. The second and fourth phrases are in contrasting relationship.
3. The fourth phrase contains a substantial phrase extension.
4. The second phrase is parallel to the first.
5. The melody line (uppermost voice) of the first and third phrases contains a sequence.
6. The third and fourth phrases are in modified repeated relationship.
7. The complete excerpt is a double period.

Cadences

8. The only perfect authentic cadence occurs at the end of the excerpt.
9. The second and fourth phrases end with different cadence types.
10. The first and second cadences are of different types.

Harmony and Nonharmonic Tones

11. The first phrase contains only tonic and dominant harmony.
12. The second phrase contains only tonic and dominant harmony.
13. The excerpt modulates to the dominant.
14. The harmonic rhythm is consistently three chords only (two chord *changes* per phrase).
15. The first phrase contains two prominent escape tones (uppermost voice).
16. The first phrase contains two appoggiaturas (in the uppermost voice).
17. The final cadence contains both a suspension and a retardation.

Miscellaneous

18. The third phrase contains an Alberti bass figure.
19. The complete excerpt contains an example of change of mode.
20. An ostinato figure the length of a phrase is heard throughout the excerpt (four times).

Harmony 14D

Harmonic Dictation: Chorale Phrases Containing Secondary Dominants

Student text: Page 210.

Each exercise consists of a chorale phrase.

Numbers	No. of Chords	Position	Nonharmonic Tones
1–6	4	Root position only	Occasional passing tone and suspension
7–12	6–9	Root position and inversions	Several—any type

For numbers 1—6 (practice outside of class):

It will help you to identify secondary dominants if you know the possibilities and common patterns. Numbers 1—6 contain no secondary leading-tone chords or inversions, so you should concentrate on the following:

Major Triad or Dominant 7th Sounding 7th Chord on Scale Step:	Means a Secondary Dominant of:
1	IV
2	V
3	vi (VI in minor)
6	ii

The following procedure is recommended:

1. As you listen to each chord try to match the pitch of the root (bass pitch) by *thinking* it rather than *singing* it.
2. Immediately recall the complete succession of chord roots.
3. Associate the root pitches with solfeggio syllables or numbers.
4. Convert the syllables or numbers to actual pitches, and write out the bass notes on the staves provided.
5. Listen for major or major-minor sounds above each root—where you would normally expect minor triads and nondominant sounding 7th chords. In light pencil indicate these with a "V/" or "V⁷/." You can complete the analysis later when you have more information.
6. If your instructor requests, in successive listenings pick out the soprano, alto, and tenor parts. Relate each to syllables or scale numbers.

7. Convert the syllables or numbers to actual pitches, and add the notes to the staves.

8. When you have completed the phrase, make sure you have placed the correct analysis symbols under those chords you determined to be secondary dominants (see step 5). Complete the analysis.

To the Instructor:

For marginal students, play each of the four chords a bit slower, allowing them more time to pick out secondary dominants. Numbers 1—6 are well within the grasp of all class members if they will use a carefully designed strategy.

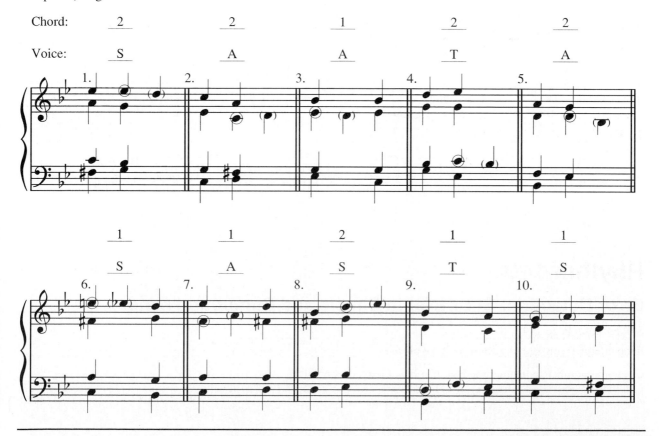

11. Das alter Jahr vergangen ist
(The old year has passed away)

12. Warum betrübst du dich, mein Herz
(Why do you grieve, my heart?)

em: V   i⁶ V⁶/VII VII III⁶   VII vii°⁷ (V⁶) i   am: i   i⁶   i⁶   V   vii°⁷/iv iv vii°⁷/V V
                                        V

Harmony 14E

Error Detection: Triads and 7th Chords

Student text: Page 212.

Each exercise consists of two chords in four parts.

1. As played by the instructor, one note in each exercise is incorrect. Errors may occur in the soprano, alto, or tenor voices.
2. Indicate the chord (no. 1 or no. 2) containing the error.
3. Also, indicate the voice where the error occurs:
    S = soprano   A = alto   T = tenor

To the Instructor:

Play both chords, including the circled note, two or three times. The note seen by the student is placed in parentheses to the right of the circled note. If students have initial difficulty with this type of drill, roll the first few chords (bass to soprano) to get them started.

Rhythm 14A
Rhythmic Dictation: Subtriplet in Simple and Compound Meter

Student text: Page 213.

Each exercise consists of a short phrase or melody.

Complete the rhythm of each exercise on a neutral pitch.

To the Instructor:

Play each exercise three or four times at a moderate tempo. Ask class members to clap the rhythm either of the entire phrase or at least a small section.

Rhythm 14B

Error Detection: Subtriplet in Simple and Compound Meter

Student text: Page 214.

Each exercise consists of a short melodic phrase.

Circle the number indicating the beat that is *not* played as notated.

Play only one or two times at performance tempo.

*Circle indicates the beat that disagrees with the workbook.

Transcription 14

Challenging Keyboard Music

Refer to instructions found in Transcription 1 (page 25).

Note: * = given material

Johann Christoph Friedrich Bach: *Anglaise*

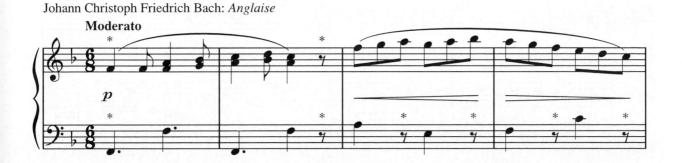

G. P. Telemann: *Christ lag in Todesbanden*

Allegro

Recorded Example 29

Unit 15

Melody 15A

Melodic Dictation: Nondiatonic Tones

Student text: Page 219.

Each exercise consists of a short melodic excerpt containing one or two nondiatonic tones often suggesting secondary dominant harmony.

Suggested procedure for each melody (outside of class):

1. Listen to the melody. Determine the tonic—it is always the first pitch given.
2. In your mind, construct the scale and sing or *think* it.
3. As you hear the melody again, memorize it in its entirety.
4. Be aware of one or two pitches that are nondiatonic.
5. When you have memorized the melody, sing it adding solfeggio syllables or numbers. Your instructor will tell you how to accommodate the nondiatonic pitches.
6. Convert the syllables or numbers to actual pitches, and notate the melody on the staff provided.

To the Instructor:

This set of short melodies provides students with experience in identifying nondiatonic tones unrelated to modulations. Most such notes in this assignment suggest brief secondary dominant or leading-tone harmony, and are common to melodies of the seventeenth through nineteenth centuries. Many are adapted from longer melodies from music literature. Suggested procedures for study outside of class may be used effectively in class as well.

12. Em   13. FM

14. CM

*Note or rest in workbook.

(R) means recorded.

Melody 15B

Error Detection: Five-Note Melodic Figures

Student text: Page 220.

Each exercise consists of a series of five tones with one pitch printed incorrectly. The first pitch (not lettered) is always correct.

Circle the letter (a, b, c, d) representing the incorrect pitch.

To the Instructor:

Play each series of tones two or three times. Ask class members to sing the five pitches immediately after they are played.

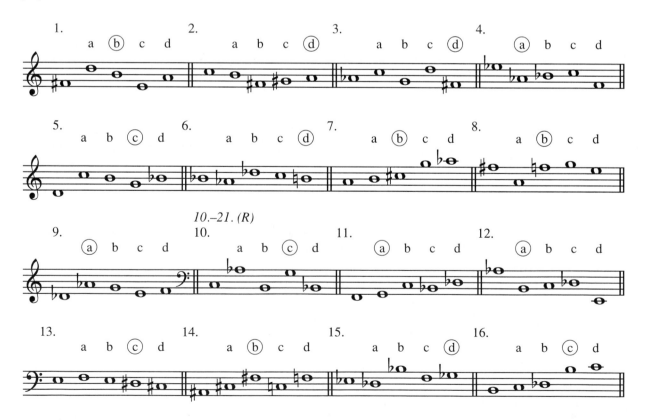

Melody 15C

Mode Identification: Dorian, Phrygian, Lydian, Mixolydian, and Aeolian Modes

Student text: Page 220.

Each exercise consists of the Dorian, Phrygian, Lydian, Mixolydian, or Aeolian scale. Recognize the mode of each melody.

See Melody 14C for information concerning these modes. The Aeolian mode is the same as the natural minor.

1. In the blank provided, name the mode you hear.

To the Instructor:

Review the modes. Explain very carefully the ways that modes differ from their major and minor counterparts. In most cases, only one tone is different from either a major or natural minor.

Play each scale two or three times at a moderate tempo. Ask class members to sing each scale immediately after it is played.

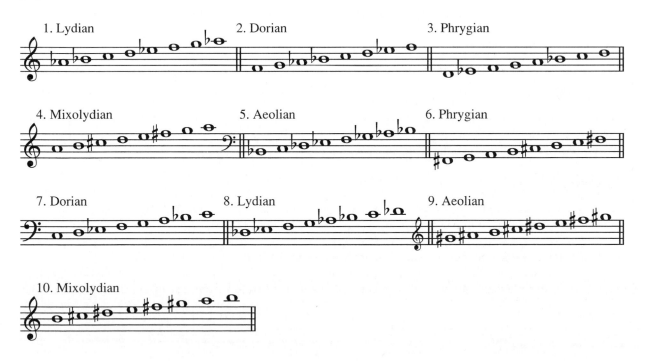

2. Numbers 11—20 consist of very short melodies utilizing the same modal scales played in numbers 1—10.
3. Write the name of the mode used in each melody.

4. The instructor may also ask you to write the key signature for each melody. The beginning note, which is also the mode *final*, is given.

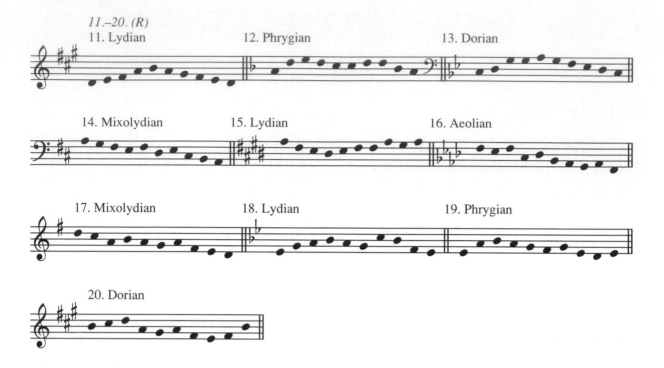

11.–20. (R)
11. Lydian   12. Phrygian   13. Dorian

14. Mixolydian   15. Lydian   16. Aeolian

17. Mixolydian   18. Lydian   19. Phrygian

20. Dorian

Melody 15D

Interval Dictation: Adding Proper Accidentals to Modal Melodies

Student text: Page 221.

Each exercise consists of a ten-note modal melody.

1. The first and last notes are correctly written, but the accidentals have otherwise been removed.
2. Write the proper accidentals for each modal melody. (Do not change the letter names of any of the notes. They are correct.)
3. Write the name of the mode in the blank above each score.

To the Instructor:

Play each melody once or twice. Ask class members to sing the scale upon which the melody is based. When students give the correct response, they are ready to write their answers.

Warn students not to work from note to note in adding the accidentals. It is not a good procedure.

A total of four or five playings may be necessary at first; but after the first few exercises, two or three should suffice.

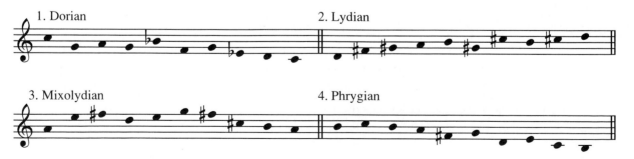

1. Dorian   2. Lydian

3. Mixolydian   4. Phrygian

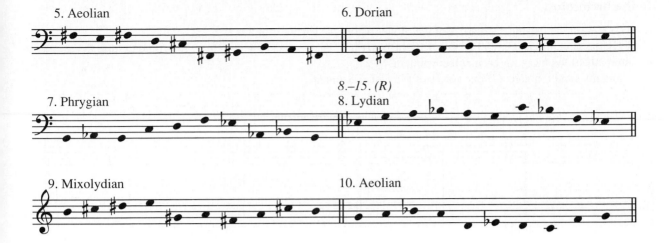

5. Aeolian   6. Dorian

7. Phrygian   8.–15. (R)
8. Lydian

9. Mixolydian   10. Aeolian

4. Exercises 11—15 are different from exercises 1—10 only in that they contain the element of rhythm.
5. The same directions apply to these as given for exercises 1—10.

11. Lydian   12. Dorian

13. Mixolydian

14. Aeolian

15. Phrygian

Melody 15E

Models and Embellishments: Harmonic Structure with Melodic and Harmonic Embellishments

Student text: Page 223.

1. The model in this section is a I-V-I progression in the major mode using four voices and containing a descending melodic line. Other chords are added to the progression and chromatic embellishments can also be found. The upper three voices are always in close position. Sing all parts of this structure before class.
2. Your instructor will play the structure followed by embellishments of that structure.
3. Write the model's embellishments on the numbered staves provided.

To the Instructor:

1. Have the students sing each voice of the model before the early examples.
2. Play the structure and embellishments in the order printed, or repeat the structure from time to time to remind students of the basis for each embellishment.
3. Students should notate all four voices of the embellishments.

Harmony 15A

Chord Function Identification: All Secondary Dominants

Student text: Page 224.

Each exercise consists of a series of four chords in block harmony.

1. In the blank provided, analyze each of the four chords.
2. All of the secondary dominants studied to date, plus that of iii, are used. All exercises are in G major.

To the Instructor:

To prepare for this set of exercises:

1. Ask class members to sing the G-major scale.
2. For numbers 1—15, make a transparent acetate copy of the following chords for an overhead projector:

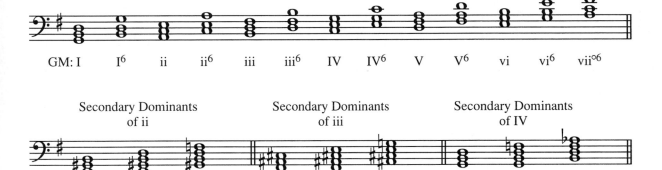

3. Point to symbols on the overhead projection, and ask class members to sing the chords they represent. For instance, select a common series like I ii⁶ vii°⁷/V V; point to each symbol as class members sing the chords in simple position (arpeggiation). Ten or fifteen minutes of class time will be well spent in this procedure. Then, progress to the exercises themselves.
4. For the first three or four exercises, ask class members to sing the chords (simple position, arpeggiated) as they are played. After the first three or four exercises, the chords should be identified without such artificial aids.

Numbers 1—15 contain root-position chords only:

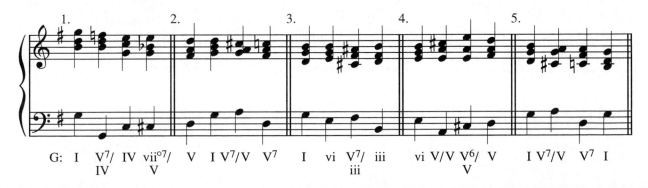

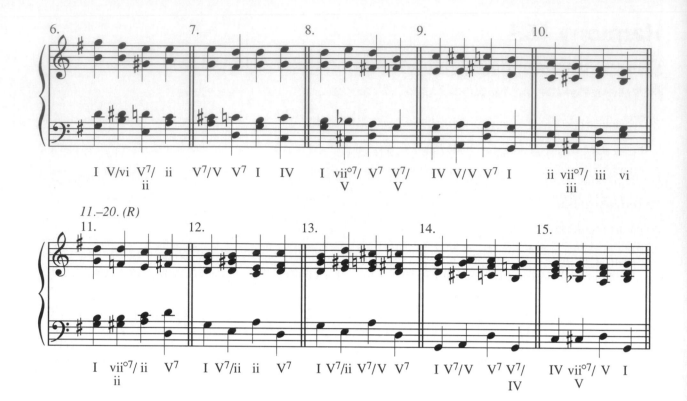

Numbers 16—25 contain inversions:

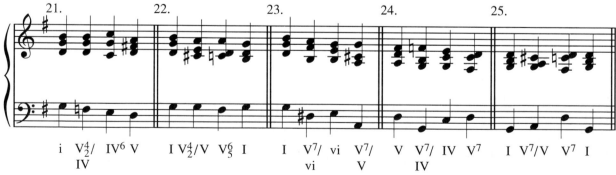

Harmony 15B

Chords in Music Literature: All Secondary Dominants and Leading Tone Chords

Student text: Page 224.

1. Each exercise consists of four examples from music literature which includes a variety of harmonic rhythms and nonharmonic tones.
2. Below you see four models (A through D). Your instructor will play each of these four models. Listen carefully and try to distinguish each—one from another. Pay close attention to the key signatures in these examples.

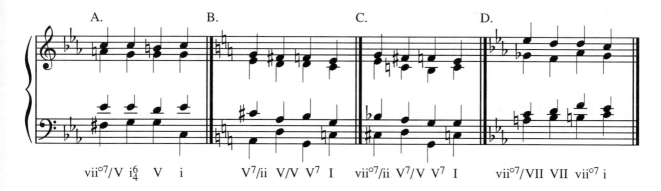

3. Your instructor will play an example (1 through 4) from music literature. The music literature example contains the same chords and same inversions as one of the four models above.

1. Beethoven: Piano Sonata, Op. 2, No. 1, II

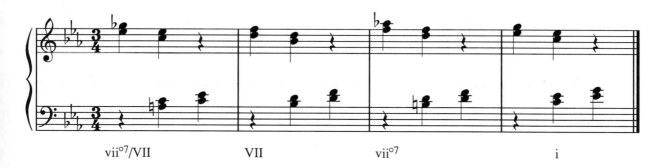

2. Beethoven: Piano Sonata, Op. 2, No. 2, III

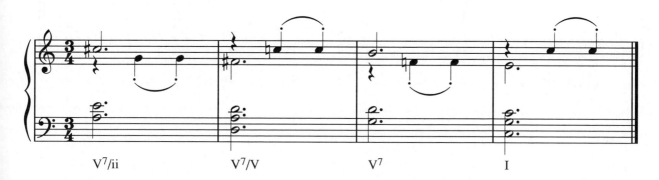

3. Beethoven: Piano Sonata, Op. 27, No. 2 (Quasi una Fantasia)

vii°⁷/V   i⁶₄   V   i

4. Verdi: Rigoletto, Act II, no. 14

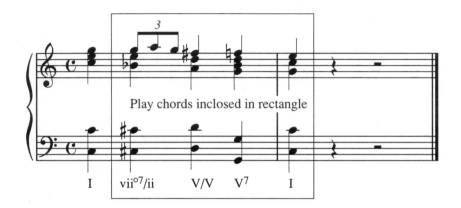

Play chords inclosed in rectangle

I   vii°⁷/ii   V/V   V⁷   I

4. When you have matched the literature example with one of the four sets of chords (A through D), place the letter in the appropriate blank below, and prepare for the next example from music literature.

    1. _____   2. _____   3. _____   4. _____

5. When the first four examples are completed, use the same procedure for models 5 through 8.

These (**E, F, G, H**) are the remaining four models. Pair them up with the examples from literature (**5, 6, 7, 8**).

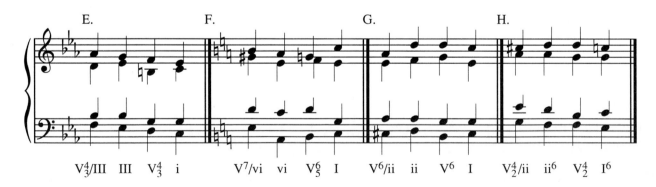

    E.   F.   G.   H.

V⁴₃/III   III   V⁴₃   i   V⁷/vi   vi   V⁶₅   I   V⁶/ii   ii   V⁶   I   V⁴₂/ii   ii⁶   V⁴₂   I⁶

    5. *(R)* _____   6. *(R)* _____   7. *(R)* _____   8. *(R)* _____

5. Mozart: Piano Sonata, K. 281

V⁶/ii   ii   V⁶   I

6. Schubert: Quintet, Op. 114 (D.667)

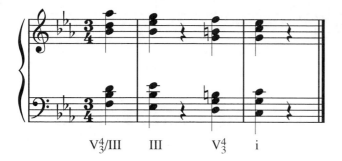

V⁴₃/III   III   V⁴₃   i

7. Tchaikovsky: Morning Prayer

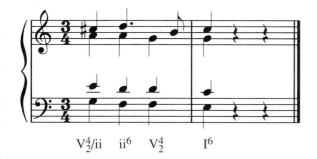

V⁴₂/ii   ii⁶   V⁴₂   I⁶

8. Schumann: Dichterliebe, Op. 48, No. 14

V⁷/vi   vi   V⁶₅   I

To the Instructor:

A complete discussion of this type of exercise and suggestions for classroom use are provided in the "To the Instructor" section of Harmony 1B.

Harmony 15C

Aural Analysis: Phrase, Key, Cadence, and Harmonic Relationships in a Five-Phrase Excerpt from a Beethoven Piano Sonata

Student text: Page 225.

The exercise consists of a single five-phrase excerpt from a Beethoven piano sonata. *(R)*

Listen to the five-phrase unit several times. Circle the *true* statements. Statements are grouped by subject matter.

To the Instructor:

Play the excerpt live in class or use the recording that accompanies this text. Allow class members sufficient time to read the statements before playing. To answer the first fifteen statements a total of five or six playings may be necessary.

For statements 16—20, it will be necessary to play the first six chords of the final phrase separately three or four times.

Although the authors have indicated the true statements according to their own frame of reference, the instructor is encouraged to challenge any answer. Indeed, the statements may be used simply to solicit class discussions. The authors encourage each instructor to make up other statements that may encourage further valuable dialogue.

Beethoven: Sonata, op. 14, no. 2 (second movement) *(R)*

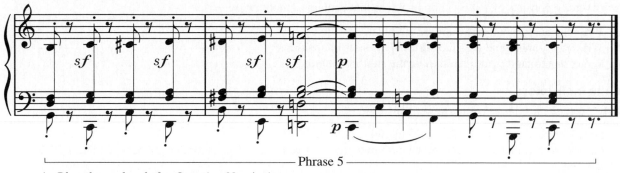

─── Phrase 5 ───

└ *Play these chords for Question No. 4.* ┘

*Note or rest in workbook.

The statements are repeated here for the convenience of the instructor:

1. Phrase relationships (only one is correct):
    a. A   AP*   B   A'   C
    b. A   A   B   B'   C
    c. A   AP   B   A   B'
    d. A   B   C   A'   D
    ⓔ A   B   B'   A'   C

* "P" refers to parallel phrase relationship.

2. Key relationships (more than one may be correct):
    ⓐ The first phrase does not modulate.
    ⓑ The excerpt contains numerous (at least ten) secondary dominants.
    c. The fourth and fifth phrases are clearly in different keys.
    d. The composition ends in a key different from the beginning.
    ⓔ The second phrase ends with an authentic cadence in (or on) the dominant.

3. Cadences (more than one may be correct):
    a. Cadences at the ends of phrases represent authentic, half, and plagal types.
    ⓑ The final cadence is authentic in the tonic key (key at the beginning of the excerpt).
    ⓒ Most phrases of this excerpt can be divided into two phrase members, each with a cadence of its own.
    ⓓ The first and fourth phrases end with different cadence types.
    e. The first cadence is decorated with a suspension.

To the Instructor:

Play the first six chords of the final phrase *separately* four or five times.

The succession of chord roots contained in the first six chords of the final phrase of the excerpt (these will be played separately for you):

4. The succession of chord roots (only one is correct):
    a. G   C   F   B♭   A♭   D♭
    b. G   C   B   E   D   G
    ⓒ G   C   A   D   B   E
    d. G   E   A   D   G   C
    e. G   D   B   F♯   D   A

Harmony 15D

Harmonic Dictation: Modulation in Chorale Phrases

Student text: Page 226.

Each exercise consists of a short chorale phrase that contains a modulation.

1. Write the analysis of each chord in the blank provided.
2. Write the soprano and bass melodies on the staff in notation.
3. Write the alto and tenor melodies on the staff in notation.

To the Instructor:

These exercises may be used in a variety of ways:

1. For identification and analysis of the harmony only
2. For identification and analysis of the harmony plus the two outer voices (soprano and bass) on the staff in notation.
3. For identification and analysis of the harmony plus four-part dictation.

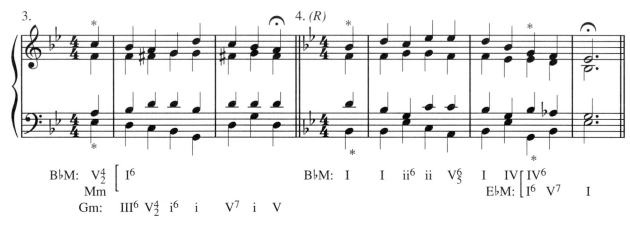

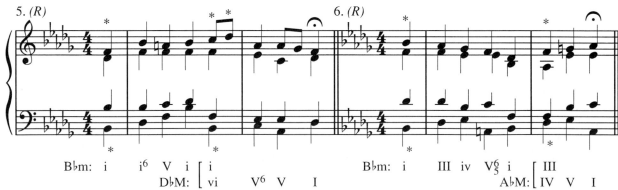

Harmony 15E

Error Detection: Triads and 7th Chords

Student text: Page 227.

Each exercise consists of three chords in four parts.

As played by the instructor, one note in each exercise is incorrect. Errors may occur in any voice.

1. Indicate the chord (no. 1, no. 2, or no. 3) containing the error.
2. Indicate the voice where the error occurs:
   S = soprano   A = alto   T = tenor   B = bass

To the Instructor:

Play all three chords, including the circled note, two or three times. The note seen by the student is placed in parentheses to the right of the circled note. If students have initial difficulty with this type of drill, roll the first few chords (bass to soprano) to get them started.

Harmony 15F

Identifying Modulations to Closely Related and Foreign Keys

Student text: Page 228.

Each exercise consists of a series of 7th chords beginning in C major and modulating to a closely related or foreign key.

1. In the blank provided, write the name of the key to which the phrase modulates. All begin in the key of C.
2. The instructor may ask some class members to provide a harmonic analysis of each chord in the excerpt. Blanks are provided for this purpose.

To the Instructor:

Play the exercise once or twice. Ask class members to sing the tonic at the beginning of the phrase (in all these exercises, this is C). Play the phrase again, and ask students to sing both the beginning tonic and the new tonic. In the first few exercises, allow class members to compare these two tones as they sing. The relationship should then be very clear. After treating the opening exercises in this manner, students should be able to incorporate this technique in the remainder without audible sounds.

Although the majority of students will do well to name only the key to which each phrase modulates, some may be able also to name the chords involved. Blanks are also provided for those ambitious students who wish to complete this additional undertaking.

Rhythm 15A

Rhythmic Dictation: More Difficult Rhythms

Student text: Page 229.

Each exercise consists of a short melody.

Complete the rhythm on a neutral pitch.

To the Instructor:

Play each exercise once or twice, and ask class members to clap the rhythm. Repeat the procedure until students can clap the rhythm accurately. Then, allow sufficient time for notating the rhythm.

Rhythm 15B

Error Detection: More Difficult Rhythmic Errors

Student text: Page 230.

Each exercise consists of a short melodic excerpt containing one error in rhythm.

Circle the number indicating the rhythm that differs from that played.

To the Instructor:

Play each exercise two or three times at a tempo as fast as the students can accommodate.

Transcription 15
Chromatic Examples

Refer to instructions found in Transcription 1 (page 25).

Note: * = given material

Recorded Example 30

J. S. Bach: "Thus Goest Thou Now, My Jesus"

M. Clementi: Prelude in C Minor

Unit 16

Melody 16A

Melodic Dictation: Nondiatonic Tones

Student text: Page 233.

Each exercise consists of a short melodic excerpt from music literature containing nondiatonic tones often suggesting momentary modulations or secondary dominant harmony.

Suggested procedure for each melody (outside of class):

1. Listen to the melody. The key is given above the staff. Figure the relationship of the first note to the tonic and sing it.
2. In your mind, construct the scale and sing or *think* it.
3. As you hear the melody again, memorize it in its entirety.
4. Be aware of some pitches that are nondiatonic.
5. When you have memorized the melody, sing it (in any register) adding solfeggio syllables or numbers. Your instructor will tell you how to accommodate the nondiatonic pitches.
6. Convert the syllables or numbers to actual pitches, and notate the melody on the staff provided.

To the Instructor:

This set of short melodies provides students with experience in identifying nondiatonic tones and octave displacement—skips that place part of the melody in a different octave (see numbers 3, 6, and 8 especially). Most such notes in this assignment suggest brief modulations, secondary dominants or secondary leading-tone harmony and are common to melodies of the seventeenth through nineteenth centuries. All are taken directly from music literature. Suggested procedures for study outside of class may be used effectively in class as well.

11. Beethoven FM

12. Beethoven F#m–AM

Melody 16B

Error Detection: Short Melodic Segments Based on Intervals

Student text: Page 234.

Each exercise consists of a series of six pitches. One of the pitches is different from that played.

The first note of the series is always correct.

Circle the letter representing the pitch that is different from that played.

To the Instructor:

After playing a melody two or three times, ask class members to sing it. Then, play the melody once or twice more.

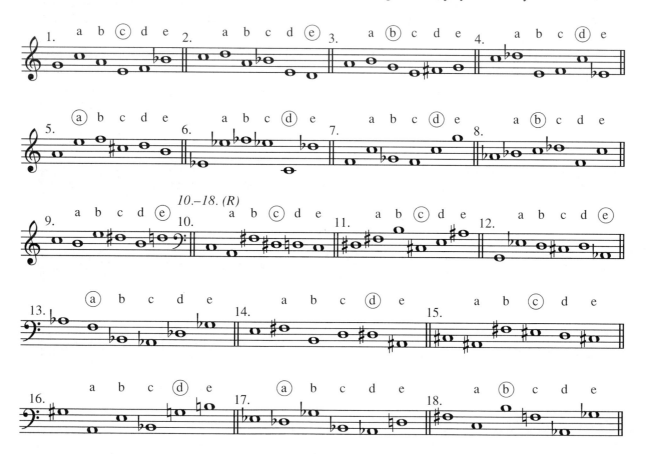

Melody 16C

Melodic Dictation: Typical Blues Figures

Student text: Page 234.

Each exercise consists of two measures of melody characteristic of the blues.

BLUES A black-American song of lament supported by I, IV, and V harmony, and extending usually to twelve measures—although eight-, sixteen-, twenty-four-, and thirty-two-bar blues are not uncommon.

BLUES SCALE A major scale with an added flat 3rd and flat 7th.

flat 3rd   flat 7th

These melodies may contain combinations of the natural 3rd, the flat 3rd, the natural 7th, and the flat 7th. Although the following are only two measures long, they contain typical figures found in blues compositions.

Complete each melody on the staff in notation.

To the Instructor:

Place the blues scale on the board, and ask students to sing it as a scale. Then, ask them to sing specific tones of the scale as you point to the notes. When the scale is familiar to students, begin the exercises, playing each melody three or four times at a moderate tempo. If the rhythm proves difficult, ask class members to clap each separately.

Melody 16D

Interval Dictation: Two-Voice Modal Compositions

Student text: Page 235.

Each exercise consists of a short excerpt from a two-voice composition of the sixteenth century.

Complete the melodies on the staff in notation.

Play the two melodies, balanced so that neither stands out separately. Three or four repetitions may be necessary. After class members have completed the melodies on the staff, ask them to sing the entire excerpt, assigning a balanced number to sing each voice. The X's indicate notes students should add.

1. Palestrina: Mass, *Ecce Sacerdos Magnus* (Credo)

2. Palestrina: Mass, *Ecce Sacerdos Magnus* (Credo)

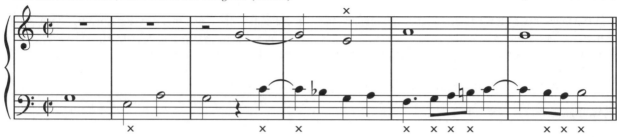

3. Palestrina: Mass, *Gabriel Archangelus* (Credo)

4. Palestrina: Mass, *Gabriel Archangelus* (Sanctus)

5. Palestrina: Mass, *Gabriel Archangelus* (Sanctus)

6. Palestrina: Mass, *Gabriel Archangelus* (Agnus Dei)

Melody 16E

Models and Embellishments: Harmonic Structure with Melodic and Harmonic Embellishments

Student text: Page 237.

1. The model in this section is a I-V-I progression in the minor mode using four voices and containing a decending melodic line. Other chords are added to the progression and chromatic embellishments can also be found. The upper three voices are always in close position. Sing all parts of this structure before class.
2. Your instructor will play the structure followed by embellishments of that structure.
3 Write the model's embellishments on the numbered staves provided.

To the Instructor:

1. Have the students sing each voice of the model before the early examples.
2. Play the structure and embellishments in the order printed, or repeat the structure from time to time to remind students of the basis for each embellishment.
3. Students should notate all voices of the embellishments.

Harmony 16A

Chord Function Identification: German and French Augmented 6th Chords and the Neapolitan 6th Chord

Student text: Page 238.

Each exercise consists of four chords in four-part harmony.

Analyze each of the four chords in the blanks provided, .

New chords:

Gm: Gr⁶   Fr⁶   N⁶

To the Instructor:

Before beginning this section, the new chords should be thoroughly explained and discussed in the class.

While many approaches are effective, the authors suggest that the usual procedure for singing chord roots and then bass notes be suspended when listening for augmented 6th chords. Instead, students should listen for:

1. The 6th scale degree in the bass voice
2. The particular sound of the German and French augmented 6th chords
3. The nature of the resolution (to the V chord or its embellishment, the i⁶₄).

For the Neapolitan 6th chord, students should be aware of:

1. The 4th scale degree in the bass voice
2. A major triad in first inversion

Numbers 1—25 contain inversions:

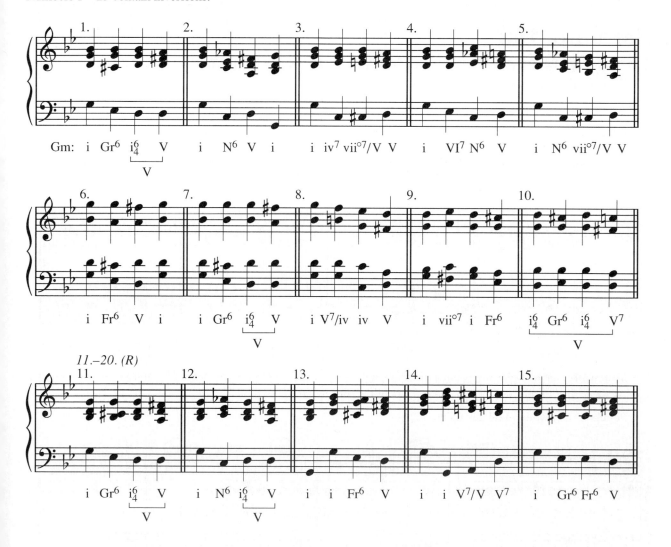

i   i⁶ N⁶   V   i V⁷/iv iv⁶ V   i   Fr⁶   V⁷ i   i   iv⁶ Fr⁶ V   i   VI⁷ i⁶₄   V

i   Gr⁶ Fr⁶ V   i   Gr⁶ i⁶₄ vii°⁷/V i⁶₄ V⁷ i   i   ii°⁶   N⁶ vii°⁷/V i⁶₄ V   i   i⁶ N⁶ V

Harmony 16B

Chords in Music Literature: Neapolitan 6th Chords and Augmented 6th Chords

Student text: Page 239.

1. Each exercise consists of four examples from music literature which includes a variety of harmonic rhythms and nonharmonic tones.
2. Below you see four models (A through D). Your instructor will play each of these four models. Listen carefully and try to distinguish each—one from another.

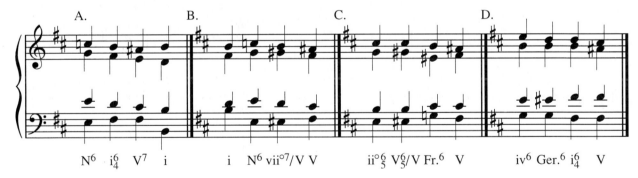

N⁶   i⁶₄   V⁷   i   i   N⁶ vii°⁷/V V   ii°⁶₅ V⁶₅/V Fr.⁶   V   iv⁶ Ger.⁶ i⁶₄   V

3. Your instructor will play an example (1 through 4) from music literature. The music literature example contains the same chords and same inversions as one of the four models above.

1. Schubert: Der Müller und der Bach

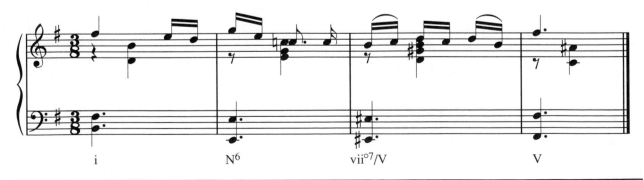

i   N⁶   vii°⁷/V   V

2. Schubert: Symphony in C

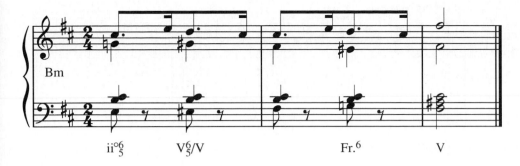

ii^{o6}_5 V^6_5/V Fr.^{6} V

3. Mozart: Piano Concerto, K. 488

N^6 i^6_4 V^7 i

4. Mozart: Theme with Variations, K. 284

iv^6 Ger.^{6} i^6_4 V

4. When you have matched the literature example with one of the four sets of chords (A through D), place the letter in the appropriate blank below, and prepare for the next example from music literature.

1. _____ 2. _____ 3. _____ 4. _____

5. When the first four examples are completed, use the same procedure for models 5 through 8.

These (**E, F, G, H**) are the remaining four models. Pair them up with the examples from literature (**5, 6, 7, 8**).

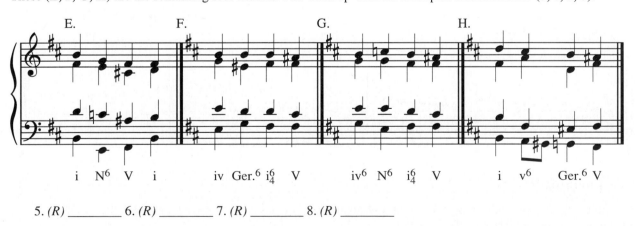

E.   F.   G.   H.

i N^6 V   i   iv   Ger.^{6} i^6_4 V iv^6 N^6 i^6_4 V   i v^6 Ger.^{6} V

5. *(R)* _____ 6. *(R)* _____ 7. *(R)* _____ 8. *(R)* _____

5. Verdi: Il Trovatore, Act II, no. 8

Bm

iv⁶   N⁶   i⁶₄   V

6. Schubert: Piano Sonata, Op. 42

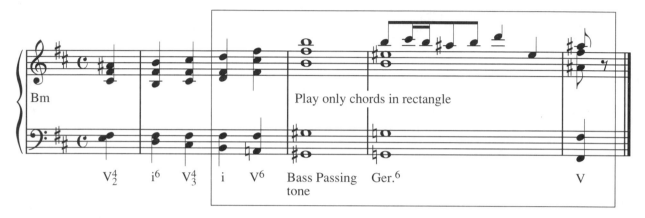

Bm

Play only chords in rectangle

V⁴₂   i⁶   V⁴₃   i   V⁶   Bass Passing tone   Ger.⁶   V

7. Schubert: Der Müller und der Bach

i   N⁶   V   i

8. Mozart: Piano Sonata, K281, III

Bm

iv   Ger.⁶   i⁶₄   V

To the Instructor:

A complete discussion of this type of exercise and suggestions for classroom use are provided in the "To the Instructor" section of Harmony 1B.

Harmony 16C

Aural Analysis: Binary, Rounded Binary, and Three-Part Forms

Student text: Page 240.

Each exercise consists of a complete composition in binary, rounded binary (incipient three-part), or three-part form.

The measure numbers for each composition are given. The instructor will count one measure before beginning to play so that you can follow the composition from the given numbers.

1. Bracket the phrases above the numbers. (The first phrase of each composition is correctly bracketed.)
2. Indicate the phrase relationships above the brackets.
3. Indicate the type of cadence at the end of each phrase. (This is given for the first phrase of each composition.)
4. Indicate the key of each cadence (given for the first phrase).
5. Indicate any melodic sequences or repetitions. (These are also given for the first phrase of each composition.)
6. Indicate the overall form of the composition (binary, rounded binary, or three-part form).

To the Instructor:

This section may be used in a variety of ways. The instructor may elect any or all of the six assignments for class members to complete. The more assignments requested, the more repetitions of the music required.

Each of the compositions in this section is included in the tapes that accompany the text, although live performance is preferred. Play each composition as many times as students require.

Repeat signs have been removed from composition nos. 2 and 3 for economy of class time.

1. Kuhlau: Sonatina, op. 88, no. 2 *(R)*   Rounded binary

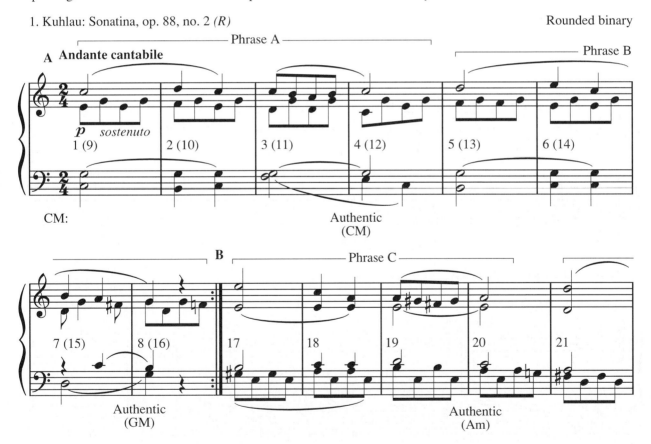

2. Handel: "Sarabande" from Suite VII for Keyboard *(R)*　　　　　Two-part form

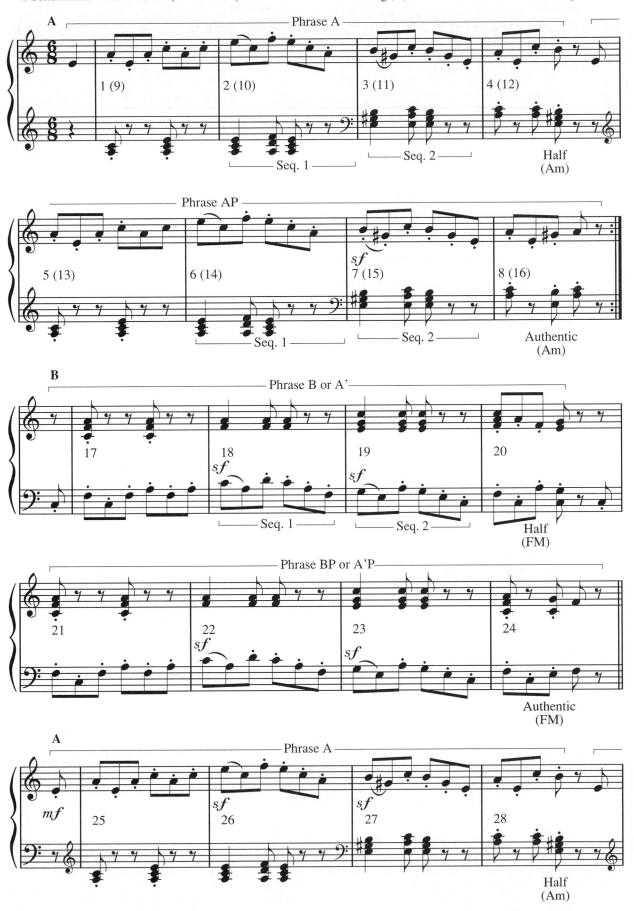

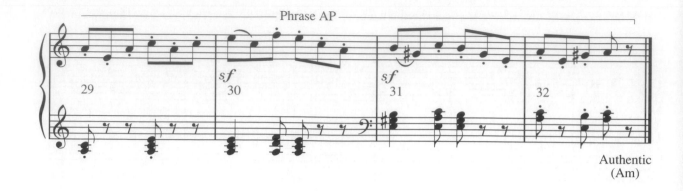

Authentic
(Am)

Harmony 16D

Harmonic Dictation: Chorale Phrases Containing Neapolitan 6th and Augmented 6th Chords

Student text: Page 242.

Each exercise consists of a chorale phrase. Except for the Neapolitan (normally found in first inversion) and augmented 6th chords (bass note a major 3rd below the tonic), the content of the phrases is:

Numbers	Position
1–4	Root position only
5–7	Root position and inversions

For numbers 1–4 (practice outside of class):

1. In numbers 1–4 the Neapolitan and augmented 6th chords are always treated in the most conventional manner.

    Neapolitan 6th chord:
    a. Major triad, the root of which is a minor 2nd above the tonic.
    b. Bass note is the 4th scale degree.
    c. Proceeds to the V chord, sometimes through its embellishment, the tonic $^6_4$. If required by your instructor, show this embellishment with brackets (See Harmony 9A.)

    Augmented 6th chords:
    a. Bass note is a major 3rd below the tonic.
    b. Italian and French types often proceed directly to V.
    c. The German type will always progress to V, but through the cadential tonic $^6_4$. If required by your instructor show this embellishment with brackets. (See Harmony 9A.)
    d. Italian 6th sounds like a dominant 7th without its 5th factor.
    e. French 6th does not sound like any diatonic chord, but it is a whole-tone chord—it contains only whole steps (no half steps).
2. A good way to identify the unique features of each augmented 6th chord is to play a number of them on the piano until you distinguish among the three types.
3. Numbers 5–7 contain root position and inversions.
4. Complete these phrases using the procedure in melody 14B.

To the Instructor:

This assignment should be undertaken only when the preceding section (Harmony 16A) is thoroughly digested. With proper preparation, phrases 1–4 should be well within the grasp of all class members. Assign phrases 5–7 to challenge more accomplished students.

Except for the Neapolitan and augmented 6th chords, the first four chorale phrases contain only root-position chords.

The following three chorale phrases include an occasional inversion:

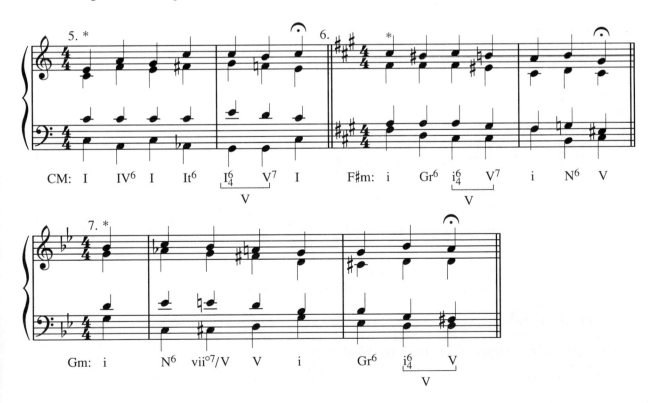

Harmony 16E

Error Detection: Triads and 7th Chords

Student text: Page 244.

Each exercise consists of three chords in four parts.

As played by the instructor, one note in each exercise is incorrect. Errors may occur in any voice.

1. Indicate the chord (no. 1, no. 2, or no. 3) containing the error.
2. Also, indicate the voice where the error occurs:
   S = soprano   A = alto   T = tenor   B = bass

To the Instructor:

Play all three chords including the circled note, two or three times. The note seen by the student is placed in parentheses to the right of the circled note:

Rhythm 16A

Rhythmic Dictation: Changing Meters

Student text: Page 244.

Each exercise consists of a short melody that employs changing meters.

Complete the rhythm on a neutral pitch and complete any incomplete changing meters.

To the Instructor:

After playing an exercise two or three times, ask class members to clap the rhythm. If the exercise is too long for this, divide it into sections.

Rhythm 16B

Error Detection: Review

Student text: Page 245.

Each exercise consists of a short melodic excerpt containing one error in rhythm.

Circle the number indicating the beat that is *not* played as notated.

To the Instructor:

Play each exercise two or three times at as fast a tempo as can be grasped by students.

1.

2.

3.

4.

5.

6.

7.

8.

Transcription 16

Advanced Chromatic Examples

Refer to instructions found in Transcription 1 (page 25).

Note: * = given material

Recorded Example 32

J. S. Bach: "Sarabande" from Cello Suite no. 5

Recorded Example 33

J. T. Kolosick: "Halloween"

Appendix _____

Because of the large number of revisions in the fifth edition, the authors have provided this chart showing the derivation of the material for each unit. This chart will help in revising syllabi based on the fourth edition.

M-1A	M1C	M-3A	M3B	M-5A	Same	M-7A	M7B
M-1B	M1A	M-3B	M1B	M-5B	M4B	M-7B	M8B
M-1C	M2A	M-3C	M5C	M-5C	M3C	M-7C	M6C
M-1D	Same	M-3D	M3E	M-5D	Same	M-7D	Same
M-1E	Same	M-3E	M4E	M-5E	M6E	M-7E	M8E
H-1A	New	H-3A	New	H-5A	New	H-7A	New
H-1B	New	H-3B	New	H-5B	New	H-7B	New
H-1C	H4B	H-3C	Same	H-5C	Same	H-7C	H6C
H-1D	Same	H-3D	H2D	H-5D	H5B	H-7D	H6B
H-1E	H1B	H-3E	H4D	H-5E	H2F	H-7E	H6E
H-1F	H1C	R-3A	R3B	R-5A	Same	R-7A	Same
R-1A	Same	R-3B	R3A	R-5B	Same	R-7B	Same
T-1	Same	T-3	Same	T-5	Same	T-7	Same
M-2A	M2B	M-4A	Same	M-6A	Same	M-8A	Same
M-2B	M3D	M-4B	M5B	M-6B	M7A	M-8B	M9B
M-2C	M3A	M-4C	M6B	M-6C	M4C	M-8C	M7C
M-2D	Same	M-4D	Same	M-6D	Same	M-8D	Same
M-2E	Same	M-4E	M5E	M-6E	M7E	M-8E	M9E
H-2A	New	H-4A	New	H-6A	New	H-8A	New
H-2B	New	H-4B	New	H-6B	New	H-8B	New
H-2C	H2E	H-4C	H3E	H-6C	H5D	H-8C	H9C
H-2D	H2C	H-4D	H3B	H-6D	H4C	H-8D	H7C
H-2E	H2B	H-4E	H6D	H-6E	H4E	H-8E	H7D
H-2F	H3D	R-4A	H4B	R-6A	Same	R-8A	Same
R-2A	Same	R-4B	H4A	R-6B	Same	R-8B	Same
T-2	Same	T-4	Same	T-6	Same	T-8	Same

M-9A	Same	M-11A	New	M-13A	M12A	M-15A	Same
M-9B	M10B	M-11B	M12B	M-13B	M14C	M-15B	M13D
M-9C	M8C	M-11C	M10A	M-13C	M16B	M-15C	M13A
M-9D	M10D	M-11D	Same	M-13D	M14D	M-15D	M13B
M-9E	M10E	M-11E	M12D	M-13E	Same	M-15E	Same
H-9A	New	H-11A	New	H-13A	New	H-15A	New
H-9B	New	H-11B	New	H-13B	New	H-15B	New
H-9C	H8C	H-11C	H9B	H-13C	H11C	H-15C	H13C
H-9D	H8B	H-11D	H11B	H-13D	H13B	H-15D	H14C
H-9E	H8D	H-11E	H12C	H-13E	H12E	H-15E	H14D
R-9A	Same	R-11A	R-11B	R-13A	Same	H-15F	H12B
T-9	Same	R-11B	R-11A	R-13B	Same	R-15A	Same
		T-11	Same	T-13	Same	R-15B	Same
						T-15	Same

M-10A	M10C	M-12A	M11A	M-14A	Same		
M-10B	M11B	M-12B	M9C	M-14B	M15B	M-16A	Same
M-10C	M11C	M-12C	M14B	M-14C	M2C	M-16B	M16C
M-10D	M9D	M-12D	M12C	M-14D	M15D	M-16C	M15C
M-10E	M11E	M-12E	Same	M-14E	Same	M-16D	M13C
H-10A	New	H-12A	New	H-14A	New	M-16E	M16D
H-10B	New	H-12B	New	H-14B	New	H-16A	New
H-10C	H7B	H-12C	H10D	H-14C	H12D	H-16B	New
H-10D	H10C	H-12D	H11D	H-14D	H14B	H-16C	H15B
H-10E	H10B	H-12E	H16D	H-14E	H13D	H-16D	H16B
R-10A	Same	R-12A	Same	R-14A	Same	H-16E	H16C
R-10B	Same	R-12B	Same	R-14B	Same	R-16A	Same
T-10	Same	T-12	Same	T-14	Same	R-16B	Same
						T-16	Same